The
Joyful
Home
Cook

HarperCollins*Publishers*
1 London Bridge Street,
London, SE1 9GF

www.harpercollins.co.uk

First published by HarperCollins*Publishers* 2019

Text © Rosie Birkett, 2019
Photography © Helen Cathcart, 2019

10 9 8 7 6 5 4 3 2 1

A catalogue record of this book is available from
the British Library.

ISBN: 978-0-00-831427-9

Food styling: Becks Wilkinson
Prop styling: Linda Berlin

Printed and bound by GPS Group

For Chrissy – the original JHC
And for Otis: today's treasure is creativity

Cook's Notes:

- To sterilise your jars, wash them (and their
lids) in hot, soapy water or in a dishwasher
then rinse and completely dry in a low
oven for 10–15 minutes (dry lids with a clean
tea towel if they aren't heatproof)
- All eggs are medium organic, unless
otherwise stated
- All milk is whole, unless otherwise stated
- All butter is salted, unless otherwise stated
- All olive oil is extra-virgin
- All salt is sea salt flakes (I like Maldon)
unless otherwise stated
- All recipes have been tested in a fan oven

The Joyful Home Cook

ROSIE BIRKETT

HarperCollins*Publishers*

Contents

Introduction

Knowing how to cook and eat well is not only one of life's most essential and great pleasures, it is a tonic for daily life. Engaging your senses, working with your hands and letting your mind unwind as you gently caramelise onions in butter until they smell so good you're compelled to eat them straight from the pan: this is the magic of home cooking. And it should be fun, too. Where there's cooking there's often – delete as appropriate – lovers/friends/family/kids/dogs/wine/music. There's discussion and debate, sometimes drama. The kitchen fills with the scent of good food, the windows steam up, the glasses brim, and the warm, fuzzy mess of our lives unfolds over plates of food greedily scraped clean.

Cooking is one of the most enriching and creative things we can do for ourselves and for those we love, and as something that we have to do most days, it should be joyful. For me, that means food prepared with a little thought and care. It could be as simple as a thick slice of homemade toast, soaking with really good butter and topped with a couple of excellent preserved anchovies; or clouds of golden meringue deep with the molasses kick of muscovado sugar. First and foremost, it's about flavour.

As a food and cookery writer, it's my job to obsess over food, write about it, create recipes, and I care immensely about every morsel I pop into my greedy, not-so-little mouth and the mouths of those in my vicinity. This book celebrates the possibilities and pleasures that homemade food can bring us when we take the time to prepare and cook good things.

Whether you're planning a weekend slow-cooking project or have hurriedly squirrelled a few ingredients into your post-work shopping basket, here are recipes to enliven your cooking. Across these pages you'll find ideas, tips, stories, simple seasonal suggestions and – most importantly – inspiring but achievable recipes that will help you coax the most flavour you possibly can out of everyday ingredients. As well as showing you how to make simple, celebratory springtime lunches, lazy summer picnics, special suppers, comforting soul food and sumptuous seasonal desserts, I want to arm you with fun and satisfying skills that will ultimately help you become a more creative, intuitive and resourceful cook.

I've included some gratifying and straightforward DIY techniques that will allow you, should you wish, to be a bit more self-sufficient at home. I show how methods like smoking, curing and brining can bring the best out in meat and fish in recipes like the Cured Smoked Sea Trout on page 136 and the Whole Brined, Spatchcocked Barbecue Chicken on page 112. You'll find recipes for flavourful pastries, fresh pasta and slow-fermentation doughs for breads and pizza, that can form the basis of so many fantastic meals, as well as homemade condiments, crispy breadcrumbs and flavoured butters and fresh cheeses that can be adapted throughout the year.

I've shared ideas for maximising seasonal produce, from making Wild Garlic Pesto (page 263), to preparing quick jams and poached fruit to spruce up your desserts, and preserves like sweet Pickled Peaches (page 153), My 'Kind Of' Kimchi (page 145) and other tangy fermented vegetables and fruit-infused spirits (pages 160–163). These flavour-packed foods will help keep your kitchen well stocked throughout the year and add extra 'wow' to your dishes. They also make fantastic edible gifts for friends.

And so that these gifts keep on giving, I've included plenty of ideas for how to use everything up so nothing is wasted, as well nifty ways of utilising any by-products. Many of the recipes feed into one another, so when you've had a go at making the Labneh on page 256, you'll wind up with tangy whey, which you can use to brine the juicy lamb chops on page 115. And once you've tasted how next-level the parsnips glazed in leftover rhubarb poaching liquor are (page 197), you'll never find yourself pouring it away again. Surplus sourdough starter goes into my squishy, sour crumpets and bright pink beetroot blinis (pages 27 and 29). And when you end up with a batch of sourdough crumpets sitting patiently in your freezer, waiting to be defrosted, toasted and slathered with butter, Future You will thank Present You for your efforts.

THE WAY I COOK

As you cook from the book, you will get used to my straightforward, ingredient-led approach; the way I combine, contrast and layer flavours and textures to get the most out of ingredients. You will find repeated flourishes and tricks that I hope will start to run through your cooking: a tang of sharp pickled onion or funk of homemade ferment here, the sweet, juiciness of a thinly sliced sugarsnap pea or crunch of Savoury Granola (page 262) there.

I've always plumped for the underdog. There's something for me in rooting for the unloved and underrepresented, which is why in the pages of this book you're not going to find yet another recipe for roast forerib of beef or chocolate mousse. Instead, I want to introduce or reacquaint you with ingredients you might not have used before, or don't use that often, but that are readily and easily available, and that can bring so much to your kitchen. Things like buttermilk – once a staple in English cookery – whey, pickled walnuts, fregola and buckwheat: all versatile ingredients worth getting in if you don't have them already.

I grew up in rural Kent with parents who bordered on obsessive when it came to food and drink: my mother an astonishing home cook, my late father a passionate grower of veg, keen forager and even more voracious eater. My mum's simple, delicious home-cooked meals were the heartbeat of family life. Eating vegetables that my dad grew himself, and gathering field mushrooms with him on autumn mornings, gave me a precious early insight into the connection between food and the land, and how much flavour is in an ingredient when it's at its prime. My style of cooking reflects this, often putting seasonal veg at the centre of the plate.

Now I live in a big city, but I never cease to be excited by the arrival of the first green tips of asparagus (to be drenched in spiced butter and tiny brown shrimps as on page 14) in spring, or a late summer glut of ripe tomatoes (to be baked into the galette on page 117), and I've given ideas and recipes to encourage this appreciation of seasonality, wherever you live. Connecting to our landscape through our cooking and eating gives a sense of enormous wellbeing, and the food I make is always led by which ingredients are at their freshest and most flavourful, plentiful and affordable. You'll notice that quite a few ingredients crop up more than once, and will find many ways with seasonal favourites like celeriac, runner and broad beans, beetroot and fennel.

I'm a total allotment novice, and have started growing my own vegetables and herbs with enthusiasm and varying degrees of success, often sharing most of it with the allotment's rather persistent wildlife. I'm not anywhere near the point where I'm growing enough to live off, but having a go at growing and harvesting my own plants made me value ingredients in a new way. When you harvest even a half-nibbled leaf of vividly earthy chard straight from the ground and notice how much more flavourful it tastes, you realise what goes into producing food and feel more inclined to savour the ingredient. There are a couple of recipes where I've name-checked allotment produce (the pasties on page 40 and Allotment Greens and Anchovy Orecchiette on page 68), because I thought it might be helpful for you to know what a newbie like me has found easiest to grow and cook with.

If you don't already, have a go at growing some of your own food, even if you have no outdoor space. Herbs and salad leaves are so easy to grow in a window box or container outside the front or back door, and can bring so much vibrancy to your cooking. From seed, I've successfully grown lovage (if you're not familiar with it, it has a wonderful spicy, curry leaf-meets-celery flavour and comes back year after year), chervil, tarragon, borage (tastes like cucumber and has gorgeous blue and pink flowers), sage and thyme. Investing in a rosemary plant and bay tree is also helpful. Our bay tree is meagre and dog-eared, often battered by the bin men and attacked by slugs, but it's still consistently provides enough fresh bay leaves for all my cooking.

Foraging isn't just for men in waxed hats who can identify any mushroom at twenty paces. When I walk the dog down the canal, inhaling the heady scent of elderflower in May and June, it's impossible to resist grabbing fragrant fistfuls for the strawberry tarts on the cover of this book, or to infuse vinegar. On the coast, I'll look for flowering stems of wild fennel – their golden pollen is like an extra seasoning of intense anise for seafood or juicy, ripe stone fruit. There's something incredibly exciting about picking wild ingredients, and

they bring intense, hyper-local and unique flavours to your cooking. It goes without saying that you should never eat an ingredient if you're not 100 per cent sure about it.

While fresh seasonal produce forms the backbone of my cooking style, as part of my job I've been lucky enough to travel and report on different cuisines, meeting many chefs and food producers around the world. So naturally, a number of enlivening international ingredients have found their way into my cooking and are now firm kitchen staples: things like harissa, tahini, tamarind sauce, pomegranate molasses, fish sauce and grains and pulses such as freekeh and lentils. If some of these ingredients are more unfamiliar or a little harder to source, I promise they will delight and inspire your cooking from here on in, and not just gather dust in the cupboard.

CHERISH THE CRAFT OF COOKING

There is an increasing appetite to understand the craft and processes behind much of the food we love, and I want to demystify techniques like simple sourdough bakery, fermenting, smoking, curing and brining, and making simple homemade fresh cheeses. They are all age-old techniques that have been recently re-embraced by restaurant chefs, but they mostly originated from domestic kitchens, and we are now reconnecting with them as home cooks.

In particular, I'm excited about the fermented recipes. What I love most about the process is that anyone can do it in any home kitchen: you don't need any fancy kit. It's as simple as salt, ingredients and patience. That naturally occurring wild yeasts and bacteria we can't see work together to transform ingredients into something fizzing, tangy and delicious can feel miraculous, and sometimes a

little nerve-wracking, but it's the most natural of processes, and one which we can control. The resulting foods are packed full of good bacteria, making them great for our guts and digestion, and their flavours are quite literally alive and completely revelatory: just wait until you try Fermented Green Chillies (page 146), and the tangy spiciness they will add to your pizzas, salads and the addictive cheesy cornbread on page 123.

Mastering sourdough at home has been life-changing for me, so I was determined to include a really accessible, straightforward recipe (page 22). It's my failsafe method for a steadfast, tasty bread, and you only need flour, water, a bowl and a lidded, ovenproof pot or casserole dish: no special proving basket is required (though if you have one, of course put it to use). If you've never made it before, I can't wait for you to experience the thrill of cutting the hefty crust of your first loaf of homemade sourdough, to spread with butter while it's still warm because you're so impatient.

Home cooking is, by its nature, not about perfection; things can be improved upon, tweaked to suit a person's palate, or adapted to use up what's in the fridge or storecupboard and I wholeheartedly encourage this. It's about thought, care, resourcefulness and creativity, and making these recipes your own. But most of all it's about slowing down and enjoying the process, learning and gaining confidence, experimenting and taking risks. Sure, sometimes things go a little wrong, but try and be kind to yourself. If homemade pastry rips, patch it up – it will still taste better than anything you could have bought. In my experience of cooking for friends and family at home, and paying guests at my pop-ups, most folk will be a little moved, grateful and happy when you put a plate of something tasty and thoughtfully prepared in front of them.

So often – particularly for women – the conversation around food and eating is an anxious, confusing, shame-filled one, with more of an emphasis on what to deny yourself than what to enjoy. Let's shift the conversation back to what's delicious, what's worth cooking and eating, and how much happiness and satisfaction we can experience by getting to grips with the craft of cooking, spending a bit of time in the kitchen handling – and cooking with – beautiful ingredients. I'm a big believer that more wellbeing can be gained from spending time enjoying the creative process of making food for those you love, and connecting to nature and seasonality through your cooking, than stressing about how many calories are in things.

I hope these recipes will bring joy to your table, your favourite comfy chair, the garden, the beach, your bed – wherever it is you choose to eat them, and with whomever you choose to share them. Life can be tough, chaotic and often unfathomable. So many things are outside of our control, so let's take the light where we can, and make something good for supper.

A NOTE ON SOURCING

To be able to write a book about the joys of good food, and talk to you from these pages in the intimacy of your home kitchen is a huge privilege, and not something I take lightly. It would feel disingenuous to not address the environmental and ethical implications of our consumer choices as home cooks, and while I don't want to preach to you (because I am sure you already consider these things), I thought it might be helpful to share some thoughts. To borrow some wise words from the brilliant writer and activist Wendell Berry, 'eating is an agricultural act', and it's important and empowering to understand how the way we shop, cook and eat affects the world around us, as well as our own health. Knowing where our ingredients come from and how they're produced helps us to make better decisions with a more positive impact, and ultimately make more joyful food.

While I do still enjoy cooking and eating meat, we're all becoming increasingly aware that the human appetite for meat and dairy is having a hugely destructive impact on our world. Like many people, I've massively reduced my meat consumption over the past few years. Both consciously and because my cooking style naturally gravitates towards making the most of seasonal vegetables, grains and pulses, along with sustainable fish and seafood.

I live by the idea that 'meat is a treat', so when I buy it I am happy to spend more on something that has been produced in as natural and sustainable a way as possible, and the same goes for dairy, poultry and eggs. The slow-grown, organic chicken you splurge on can be celebrated from its first glorious roasting to the last drop of its golden stock, which will elevate a dish of Wild Garlic Gnocchi (page 97), or a warming chicken soup laced with ginger (page 171).

Slow-grown animals have a better flavour because they've had time to lay down natural fat, and those reared with space to roam and graze, and slaughtered nearer to where they've lived are less stressed and therefore taste better, because stress hormones like cortisol and adrenaline present at the time of slaughter have a negative impact on the flavour and nutritional value of the meat. It makes sense that what an animal eats will affect the way it tastes, and animals that graze and forage on grassy, diverse, wildflower-rich pastures have a superior flavour. A great example of this is salt marsh lamb, one of my all-time favourite meats, which has a unique herbaceous flavour and minerality, as it grazes on coastal pastures and estuary salt marshes. Look out for it in June and July. You can read more about pasture-fed farming at www.pastureforlife.org.

It's worth tracking down a good local butcher or farm shop where you can find out about the provenance of their meat – if you don't have the luxury of either of these, there are plenty of helpful online resources where you can read more about ethical meat (check out bicbim.co.uk), and some fantastic direct farm-to-table box schemes such as farmdrop.com and greenpasturefarms.co.uk. If the supermarket is your main port of call, look out for RSPCA assured and the organic label. While there are plenty of farmers doing things well without being officially certified as 'organic', I do believe in the organic certification as a guarantee that it has been farmed or raised in the most natural way possible – in healthy, fertile soils that promote biodiversity rather than chemical-led monocultures, without routine use of antibiotics or chemical pesticides. It's a good barometer of quality, animal welfare and care and that means, particularly in the supermarket, that it's an easy way for us as consumers to make better choices.

You'll notice that there are plenty of fish and seafood recipes in the book: I wrote much of it on the Kent coast, where my mum lives, and couldn't help but feel inspired by the incredible haul at the local fishmonger Jenkins & Son. I have tried to use species that are broadly more sustainable and in line with MSC (Marine Stewardship Council) recommendations, but because monitored fish stocks are constantly changing, and vary regionally, talk to your local fishmonger about what's in season, sustainable and plentiful in your area. Look out for fish that is line-caught, squid caught by jig, and species that are certified with a blue label by the MSC, and try and avoid any fish or seafood that has been trawled – this method of fishing destroys the flora and fauna of the seabed.

I also hope that by including recipes for making your own fresh cheese and butters, I'll show you that it's worth investing in fewer, better quality dairy products. Although milk, cream and butter are things we have come to take for granted, they vary greatly in terms of flavour and quality according to how they've been produced. Again, plump for organic if you can, and keep an eye out for smaller-scale producers – these guys tend to pour their heart and soul into their animals and their products, and it all comes through in the flavour.

Brunch,
Lunch
and Bites

We begin this chapter in spring, and there couldn't be a better way to welcome those first warmer, lighter days than with celebratory dishes of new season asparagus, Jersey Royal potatoes and wild garlic. These ingredients pop up throughout the book, and lend themselves well to the brunchy dishes, bright salads and smaller lunch plates here.

Food is what gets me out of bed, and I'm a toast girl most days, opting for a slice of homemade toasted sourdough, spread thickly with butter, sometimes topped with a fried egg and kimchi. This, then, is the place to introduce you to my simple sourdough (page 24) – a rustic, naturally leavened loaf to base many happy meals around, and a starting off point, I hope, for many experiments. You can use it for the Wild Mushrooms on Toast (page 20). You'll also find snacks and dips in this chapter because – while I'm all for buying in crisps – it's good to have a couple of homemade goodies up your hosting sleeve, too. Cue crispy spring croquettes, filled with a verdant béchamel that marries one of my favourite herbs – lovage – with peas (page 42). These nuggets of spring, served with a garden salad, are a strong start to any meal.

New season asparagus
with spiced butter and brown shrimp

Right at the start of asparagus season, at the end of April, there is very little that can improve on the flavour and tenderness of these perfect first spears, but asparagus and butter are always a good idea, so why not throw in some irresistible little brown shrimp too? This is a sort of potted shrimp situation with pools of mace-spiked butter, poured over freshly poached asparagus. The result is something so memorable and magnificent I didn't feel sheepish serving it to a very brilliant chef for lunch. He loved it. It's perfect as a celebratory spring lunch, but could work well as a show-stopping sharing starter, too. If you can, make this dish when the early asparagus comes through at the end of April (though later in the season it will still be ridiculously good).

60g unsalted butter
½ tsp sea salt
½ tsp cayenne pepper
½ tsp ground mace
¼ tsp pink peppercorns, lightly crushed in a pestle and mortar
500g asparagus spears, trimmed
200g peeled brown shrimp
2 leaves of wild garlic, or a handful finely shredded chervil or chives
juice of 1 lemon
a few wild garlic or chive flowers (optional)
chunks of crusty white bread, to serve

1. Warm a large platter or plate in the oven.

2. Gently melt the butter in a small saucepan over a low heat, then stir in the salt, spices and peppercorns. Stir to combine, then remove from the heat while you cook the asparagus.

3. Bring a few centimetres of salted water to the boil in a saucepan wide enough to hold the asparagus without crowding it. Add the asparagus and poach for 2–3 minutes, until a knife blade inserted into the thickest part of a spear can be pulled out with no resistance. While it's poaching, return the spiced butter pan to the heat and add the shrimp, wild garlic or herbs and lemon juice, basting the shrimps in the butter. Taste for seasoning. Drain the asparagus and pile onto the warm platter, then pour over the shrimps and butter. Garnish with the flowers, if using, and serve with chunks of crusty bread to dip in the butter.

TIP: If you don't eat shellfish, leave out the shrimp and top with crushed roasted hazelnuts or the Savoury Granola on page 262.

Three-cornered leek and scrambled eggs on toast

Serves 2

Three-cornered leeks often get mistaken for wild garlic, thanks to their allium scent, green stems and pretty white flowers, but they are easy to tell apart. Where wild garlic has fat, flat green leaves and open, star-shaped flowers in clusters, these wild leeks have hollow, three-cornered stalks and droopy, edible bell-shaped flowers, similar to bluebells, except they are white with green stripes running down them. They are in season in the UK from spring until early summer, and have a gentle, mellow green onion-chive flavour which is lovely layered into green salads, added to wilted greens or stir fries. If you can't find wild leeks use baby leeks, chives or spring onions instead.

4 eggs
25g salted butter, diced, plus extra for spreading
50g three-cornered leek, baby leek or spring onion, washed and roughly chopped
2 slices of sourdough (shop-bought or see recipe on page 24)
pink peppercorns or dried chilli flakes, to taste
sea salt and freshly ground black pepper
three-cornered leek or chive flowers, to serve (optional)

1. Crack the eggs into a bowl or jug. Whisk lightly with a fork, just to break up the yolks, then stir in three-quarters of the diced butter.

2. Heat a small non-stick frying pan over a medium heat. Add the remaining butter to the pan, followed by the three-cornered leek. Season with salt and cook for a minute or two, stirring, until it has wilted into the melted butter. Toast the bread and warm two plates.

3. Add the egg mixture to the pan with the leeks and cook, stirring, until all the butter has melted and the eggs are coagulated but still silky and creamy. Butter the toast and top with the scrambled eggs, season with salt and some freshly ground pink or black peppercorns or chilli flakes and garnish with some of the three-cornered leek flowers, if you can find some.

Kimchi and sweetcorn fritters
with chilli maple syrup

Serves 2
(makes 4–6 fritters)

Sweetcorn fritters have been a staple since childhood. My mum used to make them to go with her 'chicken Maryland' – basically spiced fried chicken. My sister and I used to fight over the fritters, so I've given them a recipe in their own right, which makes a great brunch dish and also happens to be gluten free. I've added the fire and spice in the form of kimchi, which gives them a lovely sour crunch and an addictive, chilli-spiked maple syrup. Add fried eggs, avocado and streaky bacon to this to make it a brunch for four, otherwise serve two fritters per person with some avocado on the side.

2 eggs
3 tbsp water
½ tbsp soy sauce
65g rice flour
¼ tsp baking powder
½ tsp smoked paprika
½ tsp ground turmeric
100g My 'Kind Of' Kimchi (page 145), or shop-bought kimchi, drained and finely chopped
165g drained tinned or frozen sweetcorn (or fresh corn boiled and cut from the cob)
2 spring onions, thinly sliced
2 tbsp coconut, rapeseed or vegetable oil
1 avocado, halved and stoned
sea salt flakes

For the chilli maple syrup
80ml maple syrup
½ tsp dried chilli flakes (preferably Urfa chilli flakes), or 1 fresh bird's-eye chilli, deseeded and finely chopped
10ml dark soy sauce
1 tsp black sesame seeds
spring onion greens

1. Crack the eggs into a bowl, add the water and soy sauce and whisk to combine. Sift in the flour, baking powder and spices and whisk to form a smooth batter. Leave the batter to sit for a few minutes while you make the syrup.

2. Put the maple syrup, chilli flakes, soy sauce and sesame seeds into a small saucepan and stir. Heat until really runny and warm but not reducing or bubbling. Remove from the heat.

3. Stir the kimchi, sweetcorn and spring onions into the batter and coat well to make sure everything is cloaked in the batter. Add a dash more water or soy sauce if you think it needs loosening – it should be loose enough to drop off a spoon.

4. Line a plate with kitchen paper and heat half the oil in a large non-stick frying pan over a medium-high heat. To make the fritters, spoon 2–3 dessertspoonfuls of the batter into the pan in little piles, leaving space between each pile. Use the back of the spoon to flatten them slightly and fry for 4–5 minutes, flipping them over to cook on the other side halfway through, until golden and crispy on the outside and cooked all the way through. Drain on kitchen paper and season with salt. Add the remaining oil to the pan and fry the rest of the batter, keeping the first lot warm in a low oven until you're ready to serve. Serve the fritters with the syrup poured over, and slices of avocado alongside.

Wild mushrooms on toast
with lemon and thyme seeded crumb

I made this dish for 120 people from the kitchen of a pub in Borough Market with a brigade of brilliant female food writers and chefs. We were cooking a dinner to raise money for the food poverty charity Action Against Hunger, and even though it's just fancy mushrooms on toast, it went down a storm – though the logistical effort of cleaning wild mushrooms and making toast for that many people is not something I wish to repeat!

Try to sniff out wild mushrooms, which have more of an interesting woodland flavour than standard 'shrooms, and come into season from early autumn onwards – girolles and porcini work well but if you can't find them, try chestnut or oyster. The crumb provides extra texture and lovely nuttiness thanks to the toasty, malty quality of the buckwheat. The butter and crumb can both be made in advance.

4 thick slices of sourdough
   bread (shop-bought or see
   recipe on page 24)
1 garlic clove, peeled and halved
½ tbsp rapeseed or neutral oil
500g wild mushrooms (see tip),
   cleaned (larger ones halved)
leaves from 2 sprigs of thyme
lemon juice, to taste
sea salt and freshly ground
   black pepper

For the seeded crumb
2 thick slices of sourdough
   bread (shop-bought or see
   page 24)
2 tbsp pumpkin seeds
2 tbsp buckwheat groats
2 tbsp olive oil
grated zest of 1 unwaxed lemon
leaves from 4 sprigs of thyme
½ tsp dried chilli flakes
sea salt

For the garlic and herb butter
1 shallot, peeled and quartered
1 tsp sea salt
2 garlic cloves
20g flat-leaf parsley, leaves
   picked
10g tarragon, leaves picked
1 tbsp lemon juice
70g unsalted butter, at room
   temperature, diced

1. First, make the crumb. Blitz the bread in a food processor until it forms breadcrumbs. Heat a heavy-based dry frying pan or skillet over a medium-high heat. Add the pumpkin seeds and buckwheat groats and toast for 2–3 minutes, until the buckwheat is golden and the pumpkin seeds are puffed, popped and crunchy. Transfer to a bowl and put the pan back on the hob over a medium heat. Add the olive oil along with the lemon zest, thyme and chilli flakes and stir to infuse for a minute, then add the breadcrumbs and toast them in the oil for 3–5 minutes, until golden and crunchy – it usually takes a bit longer than you'd expect. Scrape all the crumbs into the bowl with the pumpkin seeds and buckwheat. Season with sea salt. Pour into a jar or airtight container once cool, or use immediately.

2. Make the butter by blitzing the shallot, salt and garlic cloves in the small bowl of a food processor or mini chopper, followed by most of the herbs (saving a few for garnish) and the lemon juice. Season with salt and pepper, add the diced butter and blitz to make a green butter. Scrape out of the food processor and into a bowl by the hob.

3. Toast the sourdough and rub it with the garlic. Keep warm in a low oven with the plates while you cook the mushrooms.

4. Place the pan back over a medium-high heat and pour in the rapeseed or neutral oil. Add the mushrooms with the thyme and a pinch of salt and fry for a couple of minutes, until they are caramelised and losing their moisture – they will shrink a little and you want to see some nice dark colour on them. Turn the heat down slightly, add all the butter, stirring to melt, and baste the mushrooms with it. Taste, season to your liking and maybe add a little lemon juice to pique the flavours. Serve spooned over the warm toast with the crumb scattered over.

TIP: Look out for a mix of girolles, chestnut, oyster, blewit, black trompette and cep/porcini. If you love wild mushrooms as much as I do, it's worth investing in a mushroom brush, but you can also use a damp kitchen towel to get rid of any dirt or grit.

Simple sourdough

Proper sourdough bread is a truly magnificent thing. It's bread made the old-fashioned way, slowly and reverently, without the use of any industrially produced yeast, but rather leavened or raised with a starter culture made from naturally occurring yeasts and bacteria that awaken when flour and water are mixed together. The resulting fermentation yields something altogether more flavourful and satisfying than mass-produced bread, and in recent years we've seen a sourdough revolution, a movement of artisan bakers the world over who are re-embracing the craft of making slow-fermented doughs and beautiful, delicious and nutritious loaves. A really good loaf of sourdough takes time to make, but it becomes the basis for so many good, quick meals that it more than pays you back for the time you've invested.

Now, while I do think that squishy white bread still has a place – I can't imagine a bacon sandwich made with sourdough or, worse still, a chip butty – after interviewing bakers and chefs and tasting this delicious style of bread at many restaurants over the years, I became fascinated by the process, and obsessed with mastering the art of making sourdough at home. The idea that it was possible to raise an army of hard-working yeast who would obligingly leaven loaves of bread, producing gut-friendly acids that make that bread easier on the digestion, more nutritious and tasty in the process, had me hooked.

There are books and courses dedicated to sourdough, and if you want to delve deeper I'd recommend these books for further reading – *Do Sourdough* by Andrew Whitley, *The Handmade Loaf* by Dan Lepard, and *Flour, Water, Salt, Yeast* by Ken Forkish – but please don't be intimidated. For centuries people have been making bread this way, simply using flour and water, without technical equipment, and once you begin to wrap your head around the process, anyone can bake loaves at home, and really enjoy the journey of discovering what works for you.

The gist of it is that you create a leaven by mixing together good-quality flour and water. The yeasts and bacteria already present in the flour thrive and multiply in this wet environment, feasting on the sugars in the flour and creating carbon dioxide (the bubbles that will eventually raise your bread), and lactic acid, which give the bread its signature sour flavour. You have to feed the starter initially to help the network of yeasts and lactobacilli become strong, and once this starter is a happy and lively culture, you introduce it to more flour and water and allow it to continue its work, creating a fermented and flavourful dough that is then baked into delicious bread.

This is a simple, entry level recipe and it's relatively hands off. The trick is to let the bread work around your schedule, rather than keeping you prisoner. This method consistently delivers loaves of good bread that I base many meals around, and I hope you will too. You will need a few things to get started, but none of them are outrageously expensive or unattainable: an ovenproof ceramic or cast-iron pot to bake your bread in, good-quality organic wholegrain rye flour, some digital scales and a sharp knife or razor blade for slashing the dough before baking. I use a casserole pot I found in a charity shop to bake mine, but you could use a small Le Creuset, a Pyrex dish with a lid or a stewing pot. Please use this as a jumping off point for your sourdough experiments. I'm convinced, when you see what a natural, simple and satisfying process it is, you too will be hooked.

My simple rye flour starter

The first step is to create a happy starter to levain your bread. All you need in order to make your own is some really good-quality wholegrain flour, some filtered water and a sterilised jar.

You need to make the starter about a week before you want to make your bread and you will have to tend to it – for literally a couple of minutes – every day to start with. You should only have to do this once, and then you can keep your starter dormant in the fridge, refreshing it a day before you want to make bread. A good-quality, organic wholegrain rye flour starter creates beautifully leavened and tasty, wholesome bread, but as you get more confident with sourdough you can start to play around with different starters such as wheat and spelt. Wholegrain flours are better for making starters as the bran of the wheat grain is rich in bacterias and yeasts and organic flour is always a better option as there are no yeast and bacteria-killing chemical pesticides and fungicides involved in its production.

1. In a jar, mix 2 heaped teaspoons (about 20g) of rye flour with 40ml lukewarm filtered or spring water to make a thin, pourable mixture. I use a butter knife to mix the flour and water together, incorporating as much air as possible. Scrape down the sides of the jar, rest the lid on top of the jar so that it's sealed but not tightly closed, and leave in a warm place. In the summer you should be fine to leave your jar anywhere, but in colder months you'll want to seek out a warm spot on a shelf above a radiator or in an airing cupboard as the starter needs a certain level of warmth to get going. Just don't forget about it! I set a reminder on my phone to feed mine as I'm a bit forgetful.

2. The next day, add the same amount of water and flour again, mixing and repeating the cycle. Repeat again on the third and fourth day, but this time using 40g flour and 40ml water each day. By the fourth day, you should be seeing some promising signs of life in the form of small bubbles.

3. On the fifth day, tip off 100g of the starter (to use in the Sour Cream Sourdough Crumpets on page 27) and replace what you've lost with with 50g each of flour and water. Leave this to ferment for 12 hours, or until it's looking really nice and bubbly and smelling good and yeasty. By the sixth day you should be good to get baking – see recipe overleaf. Once you've used your starter for the recipe overleaf, keep the rest (there should be about 150g) in the fridge, refreshing as per the recipe below each time you want to bake.

TIP: Always scrape down the sides of your jar before you put the starter back in the fridge to make it less likely to go mouldy.

REFRESHING YOUR STARTER FOR BAKING
Every time you want to bake a loaf of sourdough, you now have the wherewithal, but you will need to refresh and replenish your starter a couple of days ahead to do this as it will get sluggish in the fridge. Just tip your starter into a bowl, add 100g each of wholegrain rye flour and lukewarm filtered or spring water and allow it to ferment overnight at room temperature. Set aside about 100g of this mix in a jar to put back in the fridge for next time, and use the rest to bake your bread and make the crumpets on page 27. If you have any spare, give it to a friend and spread the sourdough love.

Sourdough loaf

If you want to make and bake your sourdough loaf on the same day, you need to start in the morning and bear in mind that the dough will need at least 6 hours to ferment before you bake. I prefer how the flavour develops with an overnight fermentation in the fridge, but sometimes we don't think that far ahead. How long you'll need for the fermentation will depend on how warm your kitchen is and the time of year etc., so you'll have to play some of this by ear, but I've found the only way to crack it is to keep baking until you get a feel for it.

300ml lukewarm water
130g rye starter
390g flour (310g plain/20g rye/60g spelt)
10g sea salt

Optional additions
20g each of linseed, buckwheat, white sesame seeds, walnuts, flax or pumpkin seeds – or a mixture of all of the above. Basically, whatever you fancy or have in your cupboard that needs using

1. Measure your water into a bowl, spoon in the starter and whisk with a fork until dispersed and no lumps remain. Mix the flours, salt and any seeds or nuts in another bowl. Make a shallow well in the flour and pour in the starter mixture. Using a blunt knife, whisk the liquid into the dough, rotating the bowl and cutting through until you have a well combined, sticky ball. Add a little more water if the dough is not coming together. Leave to rest for 30–40 minutes. This process is known as autolyse – while the dough rests, the flour fully absorbs the water, hydrating and kick-starting enzymes that will stimulate gluten development. Don't skip this step!

2. Still working in the bowl (the dough will be very sticky and wet) use wet fingers or a silicone spatula to dig under the edge of the dough and bring that edge up over the ball. Turn the bowl clockwise and repeat the lifting, stretching and pulling motion a good 10–15 times round the bowl. Cover and leave for 30 minutes, then repeat the lifting, stretching and pulling motion another 15–20 times. This is to develop the gluten structure of the bread. If you are baking the bread the same day, cover the bowl with a tea towel and leave it somewhere warm, like on a shelf above a radiator, for at least 5 hours. Otherwise (and preferably) leave it overnight in the fridge, covering the bowl with cling film – this will give the bread a fantastic depth of flavour.

3. If it's been in the fridge, take it out and allow it to warm up for about 20 minutes. Use wet fingers or a clean spatula to repeat the lifting, stretching and pulling motion 12–14 times around the bowl, scraping any dough that sticks to the side of the bowl back into the dough – the aim here is to create air inside the bread so don't push down too hard. If it's too tense to stretch and pull this many times then don't overwork it.

4. Leave the dough for 40 minutes somewhere warm, covered. Repeat the lift and pull motion 10 more times – you should feel now that the dough has some real tension in it.

5. Brush a large sheet of baking parchment with a little olive oil, followed by a little water, and dust with a thin layer of flour. Using a spatula or dough scraper, and without pushing too much air out, gently scrape the dough out of the bowl onto the parchment. Wet your hands slightly and tuck any stray bits under the bottom of the dough to form a neat ball. Dust it lightly with flour.

6. Grab hold of the parchment and lift it, along with the dough, back into a bowl. Dust lightly with a little flour and leave to prove for 45 minutes – 2 hours, until visibly puffed up and almost doubled in size.

7. Preheat the oven to 250°C/230°C fan/gas 9 (or its hottest setting) and put a round, lidded ovenproof pot or casserole dish in there to warm up.

8. Once the dough has proved, remove the pot or casserole dish from the oven (wearing oven gloves and being very careful as it will be stinking hot), place it on a heatproof surface and take the lid off. Now quickly lift the parchment and dough into the pot. Use the spatula to smooth the paper away from the dough and up the edge of the pot. Scatter the top of the dough with a little water and use a very sharp knife to make slashes in the top of the dough to help it rise. I do four in a square about 5cm in from the outer circumference. This gives the steam that builds up inside somewhere to go. If you forget, the bread will naturally break open, which is fine.

9. Cover and bake in the oven for 30 minutes, then lift the lid off. Your bread should be risen and smelling good. Depending on how golden the crust is looking, you might want to turn your oven down to nearer 200°C/180°C fan/gas 6, but if it's still reasonably pale don't do this. Bake the bread for another 5-10 minutes, or until golden and crisp.

10. Once you're happy that your loaf is baked, remove it from the dish and quickly peel off the parchment. Transfer the bread to a wire rack and allow to cool before slicing and tasting. However tempting the smell of the freshly baked bread is, try not to slice it until it's completely cool as this can squish the crumb.

Sour cream sourdough crumpets

Makes 6-8 crumpets

These guys are unlike any crumpet you can buy in the shops. They are made using the rye sourdough starter from page 23, along with a little buckwheat flour – a nod to crumpet heritage, as they were traditionally made with buckwheat – and fermented slowly to develop their characteristic bubbles and an incredible sour flavour. The batter is further enriched with sour cream and bicarbonate of soda to help things along just before cooking.

I make them every time I refresh my sourdough starter, and keep a stash in the freezer to bust out for breakfast and snacks. Make sure you are using lively refreshed sourdough starter or your crumpets won't bubble (follow the starter refreshment steps on page 23). They are incredibly satisfying to make, but there is a knack to it. The key is patience. And you'll need crumpet rings. Eat them with homemade butter (page 259) and jams and clotted cream or with wild medlar jelly (page 156) and a slice of cheese. They are also brilliant for breakfast topped with smashed avocado, a poached egg and My 'Kind Of' Kimchi (page 145) but really, the possibilities are endless.

50g Sourdough Starter (page 23) or 1 sachet fast-action dried yeast
2 tsp caster sugar
200ml lukewarm water
175g plain flour (or 150g plain and 25g buckwheat flour)
1 tsp fine sea salt
½ tbsp sour cream
½ tsp bicarbonate of soda
splash of milk (optional)
a little neutral oil and butter, for greasing

1. In a jug, mix your starter and sugar with the water to dissolve it, whisking out any lumps.

2. Combine the flour(s) and salt in a bowl and make a well in the middle. Slowly pour the wet mix into the well in the flour and briefly mix with a whisk to combine to a smooth batter. Don't overmix – you're not trying to create gluten as this will make the crumpets more bread-like. Cover the bowl with cling film and leave to ferment in a warm place for at least 6 hours (or preferably overnight in the fridge). How long you can leave it will depend on your patience, but I sometimes leave the batter for 2 days in the fridge – the flavour develops and gets more sour the longer you leave it.

3. After the mix has fermented, mix the sour cream with the bicarbonate of soda then add to the batter, thoroughly whisking out any lumps until you have a batter the consistency of very thick double cream. If the batter isn't pourable, loosen it with a little splash of milk. Leave for 30 more minutes.

4. Grease a flat, non-stick frying pan or hot plate with a little neutral oil or oil and butter and place over a high heat on a medium-sized gas hob burner. Grease two egg or crumpet rings and pour 2½ tablespoons of batter into each ring.

5. Cook over a medium-high heat for 1 minute (watch the clock – if you leave them any longer the bottom will burn), until bubbles have popped through on the surface and the mixture is starting to set. Turn the heat down to low and cook for a further 5–8 minutes (this will depend on how full the rings are), until set on top – there should be plenty of holes at this point and the batter should be pulling away from the crumpet ring. Using tongs, lift off the

Recipe continues over the page

crumpet rings and flip the crumpets over, turn the heat up again and cook for a minute until golden on top, then transfer to a wire rack to cool. Grease the pan in between batter additions to keep it from sticking.

6. Once all the crumpets are made and cooled, grill or toast them to perfection, or, if you're doing lots at once, you could roast them in a hot oven for 3 minutes. Slather with butter and jam, or Marmite and cheese, smashed avocado and kimchi, or tahini with really good honey, or peanut butter... you get the drift. These keep well wrapped in cling film in the fridge for a couple of days (not longer, as the sour cream with moulder). I also I like to make them ahead and freeze them.

TIP: If you're vegan, you can swap the sour cream for water and fry the crumpets in oil rather than butter.

WHAT TO DO IF...

There are no holes: this means the batter hasn't fermented enough and needs longer (the time it takes to ferment depends on the weather and humidity); also, check that your starter is alive and well. Try incorporating a little extra sugar just before frying, too.

The bottom is burned: you filled the ring too full or cooked it at too high a heat at the start. Try using a little less batter and keep an eye on the time you cook it over the higher heat. There is an art to making crumpets so don't be hard on yourself if it takes a few attempts to get it right. It's a bit like making pancakes – you'll get better as you go and while it can be a little tricky to get right, I promise you it is so worth it. Also, remember all the bottoms will be pretty dark as that's just the nature of crumpets. As long as they're not black you're good to go.

The crumpets are wet in the middle: homemade crumpets should be squishy and moist in the middle but not too wet! Did you skip the cooling stage and dive straight in?

Beetroot and horseradish blinis

Makes 15–20 blinis

You can use the crumpet batter to make plain blinis, or this beetroot version. These are great topped with sour cream, the smoked trout on page 136 and dill.

1 quantity Sour Cream
    Sourdough Crumpet mix

**For the beetroot and
    horseradish purée**
2 roasted beetroots (shop-
    bought or see page 139),
    roughly chopped
1 tbsp creamed horseradish (or
    ½ tbsp freshly grated)
1 tbsp rapeseed oil
sea salt and freshly ground
    black pepper

1. Place the beetroot in a blender, food processor or Nutribullet with the horseradish and rapeseed oil and blitz to a smooth purée. Season to taste with salt and pepper.

2. Stir in 1 tablespoon of beetroot and horseradish purée when you add the bicarbonate of soda in the crumpet method on page 27 – it will make the mix bright pink.

3. To cook the blinis, grease a flat, non-stick frying pan or hot plate as on page 27 with a little butter and oil and set over a medium heat. Add 1 teaspoon of the batter to the pan and cook for a couple of minutes (cook a few at once if your pan is big enough), until bubbles appear on the surface, then flip over and cook for a bit longer. Transfer to a plate lined with kitchen paper and repeat with the rest of the batter. Keep warm and serve, or allow to cool, then put in the oven at 200°C/180°C fan/gas 6 for 5 minutes to heat up.

TIP: You don't use all the beetroot and horseradish purée in step 2, so keep it in a jar for eating on toast with smoked fish, salt beef etc., or use in salads.

Broad bean and raw courgette salad
with ricotta

Serves 4 as a side

This salad screams early summer, with its nutty raw courgette ribbons, vivid green broad beans, lemon juice and sprightly fresh herbs. I use smaller, firmer courgettes for this as they are the stars of the show. If you grow your own and have any courgette flowers, tear them up and add them for extra colour. This makes a really special al fresco lunch, and is nice piled onto the warm yoghurt flatbreads on page 39.

2 medium courgettes, peeled into long thin ribbons with a vegetable peeler
handful of mint leaves
handful of basil leaves
2 tbsp extra-virgin olive oil
grated zest and juice of ½ unwaxed lemon
1 tsp runny honey
1 garlic clove, grated
pinch of dried chilli flakes or 1 fresh red chilli, desseded and finely chopped (optional)
100g podded fresh or frozen broad beans
100g ricotta, drained in a sieve, or Fresh Curd Cheese (page 254)
sea salt and freshly ground black pepper

1. Put the courgette ribbons in a bowl with half the herbs.

2. Whisk the olive oil, lemon zest and juice, honey, garlic and chilli flakes (if using) in a bowl. Season with salt and pepper to taste.

3. Dress the courgette ribbons with the dressing.

4. Prepare a bowl of iced water. Bring a large saucepan of salted water to the boil and blanch the broad beans for a couple of minutes, then drain and immediately plunge them into the iced water. Once cool, drain again and squeeze the broad beans from their skins, using your nail to pierce the skin. You can skip this step if you're using super-young broad beans, as the skins are less bitter than the older ones.

5. Pile the dressed courgettes onto a platter, scatter the broad beans onto the salad and dot over the ricotta or fresh curd cheese. Garnish with the rest of the herbs and serve with any remaining dressing on the side.

TIP: Broad beans can be fiddly to peel so I usually blanch and peel them as soon as I get them, then keep them in a bowl in the fridge dressed with a teaspoon of olive oil ready to use whenever I fancy. They will keep for a few days like this.

Mackerel with buttered greens
and pickled radish

Serves 1

One of my favourite food festivals takes place in May each year on the beach in St Ives, Cornwall. The setting could not be more inspiring – you can smell the sea as you cook. This dish came together one year when I heard about a mackerel honesty box where you could buy the freshest local mackerel for pennies. A kindly local gent was known for having a mackerel 'shed' which was always stocked with ready filleted, sparklingly fresh catch just outside his house. I couldn't resist walking the streets until I found the box. I paired the mackerel fillets with freshly foraged three-cornered leek, which grows like a weed in Cornwall, and is beautiful wilted in butter and served with pan-fried mackerel. If you can't find wild leeks, use the greens of spring onions or baby leeks, thinly sliced lengthways, with a handful of spinach.

handful of samphire
1 tbsp extra-virgin olive oil
sprig of thyme
1 x medium fillet of mackerel, pin-boned
10g unsalted butter
handful of baby spinach
60g three-cornered leek (or spring onions)
½ lemon, for squeezing
sea salt and freshly ground black pepper

For the pickled radish
1 tbsp cider vinegar
2 tsp caster sugar
pinch of salt
2 radishes, thinly sliced, preferably with a mandoline

1. First, quick-pickle your radishes. Whisk the vinegar, sugar and salt in a bowl until the sugar has dissolved. Toss the radish slices through the vinegar and leave them to pickle while you cook the fish.

2. Blanch the samphire in a saucepan of boiling water for 30 seconds, then drain.

3. Heat the olive oil in a heavy-based, non-stick frying pan over a medium-high heat. Add the thyme and allow it to infuse in the oil for a few seconds, then add the mackerel fillet, skin side down. Season the flesh with salt and pepper and cook, without moving the fillet, for 3–4 minutes, until the skin is crispy and the flesh is starting to cook through and become opaque. Carefully flip the fillet over and continue cooking on the flesh side for a matter of seconds, then transfer to a plate to rest.

4. Add the butter to the pan, followed by the samphire, spinach and three-cornered leek. Season with salt and pepper and wilt the greens in the butter for 2–3 minutes, tossing to thoroughly combine. Pour away any excess liquid, squeeze over a little lemon juice and serve the mackerel on the wilted greens with the pickled radish on the side.

Brunch, Lunch and Bites

Crab, Jersey Royal and asparagus salad

Serves 2–4

This recipe unites my two favourite spring ingredients – Jersey Royal potatoes and asparagus – with creamy crab, fresh green apple and soft herbs for a celebratory salad. The dish has everything: an irresistible earthy minerality from the potatoes (which are fertilised with seaweed), buttery green goodness from the asparagus, and luxury from the crab and mayo which dresses the salad as you eat it. It's worth making your own mayonnaise (you can make it in advance, it will keep in the fridge for a few days), but if you're pressed for time, shop-bought works, too – just stir a good fresh egg yolk through it to enrich it. This is a lunch worth carving out a couple of hours for with a friend.

sprig of mint
300g Jersey Royal potatoes or new potatoes, scrubbed
300g crab meat, split into white and brown
juice of 1 lemon
pinch of cayenne pepper, plus extra for sprinkling
1 green apple, cored and finely chopped (skin on)
3 spring onions, trimmed and thinly sliced
200g asparagus spears, trimmed and each cut diagonally into 3 pieces
handful of samphire or sea purslane (optional)
1 baby gem lettuce, outer leaves separated, washed and dried, heart split in half
10g chervil leaves
10g tarragon leaves
10g flat-leaf parsley leaves
sea salt

For the mayonnaise
2 egg yolks
½ tsp sea salt
juice of ½ lemon
100ml extra-virgin rapeseed oil
200ml vegetable oil
pinch of ground white pepper

1. First, cook the potatoes. Bring a large saucepan of well salted water to the boil, add the mint and the Jersey Royals and simmer for 15 minutes, until tender – do not be afraid of overcooking them, as they are far better soft than chalky. Turn the heat off and leave them to cool down in their cooking water (this retains their earthy flavour beautifully).

2. While the potatoes cook, make the mayonnaise. Put the egg yolks, salt and lemon juice in a food processor and blitz until smooth. With the blades still turning, very, very slowly drip in the 100ml rapeseed oil, a drop at a time, until the oil starts to emulsify and the mixture looks smooth and creamy. Once the rapeseed oil is incorporated, very slowly start to drip in the vegetable oil, blitzing the whole time, until it starts to thicken. Once you've added about half the oil and it's looking thick and creamy, increase the pouring of the oil to a steady stream – making the mayonnaise will take 10–15 minutes. If it becomes too thick and stiff to work at any point, just add a few drops of water or a squeeze of lemon and blitz again. If it splits, see tip on page 71.

3. Once the mayonnaise is plump and emulsified, add 1 tablespoon of water. This will lighten the mayo and make it creamier. Add the pepper and blitz until combined. Scrape it out into a bowl, taste for seasoning and add a little more salt or lemon juice until it really sings.

4. Mix half of the mayo with the brown crab meat, a squeeze more lemon juice and the cayenne pepper. Fold in the apple and spring onion. Taste for seasoning.

5. Bring a pan of salted water to the boil, add the asparagus and cook for 3–5 minutes, until just tender. For the last minute, drop in the samphire or sea purslane to blanch. Drain immediately and refresh in iced water.

6. Spread the brown crab meat and apple mayo out on a platter. Top with the drained potatoes, lettuce (leaves and heart), samphire (or sea purslane) if using, and asparagus, building up layers and seasoning as you go with salt, pepper and lemon juice. Top with the remaining mayo, followed by the white crab meat and soft herbs. Squeeze over a touch more lemon juice, sprinkle with cayenne pepper, if you like, and serve.

Cime di rapa
with roast peppers, chickpeas and oregano-baked feta

Serves 2 as a lunch or
starter, or 4 as a side

This is a lovely veggie lunch in its own right, or a satisfying summer side to go
with a barbecue. Cime di rapa is one of my all-time favourite greens – it has
wonderfully sweet and tender leaves and a satisfying bitterness. Translating
from Italian as 'turnip tops', it is also known as broccoli rabe or rapini, and is
great in pasta dishes, on pizza or as a blanched side (dressed with plenty of
lovely extra-virgin olive oil) for roasted or barbecued meats or fish.

400g mixed tomatoes,
   roughly chopped
1 garlic clove, crushed
50ml extra-virgin olive oil,
   plus extra for drizzling
pinch of dried chilli flakes
2 sprigs of rosemary
1 x 400g tin chickpeas,
   drained
2 romano peppers (or red bell
   peppers)
200g block of feta
1 tbsp fresh oregano leaves or
   1 tsp dried oregano
pinch of coriander seeds
bunch of cime di rapa (or
   chard or cavolo nero),
   bases trimmed and leaves
   separated from stalks
sea salt and freshly ground
   black pepper

1. Preheat the oven to 220°C/200°C fan/gas 7, or if you have one, fire up the wood oven.

2. Place the tomatoes in a roasting tray with the garlic, drizzle over half the olive oil and
sprinkle with the chilli flakes, then season well with salt and pepper. Throw the rosemary
in the tray and shake everything together, then roast in the oven for 15–20 minutes, until
the tomatoes have softened and are starting to char and caramelise. Add the drained
chickpeas, toss to combine, then return to the oven for another 10 minutes, until the
chickpeas are roasted and are starting to crisp up.

3. In the meantime, char the peppers over a gas flame, on a barbecue or under the grill, until
black and soft all over. Remove from the flame, place in a bowl and cover the bowl with cling
film. Allow to cool then wipe away the blackened skin with kitchen paper (don't worry if you
can't get it all off). Remove the seeds and cut the peppers lengthways into long, thin strips.

4. Put the feta on a piece of foil and drizzle over the rest of the olive oil. Scatter over the
oregano and coriander seeds and wrap the foil around the feta. Place in the oven or on the
embers of the barbecue and cook for 10 minutes, or until starting to turn golden and tender.

5. Bring a large saucepan of well salted water to the boil. Blanche the cime di rapa stalks in the
water for a couple of minutes, then add the leaves, cooking both the leaves and stalks for a
further minute, then drain. Remove the tomatoes and chickpeas from the oven, add the red
peppers and cime di rapa and toss through. Remove the rosemary sprigs and serve with the
baked feta on top and some extra olive oil drizzled over.

Quick wild garlic yoghurt flatbreads

Makes 2 medium or
4 small flatbreads

These speedy, four-ingredient flatbreads are perfect for a quick family lunch, a pre-dinner snack or on the side of the plate with a stew or curry to soak up the juices. They get a lot of airtime in our house, particularly in spring and summer when the wood oven is lit, but you can just as easily cook them on the barbecue too, or a hot griddle or frying pan. They have a moreish sour flavour (thanks to the yoghurt, which reacts with the self-raising flour to puff them up) and are just begging to be slathered with wild garlic pesto or butter while they're warm. Experiment with some of the other flavoured butters on pages 260–61 in autumn: try brushing them with the porcini butter and topping them with fried wild mushrooms and tarragon. Don't scrimp on the yoghurt with this one, full-fat is the way to go.

210g self-raising flour, plus extra for dusting
½ tsp salt
210g full-fat natural Greek yoghurt
1 tbsp extra-virgin olive oil
4 tbsp Wild Garlic Pesto (page 263), or 30g Wild Garlic Butter (page 260), melted

1. Put the flour and salt in a bowl and combine, then spoon in the yoghurt and olive oil. Give it a stir to combine everything, then, using oiled hands, bring the mix together into a soft dough. Briefly knead and scrape around the sides of the bowl to pick up any crumbs or scraggy bits, then allow the dough to sit in the bowl for a couple of minutes. While it's resting, either heat up a cast-iron skillet over a high heat or set your grill to its highest setting. For those with a wood-fired oven, these are also great cooked in there as you would the Sourdough Pizza on page 62.

2. Lightly dust the surface with flour and tip your dough out onto it. Split the dough into two or four, depending on whether you prefer 2 medium flatbreads or 4 small. Roll each piece of dough into a smooth ball and flatten each one on the surface with the palm of your hand, then roll it out using a rolling pin to your desired thickness and shape – I like these quite thick and pillowy (about 1cm thick).

3. If using a griddle pan, place your flatbread on it and cook over the highest heat for 3–5 minutes on each side, until golden and puffed, then remove from the pan and slather the top with the wild garlic pesto (loosened with the tablespoon of oil first) or butter while the bread's hot. If using the grill, place the flatbreads under the grill and grill for about 4 minutes, until puffed and golden, then brush the tops with the wild garlic butter or pesto and return to the grill for another minute or two. If you're cooking them in the wood oven, bake them as you would a pizza and brush them afterwards with the pesto or butter. Eat while still warm.

Waste not, want not allotment greens pasties
with cumin and za'atar

Makes 4

These rustic, meat-free pasties take their lead from Greek spanakopita and are perfect for picnics. They can be made with any combination of greens you like – it's all about using up whatever you've got lurking in your fridge. I came up with them after a meagre and rather random haul of greens from my allotment; a mix of spinach, chard and kale along with some window-box herbs. The cumin in the pastry adds a pleasing earthiness, while the za'atar brings a bright blast of herbaceousness. Serve with a simple tomato salad.

1 tbsp olive oil, plus extra for drizzling
1 red onion, thinly sliced
1 garlic clove, crushed
2 slices of preserved lemon, deseeded and finely chopped (shop-bought or see page 151), or grated zest of ½ unwaxed lemon
250g mixed greens (chard, spinach, watercress, kale) and soft herbs (lovage, parsley, dill, basil, tarragon)
1 tbsp lemon juice
75g Fresh Curd Cheese (page 254), ricotta or cream cheese
100g feta, camembert or mozzarella, diced or roughly chopped
1 tsp Fermented Green Chillies (page 146) or shop-bought pickled green chillies (optional)
nutmeg, for grating
1 egg, beaten
1 tbsp za'atar
sea salt and freshly ground black pepper

For the pastry
180g light spelt (or plain) flour, and 20g wholegrain rye flour (or 200g spelt or plain flour)
100g ricotta or full-fat natural yoghurt
1 tsp fine sea salt
½ tsp ground cumin
20ml olive oil
1–3 tbsp iced water

1. First, make the pastry. Place the flour(s), ricotta, salt and cumin in the bowl of a food processor and blitz until the mixture resembles breadcrumbs. Add the olive oil and the iced water, a tablespoon at a time, sprinkling it all across the crumb and blitzing between additions until the dough clumps together (you may not need all the water). Tip the dough out into a bowl and mould it into a ball. Wrap it in greaseproof paper (rather than cling film, which makes it sweat) and leave it to rest in the fridge for at least 30 minutes.

2. Meanwhile, heat the olive oil in a non-stick frying pan over a medium heat and slide in the onion, garlic and preserved lemon or lemon zest with a pinch of salt. Cook for about 5 minutes, until softened and fragrant but not colouring, then add the greens. Season with salt, pepper and a little lemon juice, put the lid on and let them wilt down for a couple of minutes. Remove from the heat and transfer the greens to a sieve to drain, pressing down on the greens to get rid of any excess moisture. Roughly chop them, then tip into a bowl, add the cheeses and fermented chillies (if using) and toss to combine, grating over a little fresh nutmeg and salt and pepper. Leave to cool.

3. Remove the pastry from the fridge, unwrap it and divide it into four equal balls, pressing the balls into discs. Dust the surface with flour and roll each ball out to a circle about 20cm in diameter and just a little thinner than a pound coin.

4. Preheat the oven to 200°C/180°C fan/gas 6 and line a baking sheet with baking parchment.

5. Fill each circle of pastry with the cooled greens and cheese mix, leaving a 2cm border around the edge of the filling, drizzle over a little more olive oil and fold the pastry around the filling to seal. It's up to you how you do this. You can either fold one half of pastry over the filling, seal to the other half and crimp like a pasty, or you can fold the edges up into the middle like an envelope or a little bag. Once formed, place on the lined baking sheet and chill for about 10 minutes, until firm.

6. Remove the pies from the fridge and brush them with the beaten egg. Scatter over the za'atar and bake in the oven for 35–40 minutes, until the pastry is crisp and golden.

Asparagus, pea and lovage croquettes
on a garden salad

Serves 4

Broken open, these crunchy, golden croquettes reveal all the joys of spring. Oozing with a vivid green filling of peas, asparagus and fragrant, slightly spicy lovage, they are at once indulgent and virtuous, and serious fun. Here I serve them with a dollop of sour cream but they are also lovely with the homemade mayo on page 35.

For the asparagus
420ml salted water
200g asparagus spears, trimmed
juice of 1 unwaxed lemon
1 tbsp olive oil, plus extra for drizzling

For the croquettes
150g frozen peas
25g lovage leaves and stems (or flat-leaf parsley), roughly chopped
40g butter
1 tsp crushed pink peppercorns
150g plain flour
1 tbsp white wine
50g Comté or Gruyère cheese, grated
30g feta, finely crumbled
grated zest of the lemon above
150g panko breadcrumbs
4 eggs
150ml vegetable oil, plus extra for greasing

For the garden salad
2 handfuls of mixed seasonal leaves (I love sorrel, spinach and nasturtium)
handful of lovage (or flat-leaf parsley), leaves picked
handful of pea shoots
2 spring onions, trimmed and finely chopped
juice of 2 lemons or 1 tbsp elderflower vinegar (page 154)
sea salt and freshly ground black pepper

1. First, cook the asparagus. Bring the water to the boil in a saucepan. Add the asparagus and cook for 3–5 minutes, or until tender. Remove with a slotted spoon and leave to cool slightly. Reserve the water in the pan. Cut away 2cm of the bottom of each spear, very thinly slice and set aside in a bowl – this will go into the croquettes. Place the remaining tips in a separate small bowl and toss with a little of the lemon juice and olive oil for the salad.

2. For the croquettes, bring the asparagus water back up to the boil and add the peas. Cook for 1 minute, then add the lovage. Cook for 30 seconds. Take out 50g of the peas with a slotted spoon, leaving the rest in the pan of cooking water. Put the reserved peas in the bowl with the sliced asparagus set aside for the croquettes. Pour the pan contents – the peas, lovage and cooking water – into the bowl of a food processor and blitz until you have a smooth green liquid – you're going to use this for the bechamel.

3. Heat a non-stick frying pan or skillet over a medium heat. Melt the butter in the pan with the crushed pink peppercorns. Gradually stir in 60g of the flour and cook for 2–3 minutes, stirring constantly, until the mixture has thickened and is smelling nutty. Reduce the heat slightly, add the wine and blitzed pea mixture and cook, stirring, for 5–6 minutes, or until you have a thickened, smooth sauce.

4. Stir in the cheeses, lemon zest, sliced asparagus and reserved peas, stirring until the cheeses have melted in nicely. Season well with salt. Pour onto a plate or tray, allow to cool and cover with cling film. Put it in the fridge to chill in the fridge for at least 2 hours (you could leave it overnight), until well set.

5. Once the mixture is set, grab it out of the fridge. It's time to 'crumb' (or, as the French call it, 'pané') and because this is quite a chunky, veg-packed mix, you need to give the croquettes a double coating. Gather two plates, a bowl and a flat tray covered with greaseproof paper. Place the remaining flour on one plate, the breadcrumbs on the other, and crack the eggs into the bowl. Lightly beat them, then, using oiled hands so that they don't stick to the mixture, pinch off about a ping-pong-ball-sized lump of mix, roll to form it into a croquette or cylindrical shape. Repeat with all the mixture to make 10–15 croquettes, placing them on the greaseproof paper. Chill for 15 minutes. Then, using one hand and keeping the other

To serve
150g sour cream
handful of edible flowers
   (chive, wild garlic or
   nasturtium work well)
   (optional)

clean for handling the rest of the mix, dip each croquette in the flour, tossing all over to coat, followed by the egg and breadcrumbs to coat completely. Repeat the process with the rest of the croquettes, until they are all coated, then repeat once more with each one and chill them all in the fridge for 10 minutes.

6. Heat the vegetable oil in a high-sided frying pan over a high heat until it's shimmering. Place a plate lined with kitchen paper next to the hob and shallow-fry the croquettes in batches for 3–5 minutes, turning them to produce an even golden crumb, until crisp. Drain on the kitchen paper and season with salt.

7. For the salad, place the seasonal leaves, lovage and pea shoots in a salad bowl. Add the reserved asparagus spears, spring onions and lemon juice or elderflower vinegar, drizzle with a little extra oil, season with salt and pepper and toss together lightly to combine.

8. Spread the sour cream on four plates and top with the croquettes. Pile on some salad and garnish with the edible flowers.

Wild garlic/harissa cheese straws

Yes, there are plenty of very good shop-bought cheese straws out there, but I wouldn't be encouraging you to make these unless I thought they were worth it. Your guests will be in awe when you breezily tell them that the cheese straws are 'homemade, darling', and some inevitably crumble in the oven, making for bonus chef's-perk nibbles. Once you get the hang of this method, the chances are you'll be busting these out at every given opportunity and trying to feed them to everyone you know. I've included seasonal tweaks – wild garlic pesto for spring, and spicy harissa for the rest of the time. You're welcome.

225g self-raising flour, plus extra for dusting
large pinch of cayenne or red chilli powder
½ tsp sea salt
nutmeg, for grating
150g cold unsalted butter, cut into small dice
1 tsp Dijon or English mustard
100g Cheddar, Gruyère or Comte, finely grated
1–3 tbsp iced water
2 tsp Wild Garlic Pesto (page 263) or rose harissa (I like the Belazu one)
1 egg, beaten with 1 tbsp milk

1. Sift the flour, cayenne or chilli powder and salt into a bowl and grate over some nutmeg, then stir. Add the butter and lightly rub it into the flour until the mixture has the consistency of coarse breadcrumbs – it's okay if there are a few smooth flakes of butter in there. Stir through the mustard and half the cheese, then sprinkle over a tablespoon of the iced water, bringing the mixture together with your hands, squeezing until you have a smooth dough. Add a little more water if needed. Roll it around the bowl to pick up any stray crumbs or scraggy bits – you can dampen your fingers to help with this if you need to. Mould it into a ball and flatten to a disc, wrap it in greaseproof paper and chill in the fridge for at least 30 minutes.

2. Preheat the oven to 200°C/180°C fan/gas 6 and line a couple of baking trays with baking parchment.

3. Unwrap the chilled pastry and roll it out on a surface lightly dusted with flour to a large rectangle just a little longer than the length of this cookbook and about 5mm thick. Fold it in half like a book, rotate it by 90 degrees and fold it in half again, then roll it out once more to a large rectangle, just bigger than the size of this book. Spread the pesto or harissa all over the pastry, then cover with the remaining cheese. Fold the pastry in half like a book again, so the filling is contained (don't worry if some escapes out the sides), and carefully roll it out lengthways to a rectangle about the size of this book, or 15 x 22cm. Place on a baking tray, trim the ragged edges with a sharp knife, brush with egg wash and chill in the fridge for 10 minutes, or until firm.

4. Cut the chilled pastry into strips – I think 13–15cm long and 1–1.5cm wide is just perfect. Either bake them as they are, or, if you're feeling a bit swish, very gingerly pinch the ends and twist them ever so slightly to reveal the filling and underside of the pastry. Brush any exposed pastry that wasn't coated in egg wash, place the straws on the lined baking trays and bake for 12–15 minutes, or until golden and oozy. Remove from the oven, allow to cool slightly, then serve still warm, or at room temperature.

TIP: the pastry can be a little delicate to work with, but it's easy to patch up, and if they crack a bit once you've shaped them, a little extra grated cheese on top before you bake them can cover a multitude of sins. Remember, the beauty of making cheese straws yourself is that they should be perfectly imperfect.

My go-to dips

When I was a kid, it was my job to hand round dips at my parents' dinner parties and I guess I've never grown out of it. Dips are an ideal way to start a meal because they can be made ahead, are communal and a great vehicle for lovely crunchy raw vegetables or the homemade spiced crackers on page 261.

Roast squash and Parmesan 'queso'

Serves 4–6

This dip is based on the creamy, cheesy Tex Mex dip 'queso', which is usually made with shedloads of orange American cheese. Here, I make it with roasted butternut squash with charred jalapeño, and serve it with spiced, popped pumpkin seeds for some much-needed crunch.

2 garlic cloves (skin on)
1 shallot (skin on)
500g butternut squash, peeled, deseeded and cut into chunks
pinch of cumin seeds
leaves from 2 sprigs of thyme
3 tbsp olive oil
1 red jalapeño chilli
2 tbsp water
1 tsp salt
1 tbsp lemon juice
1 tbsp cream cheese
50g Parmesan (or vegetarian hard cheese) grated
sea salt and freshly ground black pepper

For the toasted pumpkin seeds
1 tbsp rapeseed oil
1 tbsp pumpkin seeds
½ tsp cayenne pepper

To serve
1 tbsp Fermented Green Chillies (page 146)
1 tbsp coriander leaves
tortilla chips, to serve

1. Preheat the oven to 200°C/180°C fan/gas 6.

2. Put the garlic cloves, shallot and butternut squash chunks in a roasting tray and season with salt and pepper. Scatter over the cumin seeds, thyme leaves and pour over the olive oil, tossing to coat everything well. Cover the tray tightly with foil and roast in the oven for 40 minutes, or until a skewer can be inserted into the squash and meet no resistance.

3. Meanwhile, heat the rapeseed oil in a frying pan over a medium-high heat and fry the pumpkin seeds for a couple of minutes until popped. Transfer to a bowl and season with cayenne and salt.

4. Scorch the jalapeño chilli over a gas flame until softened and partially blackened, then rub off the skin with kitchen towel, split it lengthways and remove the seeds.

5. Remove the squash from the oven and allow it to cool slightly for a couple of minutes, then squeeze the shallots and garlic from their skins and transfer them to the bowl of a food processor. Add the roasted squash and all the remaining ingredients (including the scorched, deseeded jalapeño) and blitz on high for a few minutes until you have a creamy, smooth dip. Season to taste and adjust the acid and salt accordingly. Scrape into a bowl and top with the fermented chillies, toasted pumpkin seeds and coriander. Serve with tortilla chips.

Charred onion and sour cream

Serves 4–6

This is an update on one of my favourite classic dips – sour cream and onion – which did the rounds at the parties of my youth, scooped hungrily into mouths on the curve of a similarly flavoured Pringle. This is great with proper potato Kettle chips.

2 tbsp rapeseed oil
4 medium white onions, thinly sliced
big pinch of sea salt
pinch of caster sugar
2 tsp pomegranate molasses
200g sour cream
50g mayonnaise
3g chives, finely chopped, plus extra snipped chives, to garnish
flatbreads or raw veg, to serve

1. Heat the oil in a heavy-based frying pan over a medium-high heat. Add the sliced onions, salt and sugar and cook, stirring every now and then, for 10–15 minutes, until the onions are charred, softened and delicious. Stir in the pomegranate molasses and allow to cool.

2. In a bowl, combine the sour cream and mayonnaise. Slide in the cooled onions and chives and stir to combine. Taste for seasoning and leave to infuse in the fridge for a couple of hours to allow for the flavours to develop (if you have time). Serve in a bowl garnished with extra chives. Serve with flatbreads or raw veg for dipping.

Broad bean, mint and feta

Serves 4–6

Broad beans are one of the first things I successfully grew on my allotment, following in my father's footsteps as he was an avid fan of the 'broads'. They are very easy to grow. You simply bury the seeds (as early as February) and after a few months the green shoots start to emerge. I make this perky dip to celebrate my allotment haul, but it's also very agreeable made with frozen broad beans that have been blanched and peeled.

500g broad beans (fresh or frozen)
2 garlic cloves, peeled
small bunch of dill fronds, reserving some for garnish
small bunch of mint leaves reserving some for garnish
2 tbsp tahini
2 tbsp extra-virgin olive oil, plus extra for drizzling
1 slice of preserved lemon (shop-bought or see page 151), chopped
100g feta
juice of 1 lemon
sea salt and ground black pepper or pink peppercorns

1. Bring a saucepan of salted water to the boil, add the broad beans and garlic and cook for 3–5 minutes, until tender. Add the herbs at the last minute just to blanch them until wilted. Drain, reserving the cooking water. Peel the broad beans and discard the skins.

2. Place the beans, garlic, cooked herbs and all the remaining ingredients in the bowl of a food processor and blitz until smooth, adding a little of the cooking water to loosen, if needed. Taste for seasoning and acid and adjust accordingly. Transfer to a bowl and leave to infuse in the fridge for a couple of hours to allow for the flavours to develop (if you have time), then serve in a bowl, drizzled with more extra-virgin olive oil and garnished with the reserved herbs and pink peppercorns.

TIP: This also makes for a lovely breakfast topped with a crispy fried egg and some rose harissa.

Chermoula cannellini bean
with crispy fried artichokes

Serves 4–6

Chermoula is traditionally a North African marinade for fish, but the zippy combination of coriander, cumin, cayenne and paprika is a fantastic way to flavour this creamy cannellini bean dip. I make a big bowl of this and top it with crispy fried artichoke hearts, which are coated in semolina and fried until crunchy and golden. Try and use the good-quality jarred artichokes that come packed in oil as they have a really fantastic piquancy to them, which works nicely against the richness of the dip. It also happens to be vegan and gluten free.

flatbreads or crispbreads, to
serve

For the dip
2 tbsp olive oil
1 tsp cumin seeds
¼ tsp coriander seeds
2 garlic cloves, crushed
1 x 400g tin cannellini beans,
drained (reserving 1 tbsp
water from the tin)
½ tsp smoked sweet paprika
½ tsp cayenne pepper
2 slices of preserved lemon
(shop-bought or see page
151), chopped
1 tbsp lemon juice
2 tbsp chopped coriander
leaves
1 tbsp flat-leaf parsley leaves,
plus extra, finely chopped,
to garnish

For the crispy artichokes
2 tbsp olive oil
3 tbsp semolina flour
½ tsp cumin seeds, ground in
a pestle and mortar
pinch of sea salt, plus
extra to serve
200g olive oil-packed cooked
artichoke hearts

1. Heat the olive oil for the dip in a large frying pan over a medium heat. Add the cumin and coriander seeds and garlic and fry for a couple of minutes until aromatic, then tip in the cannellini beans and toss everything together over the heat for a minute. Remove from the heat and transfer to the bowl of a food processor with all of the remaining dip ingredients. Blitz to a smooth paste, adding a splash of water to thin until creamy. Taste for seasoning and adjust accordingly with more salt or acid, until it really sings. Leave to infuse in the fridge for a couple of hours to allow for the flavours to develop (if you have time).

2. To make the crispy artichokes, heat the olive oil in a non-stick frying pan over a medium-high heat. Put the semolina flour, ground cumin seeds and salt in a bowl and toss to combine. Drain the artichokes from their oil and one by one coat them in the semolina. Once fully coated, slide them into the oil and fry for a couple of minutes until golden and crisp, turning them to make sure they cook evenly. Remove with a slotted spoon to a plate lined with kitchen paper and scatter with a pinch of sea salt.

3. Serve the dip topped with the crispy artichokes, with flatbreads or crispbreads for scooping.

48

Brunch, Lunch and Bites

Beetroot, coconut and curry leaf

Serves 4–6

Beetroot and coconut is a flavour combination I discovered in Sri Lanka, where beetroot curry is a staple. This vegan and gluten-free dip takes its lead from this curry (page 56) and is a winner served with crisp seeded crackers (page 261) or crisps.

500g raw beetroots, scrubbed
olive oil, for drizzling
1 tbsp coconut cream
juice of ½ lime
½ tsp red chilli powder
100g drained tinned chickpeas
1 tbsp extra-virgin coconut oil
1 tsp black mustard seeds
handful of fresh curry leaves
sea salt and freshly ground
    black pepper
crushed pink peppercorns,
    to serve

1. Preheat the oven to 200°C/180°C fan/gas 6.

2. Toss the beetroots in a roasting tray with a drizzle of olive oil and season with salt and pepper. Cover the tray with foil and roast in the oven for 1¼ hours, or until a skewer inserted into a beetroot comes out with no resistance. Remove and leave to cool, then peel the beetroots and roughly chop.

3. Place the beetroot in a blender or food processor with the coconut cream, lime juice, chilli powder, chickpeas and big pinch of salt, and blitz until you have a smooth purée.

4. Heat the coconut oil in a frying pan over a medium-high heat. Add the mustard seeds and when they start to pop, add the curry leaves and fry until crispy but not browned.

5. Season the dip with salt and pepper to taste, scoop it into bowls and top with the mustard seed and curry leaf mix. Stir and serve warm or cold, garnished with pink peppercorns.

Ras el hanout roasted chickpea

Serves 4–6

A spoonful of ras el hanout transports you straight to the spice souk. A heady, fragrant North African spice blend composed of more than 30 ingredients, it translates from the Arabic to mean 'top of the shop'.
  Serve it with warm pitta bread or yoghurt flatbreads (page 39), or as part of a meze plate with Labneh (page 256), roasted veg and freekeh.

2 x 400g tins chickpeas, rinsed
1½ tbsp rapeseed oil
2 garlic cloves (skin on)
3 tsp ras el hanout
5 tbsp extra-virgin olive oil, plus
    extra for drizzling
2 tbsp tahini
140ml cold water
1 tsp salt
2 tbsp orange juice
1 slice of Preserved Orange (page
    151), chopped, or grated zest
    of ½ orange
2 tbsp coriander leaves, finely
    chopped, plus a few whole
    leaves, to garnish

1. Preheat the oven to 200°C/180°C fan/gas 6.

2. Dry the chickpeas with a clean tea towel and put them in a large roasting tray. Add the rapeseed oil, garlic cloves, ras el hanout and a pinch of salt and toss to coat. Roast in the oven for 25 minutes.

3. Leave to cool for a few minutes after roasting, then transfer to a food processor (squeezing the garlic out of the skins first), reserving a handful of chickpeas for garnishing. Add all the other ingredients and pulse until creamy, but still slightly chunky. Transfer to a bowl, top with the remaining chickpeas and drizzle over more olive oil for good measure. Scatter over the coriander leaves and serve.

Memorable
Mains

This is the place for golden-crusted pork chops rubbed with fennel, thyme and cayenne (page 52), and squishy fried aubergine with crispy roasted chickpeas and labneh (page 59); things you can rustle up without too much trouble. Giving care and attention to those important details, however – like frying those aubergines to a silken splendour – elevates the ordinary to the extraordinary, making these meals, well, you guessed it: memorable.

As well as making the most of seasonal veg in the Burrata and Roast Root Rave Salad (page 60) and Allotment Greens Orecchiette (page 68), this chapter is alive with some of my favourite international influences, and will bring some revelations, like how off-the-charts salmon tastes when cooked gently in a marinade of tahini and preserved lemon; what fresh curry leaves can bring to your kedgeree; and how an anchovy-laced béchamel can transform our old pal broccoli. You'll put your sourdough starter to good use again to make the Sourdough Pizza (page 62) – perfect for a pizza night with pals – and your vegan mates will love you for the delicious Sri Lankan-inspired vegan curry feast you cook up for them (pages 56–57).

Pork chops rubbed with fennel, thyme and cayenne

Serves 2–4

You can't beat a succulent pork chop for a simple, satisfying meal thrown together in a matter of minutes. This effortless fennel, thyme and cayenne rub flavours the meat beautifully, and is also good as a seasoning for homemade pork burgers, or a rub for chicken. Find chunky, best-end pork loin chops with a nice layer of fat for crisping up. Serve with a bright, sharp shaved salad such as the Shaved Fennel, Radish and Pickled Peach Salad on page 209 (pictured opposite).

1 tsp fennel seeds
1 tbsp sea salt
½ tsp cayenne pepper
1 tsp caster sugar
grated zest of ½ unwaxed
    lemon
leaves from 2 sprigs of thyme
4 skinless pork best-end loin
    chops (about 250g each)

1. Toast the fennel seeds in a dry frying pan over a medium-high heat for a minute or two, until fragrant and golden. Transfer to the bowl of a food processor, or a pestle and mortar, add the salt, cayenne pepper, sugar, lemon zest and thyme and blitz or pound in the mortar until finely ground.

2. Season the flesh of the pork chops with the salt mixture, rubbing it into the meat but avoiding the fat (you'll only need about half of the salt mixture – store the rest in an airtight container and use it for other meats, or chicken). Leave the pork chops to sit in the rub at room temperature for 1 hour (if you're leaving them for any longer than that, keep them in the fridge), then gently rinse them and pat dry with kitchen paper.

3. Heat a griddle or skillet over a medium-high heat, or prepare a barbecue.

4. Grill the pork for 5 minutes on each side (or a little longer if the chops are really thick), pressing the fat against the pan or barbecue grate to render some of it out and crisp it up. If you're cooking the pork in a pan, baste it in its own fat. Remove from the heat and leave to rest for 10 minutes, then serve with a salad.

Chilli, broccoli and anchovy gratin
with pan-fried red mullet

Red mullet is one of my absolute favourite fish. Aside from being crazy beautiful, its iridescent rose-red skin has a wonderful nuttiness, and its flesh a special sweetness that requires very little from the home cook, other than a quick pan-fry. This leaves you free to lavish the broccoli with a bit of attention, and really, it's never felt sexier than it does here, cloaked in this creamy, yet deeply umami béchamel made with anchovies, garlic and chilli. Rosemary adds an aromatic edge, while sourdough breadcrumbs and pumpkin seeds provide an irresistible crunch and tang. Once you've made and tasted this gratin, I'm convinced you'll want to use it as a side dish for all manner of things, as it's also superb with meat such as rare roast beef, or salt marsh lamb, and you could even make it into a meal in itself served with a little pasta or warmed white beans.

2 small-medium red mullet, cleaned, scaled and gutted
2 tbsp olive oil
thumb-sized strip of lemon zest, pith removed
leaves from 1 sprig of thyme

For the gratin
1 large head of broccoli, broken into florets, leaves set to one side, stalk trimmed and thinly sliced
2 tbsp olive oil, plus extra for greasing
grated zest and juice of ½ unwaxed lemon
1 red jalapeño chilli, deseeded and half sliced, half diced
5 good-quality anchovy fillets in oil, chopped
1 garlic clove, crushed
2 sprigs of rosemary, leaves picked and roughly chopped
2 tbsp plain flour
glass of white wine
300ml whole milk
75ml double cream
6 tbsp anchovy breadcrumbs (page 68)
2 tbsp pumpkin seeds
sea salt and freshly ground black pepper

1. Take the mullet out of the fridge, put it on a plate, season with a little salt and leave to reach room temperature.

2. Bring a large saucepan of well salted water to a rolling boil. Add the sliced broccoli stalk and boil for a couple of minutes, then add the florets and boil for another 3 minutes, until tender, adding the leaves for 30 seconds before you drain. Drain the broccoli and toss it into an oiled roasting tray. Squeeze over a little lemon juice and scatter over the sliced chilli.

3. Return the pan to the hob and heat the olive oil over a medium-high heat. Slide in the anchovies, garlic, lemon zest, rosemary and diced chilli and fry for a few minutes, until the anchovies have melted into the oil.

4. Preheat the oven to 200°C/180°C fan/gas 6.

5. Tip the flour into the oil and stir quickly to form a paste or roux, let it cook for a minute or two, until it smells nutty, then add the white wine and cook, stirring, until smooth. Now, slowly add the milk, whisking continuously, and cook for 5–8 minutes, until the sauce has thickened, breaking up any lumps with the whisk. Add the cream and whisk to incorporate. Season with salt and pepper and pour the sauce over the broccoli. Scatter over the anchovy breadcrumbs and pumpkin seeds. Bake in the oven for 20 minutes, until bubbling. Remove from the oven and leave to rest while you cook your mullet.

6. Heat the 2 tablespoons of olive oil in a non-stick frying pan over a medium-high heat and add the lemon zest and thyme leaves, stirring for a few seconds. Slide in the fish and pan-fry, basting them with the warm oil, for about 2 minutes on each side, until the flesh is opaque and cooked through. Serve with the gratin.

Sri Lankan-style beetroot curry

The beetroot curry from the second night of our Sri Lankan honeymoon has been obsessively recreated in our kitchen ever since. Deep purple, rich with coconut and the earthy, fragrant, smoky flavours of Sri Lankan curry powder, roasted to bring out extra flavour in the spices, it's a favourite meal for when vegetarian and vegan friends are round. Sri Lankan curries centre around seasonal vegetables cooked with black mustard seeds, fresh curry leaves, roasted curry powder and, crucially, fresh coconut: its luscious oil, reviving water and rich, luxurious cream, which are all added at different stages. A tin of good-quality coconut milk and dried curry leaves make perfectly reasonable substitutes for fresh, but it is worthwhile making the roasted curry powder (page 166). This dish is adaptable to almost any vegetable glut – swap beetroot for cauliflower, parsnip or courgette, even runner beans in summer. Serve with black or basmati rice, Tomato, Coconut and Spinach Dahl and Coconut Sambol (see opposite).

400g raw beetroot, peeled and cut into thick matchsticks
1 tsp fenugreek seeds
1 tsp red chilli powder
2 tsp sea salt
2 tbsp coconut oil
1 tsp black mustard seeds
handful of fresh curry leaves (or 2 tsp dried curry leaves)
½ red or white onion, thinly sliced
1 garlic clove, crushed
⅔ green chilli, thinly sliced
1 tomato, finely chopped
1 tbsp Roasted Curry Powder (page 166)
200ml coconut milk
cooked black or basmati rice, to serve

1. Put the beetroot in a bowl with the fenugreek, chilli powder and 1 teaspoon of the salt and mix by hand.

2. Heat a non-stick frying pan or wok (with a lid to hand) over a medium-high heat. Add the coconut oil and black mustard seeds and fry until they start to sizzle and spit, then add the curry leaves, swirling them around the pan with a wooden spoon to infuse the oil. Now, slide in the onion, garlic, green chilli and the remaining salt. Cook, stirring, for a few minutes, until the onion is starting to colour, then add the beetroot and fry for a couple of minutes, stirring to combine it with the contents of the pan.

3. Add the tomato and roasted curry powder and fry for a couple of minutes, until the tomato is starting to break down and release its juice, then add the coconut milk, stirring to combine. Cover and cook, stirring every now and then, for 10–15 minutes, until the beetroot is tender and cooked through and the curry is glossy and reduced. Remove from the heat and serve with rice and yoghurt flatbreads (page 39), spinach dahl and coconut sambol on the opposite page.

Tomato, coconut and spinach dahl

Serves 4

Frugal, nourishing and brilliantly flavourful, this dahl uses two kinds of lentil for added texture, and is vegan, so everyone can enjoy it. Before I started making my own, I always imagined dahl took hours and hours to cook, but if you soak the lentils ahead, it's actually so quick to make. It's perfect with beetroot curry (opposite) but is also great with a fried egg, roasted cauliflower or broccoli, some fried smoked tofu or aubergine on top.

100g split red lentils
50g split yellow or green lentils
1 tsp salt, plus a pinch
1 tbsp ground turmeric
1 tbsp coconut oil
1 tsp black mustard seeds
handful of fresh curry leaves (or 2 tsp dried curry leaves)
½ red onion, diced
½ tsp cumin seeds
1 garlic clove, crushed
2 tomatoes, cut into wedges
5 tbsp creamy coconut milk (fresh or tinned)
2 handfuls of baby spinach leaves
sea salt and freshly ground black pepper

1. Soak the lentils together in a bowl of water for a couple of hours, then rinse, drain in a sieve and place in a saucepan. Cover with cold water (about a finger's tip above the level of the lentils), add the teaspoon of salt and the ground turmeric and bring to the boil. Simmer for 10–15 minutes, until tender but still holding their shape.

2. Meanwhile, melt the coconut oil in a frying pan or wok over a medium-high heat. Add the mustard seeds and fry until they start to sizzle and pop, then add the curry leaves, onion, cumin, garlic and pinch of salt and cook for a few more minutes, until the onion starts to colour. Add the tomatoes and cook, stirring, for about 5 minutes, until the tomatoes have collapsed and given up their juice.

3. Add 4 tablespoons of the creamy coconut milk and spinach to the dahl and simmer for another 3 minutes, then pour in the contents of the tomato pan, along with the final tablespoon of coconut milk. Stir, taste, season with salt and pepper and serve or keep warm by covering with a tea towel.

Coconut sambol

Serves 2–4

Heaped on the side of the plate and dusted onto every mouthful of curry, this spicy condiment, based on Sri Lankan pol sambol, is at once fiery, tangy with lime juice and cooling with creamy coconut. It can be made ahead and kept in the fridge.

½ red chilli, deseeded and finely chopped
½ red onion, finely chopped
¼ tsp sea salt
1 tsp freshly ground black pepper
pinch of dried chilli flakes
4 tbsp desiccated coconut or fresh coconut
juice of 1 lime

1. In a pestle and mortar, grind the chilli, red onion, salt, pepper and dried chilli flakes together until well combined and the onion releases some juice.

2. Add the coconut and grind again, then add the lime juice and mix well. Taste and season further with salt and lime if needed. Store in the fridge.

Squishy aubergine, crispy chickpea and broccoli salad
with homemade ferments

Serves 2

Something magical happens when salted aubergine is fried in plenty of oil – the aubergine at once sucks it up, creating a silken, creamy inside, while the outside of the flesh caramelises and browns, making something deeply savoury and utterly addictive. Paired with nutty roasted broccoli, cooling labneh and crispy spiced chickpeas, with an array of homemade ferments to cut through the richness of the aubergine and tahini dressing, this salad has it all. The inspiration for this dish came from one of my favourite local restaurants, The Good Egg in Stoke Newington, which specialises in Israeli food and serves 'Sabih' – a popular Israeli sandwich of fried aubergines and boiled eggs stuffed into pitta bread. Add boiled eggs to this to beef it up, or lose the labneh to keep it vegan.

1 large aubergine, cut into
    1.5-cm slices
1 tsp sea salt flakes
1 x 400g tin chickpeas, drained
½ head of broccoli, broken into
    florets, including leaves
3 tbsp rapeseed, olive or
    vegetable oil
pinch of dried chilli flakes
1 tsp smoked sweet paprika
handful of flat-leaf parsley leaves
handful of dill fronds
handful of mint leaves
1 tsp sumac
150g Labneh (page 256)
sea salt and freshly ground
    black pepper

For the dressing
20g preserved lemon, deseeded
    (shop-bought or see page 151)
1 tbsp lemon juice
4 tbsp water
2 tbsp olive oil
1 tsp honey
1 tsp salt
1 garlic clove
½ tsp cumin seeds or ground
    cumin
1 tbsp good-quality tahini

To serve
1 tbsp Fermented Turnips (page
    147), drained
1 tbsp Pink Pickled Onions
    (page 180), drained
1 tbsp Fermented Green
    Chillies (page 146), drained
2 toasted pitta breads

1. Place the aubergine slices in a sieve over the sink or a bowl and scatter the sea salt all over. Leave it to sit and drain the moisture from the aubergine for about 30 minutes.

2. Preheat the oven to 200°C/180°C fan/gas 6. Dry the chickpeas with a clean tea towel and tip them into a roasting tray. Add the broccoli, broccoli leaves, 1 tablespoon of the oil, chilli flakes, smoked paprika and some salt and pepper and toss together. Roast in the oven for 25–30 minutes, until the chickpeas are really crispy and the broccoli is crispy at the edges but tender when cut into.

3. Meanwhile, wipe off any excess water from the aubergine with kitchen paper, then heat the remaining 2 tablespoons of oil in a heavy-based frying pan or skillet over a medium-high heat. Once the oil is shimmering hot, add the aubergine slices and fry for 4–5 minutes on each side, until nicely browned on the outside and squishy in the middle. You may need to add a little more oil as you go. Transfer to a plate lined with kitchen paper and set aside.

4. To make the dressing, put all the ingredients into the bowl of a food processor and blitz until you have a loose but emulsified dressing.

5. Toss the roasted chickpeas and broccoli in a bowl with half the fresh herbs and the sumac. Season with salt and pepper and coat with a little of the dressing. Spread the labneh over a serving platter and top with the salad, then strew the fried aubergine, remaining herbs and ferments over the top. Serve with fluffy toasted pitta and the dressing on the side.

Burrata and roast root rave salad
with harissa and walnut salsa

Serves 4 as a starter,
6 as a side

This is a showstopper of a salad, perfect as a sharing platter and a great way to make a fuss of the meat-free people in your life. People always swoon for burrata, and here it lends its bursting creamy splendour to a medley of root veg, roasted until tender and caramelised and piled atop mounds of fregola (a spherical, toasted Sardinian pasta) and lentils. With a punchy salsa to spoon over the whole lot, and the burrata to tear into, it's an all-star line up of spice, sweetness and umami. If you're making it for veggies, sub the anchovies for capers or black olives.

150g puy lentils
200g fregola or giant couscous
2 large beetroots, scrubbed
olive oil, for drizzling
300g organic carrots, scrubbed
and halved lengthways
100g parsnips, scrubbed and
halved lengthways
4 banana shallots, peeled and
halved lengthways
4 slices of Preserved Orange
(page 151) or zest of 1 orange
1 tsp cumin seeds
1 tsp coriander seeds
pinch of dried chilli flakes
1 tbsp honey or maple syrup
leaves of 3 heads of chicory
2 large burrata
handful of parsley and coriander
sea salt and black pepper

For the pickled beetroot
100ml cider vinegar
5g sea salt
30g caster sugar
½ tsp each fennel, mustard
and coriander seeds
½ cinnamon stick
2 candy-striped beetroots,
peeled and thinly sliced
½ red chilli, thinly sliced
(optional)

For the walnut salsa
50g walnuts
40g tinned anchovy fillets
1 tbsp rose harissa (I love the
Belazu one)
1 tbsp flat-leaf parsley leaves
1 tbsp coriander leaves
1 tbsp orange juice
1 tbsp lemon juice
100ml olive oil

1. Cook the lentils in salted water, according to packet instructions, and the fregola separately (also in salted water) until al dente, drain both and transfer to a bowl. Pour in 1 teaspoon of olive oil and fork it through so that they don't stick together.

2. Now pickle the beetroot. Combine the vinegar, 100ml water, salt, sugar and spices (except the chilli) in a non-reactive pan and bring to the boil. Place the beetroot slices and chilli (if using) in a clean heatproof jar or jug and pour over the pickling liquor. Leave to steep.

3. Preheat the oven to 200°C/180°C fan/gas 6. Take a piece of foil big enough to wrap the beetroots and place the whole beetroots on it. Drizzle with a little olive oil and season. Wrap the beetroot in the foil, leaving a little air between them, and place on a baking tray. In a roasting tray, combine the carrots, parsnips, shallots and preserved orange or zest, pour over a little olive oil to coat, then scatter over the spices and drizzle over the honey or maple syrup. Season well with salt, give everything a good toss, then put that tray and the foiled beetroot tray in the oven, with the beetroot tray on the top rack.

4. Check the parsnips and carrots after 35 minutes. They should be browned and tender with crispy edges, but not dry, while the shallots should be nicely caramelised and sticky. When done, remove the tray from the oven. Roast the beetroots for 1 hour in total, until they are tender all the way through (use a skewer to check). Remove from the oven and leave until cool enough to handle, then use some kitchen paper or the back of a spoon to peel away the skin, and slice them into wedges.

5. To make the salsa, blitz the walnuts in a food processor briefly until coarsely chopped, then add the anchovies, harissa and herbs and blitz again to combine. Add the the orange juice, lemon juice and the olive oil. Blitz again, then taste and season with salt to taste.

6. To assemble the salad, add the chicory and herbs to the bowl of lentils and fregola, season with salt and pepper and add a splash of the beetroot pickling liquor and a little olive oil. Toss to coat, then arrange on a sharing platter. Top with the roast beetroots, carrots, shallots, parsnips and burrata, then dress with the salsa. Drain the beetroot from the pickling juice (reserving the juice for another use, see Rhubarb Poaching Liquor Roast Parsnips on page 197). Scatter over the pickled beetroot and serve with extra salsa on the side.

Sourdough pizza

**Makes 2 large or
4 small pizzas**

The process below may seem lengthy, but slow fermentation is great for developing flavour and it also changes the structure of the proteins, making them more digestible, thanks to the organic acids produced. It makes the nutrients more readily available, too, so this sourdough pizza is more nourishing than usual pizza, and – crucially – more delish!

200g '00' flour, plus extra
   for dusting
150g organic strong white
   bread flour
6g fine sea salt
45g lively or refreshed
   Sourdough Starter (page
   23) (or 7g fast-action
   dry yeast)
245ml lukewarm water
1 tsp olive oil, plus extra for
   greasing

Memorable Mains

1. Put the flours and salt in a large bowl and stir to combine. Make a well in the middle and add in your starter and the water. Use a butter knife or wooden spoon to stir until you have a combined, scraggy dough. Leave to rest for 30–40 minutes. This process is known as autolyse. Don't be tempted to knead before you've let the dough rest; you will be rewarded for your hands-off approach with a more manageable dough.

2. Once rested, it's time to work the dough. It's going to be sticky, so I like to keep it all in the bowl I mixed it in. Using moistened or oiled fingers or a moistened silicone spatula, dig under the dough and stretch and pull the edge up over the ball. Turn the bowl clockwise and repeat the lifting, stretching and pulling about 15–20 times. Keep going until you have a ball, then coat with a little oil, cover the bowl with cling film and chill in the fridge for 12–20 hours.

3. A couple of hours before you want to bake your pizza dust your surface with plenty of flour, scrape your dough onto the surface and leave it to come up to room temperature for 15 minutes. Using a sharp knife (or dough scraper, if you have one), divide the dough into two or four, depending on whether you prefer two medium pizzas or four small – it will be super-stretchy and sticky but this is good! Line a tray with some baking parchment and brush with a little oil, then scatter over some flour, ready to prove your dough on.

4. Now it's time to shape your dough. One at a time, on your surface, gently roll your dough along the surface and over itself and into a ball, then cup your hand over it, so your fingers are lightly touching the surface, and, as if you are drawing circles, move your hand quickly in a circular motion to form a neat ball. Lift it onto the lined tray and dust with some more flour. Repeat with the other piece/pieces of dough, dust them all well with flour and cover them with a clean tea towel, then leave to prove for 2–3 hours (how long will depend on the time of year and how warm your kitchen is), until puffed and visibly doubled in size. You can get your toppings ready while the dough proves.

5. Halfway through the proving time, preheat your oven to its highest setting, or get your wood-fired oven really hot. Place a flat baking tray, pizza stone or upside down cast iron skillet in the oven to heat up, and prepare a couple of sheets of foil bigger than your finished pizzas (or a pizza peel, if you have one) with a scattering of flour.

6. After the final prove (your balls will have spread out into flatter circles but that's fine) flatten each ball and use your hands to push and spread them out into a circle. Once you have

Recipe continues over the page

a loose circular shape, use the palm of one hand in the middle of the dough to rotate it clockwise, while you use your other hand to gently stretch it out and flatten it around the edges to form a larger circle or your desired shape and thickness. Place each base onto a sheet of foil on a flat tray (or your pizza peel) and top with your desired toppings. I've included a method below for baking the pizza in a conventional oven in a way that mimics the heat of a pizza oven – give it a whirl, or, if you don't have a combined oven and grill, bake at your oven's highest setting for 10–12 minutes.

IF USING A WOOD-FIRED OVEN: Once your oven is really hot, make sure any logs are pushed right to the back, leaving space to cook the pizza. Transfer the topped pizza to the oven with a pizza peel, nudging it off the peel and onto the oven base. Cook for 3–5 minutes, rotating the pizza if necessary, until the base is puffed and charring and the topping is cooked. Repeat with the other bases.

IF USING A FAN OVEN: Turn your oven onto the highest grill setting (the combination of oven heat and grill setting mimic the pizza oven). Slide the foil with the topped pizza onto the preheated baking tray or stone. Close the door by all but 1cm and grill for 3–4 minutes, until puffed. Close the door fully, switch the oven back to its highest setting and bake for 10–12 minutes, until the crust is puffed and golden and the cheese is melted. Repeat with the other bases.

Suggested toppings

Walnut, Taleggio and radicchio bianco

2 tbsp Gorgonzola
a few leaves of radicchio or
    chicory
handful of walnuts
20g Taleggio cheese, sliced
1 tsp thyme leaves
olive oil, for drizzling

Spread the Gorgonzola onto the pizza base and scatter over the bitter leaves. Dot with the walnuts and Taleggio, scatter over the thyme and drizzle with olive oil.

Courgette and courgette flowers bianco

2 tbsp ricotta or Fresh Curd
    Cheese (page 254)
1 tsp grated unwaxed lemon
    zest
pinch of crushed pink
    peppercorns
1 medium courgette, sliced, or
    2 baby courgettes, halved
    lengthways
courgette flowers (optional)
½ ball mozzarella, sliced
olive oil, for drizzling

Mix the ricotta in a bowl with the lemon zest and pink peppercorns and spread the mixture onto the pizza base. Top with the courgettes, courgette flowers (if using) and mozzarella and drizzle with a little olive oil.

Cherry tomato, anchovies and capers

leaves from 2 sprigs of
   rosemary
1 tbsp capers
½ red chilli, thinly sliced
a little olive oil
2 tbsp Cherry Tomato Sauce
   (see below)
4 good-quality tinned anchovy
   fillets

For the cherry tomato sauce
2 tbsp olive oil
1 red onion, thinly sliced
leaves from 1 sprig of thyme
1 garlic clove, thinly sliced
pinch of salt
300g cherry tomatoes
   (preferably Datterini),
   halved
2 tsp red wine vinegar
handful of basil leaves
sea salt and freshly ground
   black pepper

1. First, make the sauce. Heat the olive oil in a heavy-based frying pan over a medium heat. Add the onion, thyme, garlic and salt and cook for 5–8 minutes, until the onion is softened and aromatic. Add the halved cherry tomatoes, vinegar and basil and cook, stirring, for another 10–15 minutes, until the tomatoes have collapsed and made a lovely silky sauce. Season with salt and pepper and stir.

2. Toss the rosemary, capers and chilli in the olive oil. Spread the cherry tomato sauce onto the pizza base and top with the anchovies, then scatter over the rosemary, chilli and capers. If you have any tomato sauce left, refrigerate it and keep it for toast or to stir through white beans.

Garlic mushrooms, chard and Italian sausage

1 tbsp olive oil, plus extra for
   drizzling
1 large field mushroom or
   2 chestnut mushrooms,
   sliced
½ garlic clove, finely chopped
   or crushed
big pinch of salt
2 tbsp Cherry Tomato Sauce
   (see above)
2 chard leaves
½ fresh Italian sausage, cut
   into 3-cm slices
1 tbsp Fermented Green
   Chillies (page 146)
shaved pecorino, to serve

1. Heat the olive oil in a frying pan over a medium-high heat, add the sliced mushroom, garlic and salt and fry briefly until they are browning and any liquid has evaporated.

2. Spread the tomato sauce onto the pizza base and top with the mushrooms, chard leaves, sliced sausage and fermented green chillies. Drizzle with olive oil and cook, then shave over some pecorino.

Kedgeree
with curry leaf oil

Serves 4–6

This is by no means the last word on kedgeree, the gently spiced rice and fish dish famously popularised in the UK by colonials returning from the British Raj – but it's my version, and I go back to it time and time again. This iteration is inspired in part by the flavours of Sri Lankan curries, with the white fish element being gently cooked in oil spiced with fresh curry and bay leaves and black mustard seeds. The resulting aromatic oil is then stirred through the rice along with the fish, parsley, dill and pink pickled onion for crunch and piquancy. It's at once fragrant, hearty and somehow delicate, and while it's known as a breakfast or brunch dish, it makes a sensational, bolstering midweek supper too. I hope you love it as much as I do. If you can, use the roasted curry powder from page 166 to stir through the rice.

300g hake fillet (you could also use pollock or cod)
4 eggs
3 tbsp coconut, rapeseed or vegetable oil, plus extra for greasing
1 tsp black mustard seeds
1 tsp fresh curry leaves
1 tbsp Roasted Curry Powder (page 166) or korma curry powder, plus 2 tsp for the cooked rice
1 tsp red chilli powder
1½ tsp ground turmeric
1 onion, thinly sliced
1 bay leaf
30g butter
100g frozen peas
1 tsp caster sugar
1 tbsp Pink Pickled Onions (page 180)
juice of 1 lemon
handful of 50/50 mix of dill fronds and flat-leaf parsley leaves, finely chopped
sea salt and freshly ground black pepper

For the rice
250g basmati rice
1 tsp sea salt
2 green cardamom pods, bruised
450ml boiling water
2 smoked mackerel fillets, skinned

1. Preheat the oven to 200°C/180°C fan/gas 6 and soak the rice in a bowl of cold water.

2. Remove the hake from the fridge, scatter the flesh with 1 teaspoon of sea salt and leave to sit for 20 minutes to come to room temperature.

3. Bring a saucepan of water to the boil. Lower the eggs into it and boil for 7 minutes, then drain and cool under cold running water. Gently tap the shell of each egg all over on a hard surface and peel. Set aside.

4. Heat the oil in a frying pan over a high heat. Once shimmering, add the mustard seeds and when they start to crackle, add the curry leaves. Stir to infuse the oil with the curry leaves and remove from the heat. Stir in the tablespoon of roasted curry powder, the chilli powder and a teaspoon of the turmeric. Allow to cool slightly.

5. Lay a sheet of foil big enough to generously wrap the fish in a roasting tray and lightly grease it with oil. Place the fish skin side down in the foil, top with the sliced onion and bay leaf and cover with the curry oil. Use your hands to combine everything, making sure the fish flesh and onion are well coated in the curry oil. Seal the foil and roast in the oven for 15 minutes.

6. Meanwhile, cook the rice. Drain the rice, rinse it under cold running water, then place it in a saucepan with the salt and cardamom and stir. Pour over the boiling water, bring to the boil and boil uncovered for 4 minutes without stirring, then turn off the heat, cover the pan with a clean, wet tea towel followed by a lid or plate. Leave to steam for 15 minutes. After 10 minutes, flake the mackerel over the rice and replace the lid (no need for the towel).

7. After 15 minutes, take the hake out of the oven, open the foil, add the butter and return to the oven, with the foil open, for another 5 minutes.

8. Cook the peas in a saucepan of ample boiling water, adding the sugar to the water, for 5–10 minutes until tender, then drain.

9. Transfer the rice and mackerel to a large bowl and drain the juices and curry oil from the hake into the bowl with the rice, discarding the bay leaf. Flake the fish from its skin and into the bowl, discarding the skin. Slide in the peas, pickled onions, lemon juice and most of the herbs. Sprinkle over the remaining turmeric and roasted curry powder, stir well to combine and season to taste.

10. Slice the eggs in half and divide the kedgeree among plates, topping with the eggs and the remaining dill and parsley.

Allotment greens orecchiette
with anchovy breadcrumbs

I am still an allotment novice, but I've managed to grow kale, chard, spinach and broad beans most consistently and plentifully. Growing your own is one thing, but harvesting is quite another – I'm in constant competition with the wildlife of the allotment, and more often than not, find myself gathering half-eaten leaves and scraps of greens that have also been sustenance for slugs, snails and birds.

I don't mind sharing, however, and when you've grown something from nothing, it instils a real sense of how precious even half a leaf can be, plus, once it's wilted, no one can ever tell. Like the pasties on page 40, this recipe is an ideal vehicle for any herbs and greens you might have languishing in the fridge. The anchovy breadcrumbs can be made in advance and kept in an airtight jar.

200g mixed greens (I like to use a mixture of kale/cavolo nero, chard and spinach)
small bunch of flat-leaf parsley, leaves and stems separated, stems finely chopped
handful of tarragon leaves
100g broad beans, blanched and shelled
1 tbsp olive oil
1 red chilli, deseeded and diced
2 garlic cloves, crushed
4 good-quality tinned anchovy fillets
1 large tomato, finely chopped
200g orecchiette
4 tbsp whey from Fresh Curd Cheese recipe on page 254 (or 1 tbsp lemon juice)
4 tbsp ricotta or Fresh Curd Cheese (page 254)
lemon juice, to taste
sea salt and freshly ground black pepper

For the anchovy breadcrumbs
2 slices of stale sourdough bread
2 tbsp olive oil
4 good-quality tinned anchovy fillets
grated zest of ½ unwaxed lemon

1. To make the anchovy breadcrumbs, blitz the bread in a food processor to form breadcrumbs. Heat the olive oil in a non-stick frying pan over a medium heat. Add the anchovies and fry for 30 seconds–1 minute, stirring, until they melt. Tip in the crumbs and lemon zest and toast for 5–6 minutes, shaking the pan and stirring, until the crumbs are crispy, golden and dry. Set aside.

2. Bring a large saucepan of salted water to a rolling boil. Blanch the greens, including the parsley and tarragon leaves, for under 1 minute, until just wilted, then use a spider or tongs to transfer to a sieve (keeping the water for the broad beans and pasta). Squeeze out the excess water, then roughly chop and set aside. Blanch the broad beans in the same water for 2 minutes, then drain and plunge into iced water to cool. Drain again and squeeze the broad beans from their skins. Set aside.

3. Heat the olive oil in a large non-stick frying pan over a medium heat. Add the parsley stems, chilli, garlic and anchovies and fry for 3–5 minutes, until the anchovies have melted and the garlic is turning golden, then add the tomato and cook for 3 minutes, until it has collapsed into the sauce. Remove from the heat briefly while you cook the pasta.

4. Cook the pasta in the water you used for the greens until al dente (about 2 minutes less than the packet instructions). Drain the pasta, retaining a cup of the cooking water.

5. Toss the greens and broad beans into the anchovy and garlic pan and season with salt and pepper and a squeeze of lemon juice. Toss in the pasta and a good slosh (about half a cup) of the pasta water, then add the whey (or lemon) and shake the pan, stirring to combine the ingredients and emulsify the contents with the oil and pasta water. Lightly fold the ricotta through the pasta. Divide between warm plates and top with the anchovy breadcrumbs.

TIP: To make it veggie, omit the anchovies from both the pasta and the crumb, replacing them in the pasta with 1 tablespoon of capers and in the crumb with the leaves from 1 sprig of thyme.

Hake with white beans, fennel and courgettes
with harissa mayo

Serves 2

Hake, an under-appreciated fish, has succulent white flesh and skin that crisps up nicely in the pan. I discovered its brilliance on a work trip to Galicia in northern Spain, where it's prized for its pearly meat. The Galicians know a thing or two about seafood, having arguably some of the most diverse and abundant marine life in Europe, and they know it's a fish that stands up well to robust flavours. This dish unites the fish with a gently yielding braise of softened fennel, courgettes and white beans with a garlic-laden, harissa-spiked aioli. The aioli is best made at least three hours before serving, so that the flavours can really develop, but if time's short you can use shop-bought mayonnaise instead, with added garlic and harissa.

4 tbsp extra-virgin olive oil
pinch of fennel seeds
½ medium fennel bulb, thinly
    sliced widthways (reserve
    any fronds)
pinch of dried chilli flakes
handful of cherry tomatoes,
    halved
1 garlic clove, finely chopped
2 medium courgettes (or 1
    large), sliced (about the
    thickness of a pound coin)
100ml white wine or sherry
1 tbsp lemon juice
1 x 400g tin cannellini beans
handful of dill fronds, chopped
leaves from 1 sprig of thyme
sea salt and freshly ground
    black pepper

For the aioli (optional)
1 egg, plus 1 egg yolk
½ tsp salt
1 tbsp Dijon mustard
3 garlic cloves
juice of ½ lemon
2 tbsp extra-virgin olive oil
300ml vegetable or
    sunflower oil
1 tbsp cold water
1 tbsp harissa

1. First, make the aioli (if using). Put the egg and egg yolk, salt, mustard, garlic and lemon juice in a food processor and blitz until well emulsified. With the blades still turning, very, very slowly drip in the 2 tablespoons of extra-virgin olive oil, a drop at a time, until the oil starts to emulsify and the mixture looks smooth and creamy. Once the olive oil is incorporated, very slowly start to drip in the vegetable or sunflower oil, blitzing the whole time, until it starts to thicken. Once you've added about half the oil and it's looking thick and creamy, increase the pouring of the oil to a steady stream – this could take 10–15 minutes. If it becomes too thick and stiff to work at any point, just add a few drops of water or a squeeze of lemon juice and blitz again.

2. Once the mayonnaise is plump and emulsified, add 1 tablespoon water and blitz again – this will lighten the aioli and make it creamier. Scrape out into a bowl and stir through the harissa, transfer to a container and chill in the fridge for at least 3 hours.

3. Take the fish out of the fridge 20 minutes before you want to cook it to let it come to room temperature and season the flesh well with sea salt. Preheat the oven to 200°C/180°C fan/gas 6.

4. Heat the 4 tablespoons of olive oil in a high-sided non-stick frying pan or skillet over a medium-high heat. Add the fennel seeds, sliced fennel and chilli flakes with a pinch of salt and cook for 5 minutes, until softened and fragrant, then add the cherry tomatoes, garlic and courgettes, season with salt and pepper and cook for a few more minutes, until softened but not browned. Pour in the wine, lemon juice and a cup of water, reduce the heat to low-medium and simmer for 15–20 minutes, until the tomatoes and courgettes are collapsing and the fennel is soft. Stir through the drained beans and chopped herbs and keep warm while you cook the hake.

For the fish

2 x hake or sea bass fillets, skin on (about 120g each) (cod and pollock also work well)
2 tbsp olive oil
20g butter
½ lemon, for squeezing

To serve

4 tbsp aioli (or good-quality mayonnaise mixed with 1 crushed garlic clove and 1 tbsp harissa)
lemon wedges

5. Heat the olive oil for the fish in an ovenproof non-stick frying pan over a low-medium heat and place the fish fillets, skin side down in the pan. Season the flesh side of the fillets with pepper. Cook gently for 6–8 minutes, until the skin is crispy (it might spit, so it's best to wear an apron), then add the butter and a squeeze of lemon juice and baste the flesh of the fish with the warm lemony butter. Transfer the pan to the oven and roast the fish for about 4 minutes, or until opaque and cooked through.

6. Divide the vegetable and bean braise between plates and top with the hake. Spoon over the aioli and serve with lemon wedges.

TIP: If the aioli splits, do not despair. Just transfer it to a bowl, clean the food processor and add a tablespoon of hot water from the tap, then repeat the dripping and blitzing with the broken mixture – it will come together. If this also fails, do not give up! Remove the broken mixture and clean the food processor, then try again with an extra egg yolk, blitzing and dripping the broken mixture in until it comes together.

Tahini roast salmon
with sugar snap gremolata

Serves 4–6

Tahini – gorgeously silken ground sesame paste – is an ingredient that has found its way firmly into my pantry, thanks to chefs like Yotam Ottolenghi who have demystified its incredible versatility. Here it's mixed with preserved lemon and used to marinade salmon, ensuring fish that is sublimely soft and buttery, with gorgeous nutty notes. The raw sugar snap gremolata is a sweet, crunchy revelation. To make a scaled-down midweek version, use two salmon fillets (about 140g each) instead, use less of the marinade and roast the fillets for 15–20 minutes. Serve with the Mujadara with Brown Butter-basted Radishes on page 74.

1 x 800g large fillet (or half a side) super-fresh, preferably organic salmon
oil, for greasing

For the marinade
1 tsp cumin seeds
15g preserved lemon rind, after flesh and pith removed (page 151)
3 tbsp olive oil
1 garlic clove
juice of ½ lemon
pinch of salt
pinch of white pepper
2 tsp honey
3 tbsp good-quality tahini (I like Belazu), at room temperature
2 tbsp warm water

For the sugar snap gremolata
8 sugar snap peas, washed and thinly sliced on the diagonal
1 spring onion, thinly sliced on the diagonal with the green ends too
1 thick, thumb-sized pared strip of unwaxed lemon zest, pith scraped off and zest very thinly sliced
½ lemon, for squeezing

1. Dry toast the cumin seeds in a frying pan until golden and fragrant. Reserve a pinch of them for the gremolata and put the rest in a food processor, along with the other marinade ingredients, except the tahini and water. Blitz to a paste, then add the tahini and water and blitz again to emulsify, adding more water if necessary – the marinade should be a little thicker than pouring cream. You can make it a few hours in advance.

2. Take the salmon out of the fridge 30 minutes before you plan to cook it, so it's at room temperature. Because you're cooking it at a low temperature, this is really important. Lightly salt the flesh of the fish when you take it out of the fridge. After 30 minutes, wipe away any excess moisture from the flesh with kitchen paper.

3. Preheat the oven to 140°C/120°C fan/gas 1 and grease a roasting dish big enough to hold the salmon with oil.

4. Smother the salmon with enough marinade to coat. You might not need it all (see tips below for how to use the rest). Place the fish skin side up in the roasting dish, cover with foil and bake for 20–30 minutes, until the flesh is tender and breaks apart in moist, buttery flakes, but is cooked through. The fish is ready when it reaches 50°C on a thermometer.

5. While the fish is cooking, combine the gremolata ingredients with the reserved cumin seeds in a bowl and squeeze over a little lemon juice. Remove the fish from the oven and serve, spooning over the delicious marinade. Top with the gremolata.

TIPS: Chill leftover marinade and use it to dress boiled greens, asparagus, roast radishes or cooked grains, or to slather on poached eggs on toast.

You can also use the marinade as a barbecue glaze. Make it as above, adding a tablespoon more olive oil. Place the salmon on a double sheet of foil, slather over the marinade and cook on the barbecue grate above glowing coals for about 20 minutes, until cooked through. If you have a lid for the barbecue you can use this to help it cook and enhance the smoky flavour.

Mujadara
with brown butter-basted radishes

Serves 4

I discovered mujadara – a traditional Middle Eastern dish of lentils, rice or bulgur wheat and caramelised onions – while researching some recipes I contributed to the charity cookbook *Cook For Syria*. While it's not particularly authentic to do so, it does lend itself well to adapting with seasonally changing veg. Change what you top it with according to what's at its best – I've made it with sweet roasted squash and asparagus before, and prefer it with rice rather than bulgur, but have a play. This version is topped with nutty brown butter-basted radishes and goes well as a side for the tahini roast salmon, as pictured on the previous page.

160g long-grain or basmati rice (or a 250g pre-cooked rice pouch)
160g puy lentils (or a 250g pre-cooked lentil pouch)
3 tbsp olive oil
2 red onions, thinly sliced
½ tsp cumin seeds
½ tsp salt
1 bay leaf
handful of coriander leaves, roughly chopped, plus whole leaves for garnish
handful of mint leaves, roughly chopped, plus whole leaves for garnish
sea salt and freshly ground black pepper

For the dressing
juice of 2 lemons
2 garlic cloves, crushed
4 tbsp olive oil
½ tsp ground cumin
½ tsp sumac

For the brown butter-basted radishes
30g salted butter, diced
200g radishes (I love the two-tone breakfast variety), greens removed and radishes halved
1 tsp sumac
squeeze of lemon juice

1. Soak the rice and lentils in separate saucepans or bowls of cold water for at least 30 minutes before you cook them.

2. While they are soaking, heat the oil in a frying pan over a low-medium heat. Add the sliced onions, cumin seeds and salt and cook gently for 25–30 minutes, until caramelised and sweet.

3. Put the drained and rinsed rice and lentils in separate saucepans of water (put a bay leaf and a teaspoon of salt in the lentil pan and ½ teaspoon of salt in the rice pan) and cook according to the packet instructions. Drain the lentils (the rice should have absorbed the water), fluff up the rice grains with a fork, then combine in a large bowl. Stir through the caramelised onions.

4. In another bowl or jug, whisk together the dressing ingredients. Dress the rice mixture and set aside for the flavours to mingle while you cook the radishes.

5. In the same frying pan you used for the onions, melt half the butter over a medium-high heat, until it's foaming and the solids are starting to turn brown and nutty. Add the radishes and toss them through the butter, then cook for about 6 minutes, adding the remaining butter as you go, until the radishes are caramelised and glazed in the butter. Sprinkle over the sumac and squeeze over the lemon juice and toss everything together to coat once more. Remove from the heat.

6. Stir the herbs through the rice and lentil mix, season with the salt, then pile onto a platter. Top with the brown butter-basted radishes and scatter over some whole herb leaves to garnish. Serve.

Sardine and fennel bucatini

Serves 4

This is my version of a Sicilian classic, which traditionally brings in some Moorish influences (Sicily was under Arab rule more than 1,000 years ago) in the form of the combination of saffron, pine nuts and sultanas, so the addition of some preserved lemon is not an entirely outrageous leap. I fell in love with the dish at a restaurant in Ortigia, and particularly adore the use of the wild fennel, an ingredient which is abundant in the UK, too. In summer, the British coastline is covered with the fragrant wild herb, and I collect it by the bagful. It has an incredibly intense, aromatic flavour which knocks shop-bought fennel out of the water, but you can use shop-bought fennel and fennel seeds together if you can't find the wild stuff.

about 100g wild fennel stems and fronds, fronds and tender stems finely chopped (hard stems retained)
½ wild fennel bulb, diced (or if no wild fennel, 1 large, regular fennel bulb, trimmed and diced, and 1 tsp fennel seeds)
2 tbsp extra-virgin olive oil
6 good-quality tinned anchovy fillets
15g preserved lemon rind (pith removed), diced (shop-bought or see recipe on page 151)
½ red onion, diced
1 tsp saffron threads
1 large tomato, chopped
1 tbsp sultanas
80g pine nuts, toasted
350g bucatini or linguine
400g filleted, butterflied sardines, tails removed and flesh finely chopped
½ lemon, for squeezing
100g anchovy breadcrumbs (page 68)
sea salt and freshly ground black pepper

1. Warm some plates in a low oven.

2. Bring a very large saucepan of well salted water to a vigorous rolling boil. Put the hard wild fennel stems in the water. If you're not using wild fennel, cut a chunk off the top of the regular fennel bulb and place that in the water. This will infuse the water with the flavour of the fennel, which in turn will infuse the pasta as it cooks.

3. Heat the olive oil in a large frying pan over a medium-high heat. Add the anchovies and preserved lemon and cook for a couple of minutes, until the anchovies have melted into the oil, then add the onion, fennel (and fennel seeds, if using), wild fennel fronds and tender stems (keeping some fronds back to garnish), with a pinch of salt and pepper and cook for about 5 minutes, until softened and aromatic. Add the saffron and tomato and cook for a couple more minutes, until the tomato is breaking down into the olive oil, then add the sultanas and pine nuts.

4. At this point, put the pasta into the pan of boiling water and cook until al dente (this is usually 2 minutes less than the time stated on the packet) – it should retain some bite but have no chalky core. When the pasta is almost ready, add the sardines to the frying pan, season with salt and pepper, and cook for 3 minutes, until almost cooked through. With the heat still on, pour a ladleful of the fennel-infused pasta water into the sardine pan then, using tongs or a spider, transfer the pasta to the sardine pan too, shaking the pan to coat the pasta and emulsify the sauce – you need the oily pan contents to meld with the pasta water, and the starch from the pasta to emulsify into a glossy sauce, so move the pasta around to release its starch and coat it in the sauce, working quickly so as to not overcook the pasta. Add a squeeze of lemon juice. Divide between the warm plates and top with extra fronds of fennel and the anchovy breadcrumbs.

TIP: You can also use good-quality tinned sardines in the place of fresh.

Braised courgettes
with dried cherry freekeh, harissa yoghurt and dukkah

Serves 4

Freekeh, a Middle Eastern staple, is fantastic for making toothsome salads, stuffings and pilafs. It's durum wheat that is harvested while still green and then roasted on a wood fire, giving it a wonderful smoky flavour. It's a great alternative to quinoa, spelt or barley, and here it's paired with slow-braised courgettes, cherries and dukkah. This makes a fantastic vegetarian main meal, or side dish with lamb or chicken kebabs.

For the braised courgettes
4 tbsp olive oil
2 garlic cloves, chopped
1 red chilli, deseeded and diced
500g small/medium courgettes (preferably yellow and green), cut into 1-cm diagonal discs
a little lemon juice, to taste

For the freekeh
1 tbsp olive oil
4 slices of Preserved Orange rind (or lemon) (page 151), or a mix of both, finely chopped
1 red onion, finely chopped
1 bay leaf
pinch of dried chilli flakes
300g cracked freekeh, soaked for 1–2 hours and drained
350ml water
handful of dill fronds, chopped
handful of mint leaves, chopped
handful of parsley leaves, chopped
2 tbsp dried cherries, soaked in 1 tbsp lemon juice for 30 minutes, or Pickled Cherries (page 152)
1 tbsp toasted pine nuts
2 tbsp olive oil

2 tbsp dukkah (shop-bought or see opposite)
sea salt and freshly ground black pepper
whole herbs, to serve

For the harissa yoghurt
150g full-fat natural yoghurt
1 tbsp tahini
1 tbsp harissa

1. Put the olive oil, garlic and chilli in a non-stick frying pan or skillet over a medium-high heat and cook, stirring to infuse the oil until the garlic is just starting to colour. Add the courgettes, season well with salt and coat in the oil, then turn the heat right down and cook for 25–30 minutes, stirring every now and then, until the courgettes are collapsing. Taste for seasoning and add a little lemon juice to lift the flavour if you think they need it.

2. While the courgettes are cooking, prepare the freekeh. Heat the olive oil and the preserved citrus in another skillet or heavy-based non-stick frying pan over a medium-high heat and cook until the citrus has melted into the oil a little. Add the onion, bay leaf, chilli flakes and a pinch of salt and fry for 5 minutes, then stir in the freekeh and toast it for a couple of minutes. Cover the freekeh with the water, bring to the boil, skim any scum from the surface and simmer for 25–30 minutes, or until all the water has been absorbed and the freekeh is cooked but retains a little bite.

3. Once cooled, mix the freekeh with the chopped herbs, the cherries (with the lemon juice, or pickled cherries) and the toasted pine nuts and olive oil and mix. Taste for seasoning and adjust if you need to.

4. Combine the harissa yoghurt ingredients in a bowl.

5. Pile the freekeh onto a platter and serve with the braised courgettes spooned over the top and the dukkah and whole herbs scattered over. Serve the harissa yoghurt alongside.

Dukkah

This is a delicious Egyptian condiment made of roasted nuts, sesame seeds and spices. It's wonderful scattered over salads, roasted veg, thick soups and fried eggs. I also love eating it scattered over griddled flatbreads with olive oil.

60g blanched, skinless
   hazelnuts
2 tbsp coriander seeds
1 tbsp cumin seeds
1 tbsp white sesame seeds
2 tsp freshly ground black
   pepper
1 tsp sea salt

1. Preheat the oven to 180°C/160°C fan/gas 4.

2. Tip the hazelnuts and seeds into a roasting tray and roast in the oven for 5–6 minutes, until toasted and golden. Tip into the bowl of a food processor and blitz to a coarse crumb, then transfer to a bowl and stir through the salt and pepper.

Special
Suppers

These are recipes for those times when you want to really indulge or impress someone, and while you can do that simply and quickly with the dreamy Dover Sole and Caramelised Grapefruit Meuniere (page 80), some of the recipes in this chapter require a bit more of your time and love. The lace-like, lovage-flecked handmade pasta filled with fresh curd cheese and served with peas and tomato (page 89) is longer in the making, but you'll enjoy the craft of it, and be rewarded with something truly lovely. Celebrate the flavour spoils of a delicious slow-grown chicken by lightly curing and confiting its legs until the skin is golden and crisp, and the flesh ultra chickeny, tender and yielding, and serve it with sour, spicy kimchi noodles (page 100), using the carcass to make broth for the handmade Wild Garlic Gnocchi (page 97). Whether it's yourself, a mate in need of some TLC, or a hot date, you (or they) will melt when you dish up Grilled Langoustines with Seaweed Butter (page 86) or the Confit Sea Trout with Peas, Broad Beans and Lovage (page 82).

Dover sole and caramelised grapefruit meunière

Serves 2

Dover sole reminds me of my earliest restaurant meals with my parents, which were few and far between, always special occasions that involved donning dresses and thick tights and sitting quietly at white linen tablecloths for hours, often in France. If Dover sole was on the menu, my mum would order it, and it would come out smelling amazing with an air of ceremony about it because it was cooked on the bone. I loved to watch her pulling the meat away from the bones – so sophisticated! – and the way she'd take her time eating it, usually pausing for a cigarette midway through at the table – can you even imagine that now?! There's more than a hint of luxury about its sweet white meat but the wonder of this dish is how quickly it's pulled together. This is a spin on the classic meunière, with crispy capers, bitter grapefruit and chopped, toasted hazelnuts that emphasise the nuttiness of the caramelised butter. Perfect seduction food, and lovely with a Campari tonic.

handful of whole, skin-on hazelnuts
3 tbsp rapeseed or groundnut oil
2 tbsp capers (preferably salt-packed capers, rinsed)
2 tbsp plain flour
2 whole medium Dover sole, descaled, trimmed and top skin removed
40g unsalted butter, diced
1 pink grapefruit or blood orange, peeled, segmented and segments finely diced (reserving a few pretty chunks for garnish)
1–2 tbsp lemon juice
pinch of ground pink peppercorns or dried chilli flakes
leaves from 2 sprigs of rosemary, chopped
handful of flat-leaf parsley, finely chopped
sea salt and freshly ground black pepper

For the wilted spinach (optional)
dash of olive oil
knob of butter
100g spinach, washed
nutmeg, for grating
lemon juice, to taste

1. Preheat the oven to 200°C/180°C fan/gas 6. Place the hazelnuts in a roasting tray and roast for 6–8 minutes, until well toasted. Remove from the oven and rub the skins off with a clean tea towel. Roughly chop and set aside.

2. Heat 1 tablespoon of the rapeseed or groundnut oil in a large non-stick frying pan over a medium-high heat. Add the capers and fry for about 2 minutes, until puffed and crisp, then transfer with a slotted spoon to a plate lined with kitchen paper to drain.

3. Put the flour on a plate and season it well with salt and pepper. Lightly dust the fish on both sides in the seasoned flour. Heat the remaining oil (in the pan you cooked the capers in) over a high heat. Add both the fish, skin side down, turn the heat down slightly, then cook for 2–3 minutes without moving them. Carefully turn them over and cook for a further minute, until the flesh is just cooked through, then transfer to a warmed plate and keep warm.

4. Add the butter to the pan, along with the chopped segmented grapefruit and the lemon juice. Cook for a couple of minutes, until the grapefruit is starting to caramelise, then add the pink peppercorns or chilli flakes, chopped hazelnuts and rosemary. Stir well to combine, taste, then add more lemon juice if you think it needs it – it needs to be reasonably sharp as the fish is so buttery. Add the capers back to the pan, followed by the fish, basting them briefly in the butter. Divide between two plates and spoon over any excess butter.

5. Now wilt the spinach (if using). Heat the olive oil and butter in a medium frying pan over a medium heat, add the spinach, and cook, stirring, until wilted. Pour away any excess liquid and season with salt, freshly grated nutmeg and a little lemon juice.

6. Serve the fish with the wilted spinach (if using) and your choice of side.

TIP: You can swap the Dover sole for 2 large lemon sole, or 2 plaice fillets (pin-boned) if you prefer.

Confit sea trout
with peas, broad beans and lovage

Serves 4–6

My mum's aunty Mary was a fantastic home cook. She was Welsh, and loved sea trout (sewin). She swore by placing it in a Tupperware, pouring a kettleful of hot water over it, and leaving it for a few minutes to cook; a sort of old-fashioned sous vide, while she made a parsley sauce. This is my update on her recipe, which gently poaches the trout in oil at a much lower temperature. Sea fish start to cook at around 40–45°C, so oil heated up to 50°C will cook the fish perfectly. There are a few stages to this, but get ahead by making the sauce earlier and finish the peas and broad beans in it while the trout is confiting. This cure is much lighter than the smoking cure later in the book – it draws out some moisture from the fish, seasons it and firms up the flesh.

Try to avoid eating sea trout between November and March as this is their spawning season.

1 side of line-caught sea trout, or Norwegian Fjord trout (about 500–600g) or 4 sea trout fillets
800ml rapeseed oil, olive oil or vegetable oil
pinch of black onion or nigella seeds, to serve

For the pickled cucumber
50ml good-quality white wine vinegar
2 tsp caster sugar
large pinch of salt
10cm piece of cucumber, peeled lengthways into elegant ribbons with a peeler or mandoline (discard the seedy, watery core)

For the cure
10g sea salt flakes
5g caster sugar
1 tsp grated unwaxed lemon zest

For the sauce
1 tbsp olive oil
knob of butter
1 bay leaf
1 shallot, sliced
¼ fennel bulb, finely chopped

1. First, pickle the cucumber. Whisk the vinegar, salt and sugar together in a bowl until dissolved. Add the cucumber ribbons, toss them in the vinegar, then allow to sit for at least 10 minutes (you can do this up to a day ahead).

2. Next, cure the trout. Combine the cure ingredients, place the trout side or fillets skin side down on a large tray and scatter the cure over the flesh. Leave at room temperature while you make the sauce (if you haven't made the sauce in advance). You only want the fish to be cured for 30 minutes or so.

3. To make the sauce, heat the olive oil and butter in a non-stick frying pan over a medium-high heat and add the bay leaf. Add the shallot, fennel and salt and fry for about 5 minutes, until softened and fragrant, then add the vermouth, turn up the heat (if necessary) to bring to the boil and reduce the liquid by one third, stirring briskly. Add the fish stock, reduce the heat a little and cook for about 8 minutes, until the liquid has reduced by half. Remove from the heat, tear the lovage sprigs into the sauce and allow to infuse for a couple of minutes off the heat, then pass it through a fine-mesh sieve. Return the sauce to the pan and add the cream, stirring to incorporate. Reduce the sauce over a medium heat until nicely thickened, then take it off the heat while you cook the peas and broad beans.

4. Bring a large saucepan of well salted water to a vigorous rolling boil. Blanch the peas for 2–4 minutes, until they are cooked through, but still a vivid green colour (the cooking time will depend on the age of the fresh peas, frozen will only need 1–2 minutes). Transfer with a slotted spoon into iced water, then repeat with the broad beans. How long they take will depend on the beans' size and age, but they should take between 3–5 minutes. Transfer the beans to a separate bowl of iced water, then peel away their skins by gently piercing the white skin with a nail and carefully squeezing out the vivid little green beans into another bowl. Drain the peas from the iced water before you finish the sauce.

pinch of salt
200ml dry vermouth (I use
 Noilly Prat)
600ml fish stock (see recipe on
 page 267 or use good-quality
 shop-bought)
4 sprigs of lovage (or tarragon
 or flat-leaf parsley), plus an
 extra 2 leaves for finishing
 the sauce
2–3 tbsp double cream
100g fresh or frozen peas
 (shelled weight)
100g fresh or frozen broad
 beans (shelled weight)
½ baby gem lettuce, thinly
 sliced
squeeze of lemon juice

5. Now it's time to cook your trout. Gently rinse the cure from the fish and pat it dry with kitchen paper. If using a side of trout, cut it into 4–6 evenly-sized portions (the number of portions will depend on the size of your fish). Pour the oil into a clean, deep saucepan and gently heat until it reaches 50°C (you'll need a kitchen thermometer for this), then remove the pan from the heat and lower in the fish fillets. Leave them in the oil for 10 minutes, then gently remove with a slotted spoon and drain on kitchen paper. The trout should be a lovely pale pink colour and come apart in beautiful buttery flakes. (You can re-use the oil for more confit if you wish, keeping it in a jar in the fridge. Just remember to label it.)

6. To finish the sauce, warm it up over a low heat and tip in the lettuce, peas and broad beans. Stir for a couple of minutes to warm through all the veg, then add a little lemon juice and the chopped fresh lovage (or other herb) to finish. Season to taste, then spoon onto plates and top with the fish. Top the fish with slivers of the cucumber pickle, drained, and garnish with a scattering of black onion or nigella seeds.

Bay and butter-roasted brill
with new potatoes

Serves 2–4

Few things are more special than roasting a whole fish on the bone to share around the table. Brill is one of my favourite fish and is truly magnificent. It's much more affordable than its cousin turbot and it's meaty but still has a clean, delicate flavour. This is roasted on fresh bay leaves from the garden, which lend the fish a subtle herbal note, and basted with fish stock and butter. It's great with a simple baby gem salad and the Grilled Langoustines on page 86.

1 large brill or turbot (1–1.2kg)
300g new potatoes (preferably Jersey Royals or Yukon Golds), scrubbed
500ml fish stock (good-quality shop-bought or see recipe on page 267)
½ tbsp good-quality white wine vinegar
30g cold unsalted butter, diced, plus a little extra for cooking the fish
6 bay leaves
1 tbsp finely chopped chives
sea salt flakes

1. Take the brill out of the fridge 30 minutes before you want to cook it so that it comes up to room temperature. Make a couple of diagonal slits (about 5mm deep) in the skin either side of the spine, then season it all over with a little sea salt.

2. Preheat the oven to 240°C/220°C fan/gas 8, or if you have a wood oven, get it lit and nice and hot.

3. Put the potatoes in a pan with 2 teaspoons of salt and cover with water so that there's about 2cm of water above the surface of the potatoes. Cover, bring to the boil, then turn down to a simmer and cook the potatoes for 15–20 minutes, or until tender. Remove from the heat but allow them to sit in their cooking water while you're cooking the fish – this will bring out the earthy flavour of the potatoes.

4. Pour the fish stock into a saucepan and bring to a rolling boil over a medium-high heat. Boil the stock rapidly until it's reduced by half and is slightly more viscous. Add the white wine vinegar then add the butter a cube at a time, whisking to emulsify. Season to taste and add a little more salt or acid to balance the sauce. You should have 250–300ml. Remove from the heat and allow the sauce to cool until it's warm rather than hot, then pour it into a roasting tray large enough to hold the fish. Add the bay leaves and sit the fish in the sauce. Dot the fish with a little more butter, then roast in the oven for 12–15 minutes, basting it every few minutes with the sauce (I find a turkey baster handy for this). Once roasted, transfer the fish carefully to a warm platter, glaze it with about half the sauce and leave the rest of the sauce in the roasting tray for the potatoes. Leave the fish to rest for a few minutes, covered loosely with foil. Meanwhile, drain the potatoes and tip them into the tray you roasted the fish in and toss them in the roasting juices. Roast them in the oven for 5–8 minutes, then transfer to a warm bowl and top with the chives.

5. Carve the fish at the table and let everyone help themselves to potatoes.

TIP: Try cooking this in a wood oven if you have one, it will bring wonderful, smoky notes.

Grilled langoustines
with seaweed butter

Langoustines, nephrops or Dublin Bay prawns are incredibly plentiful in the UK and we should be eating more of them. They make a wonderful canapé or starter for a special meal and are divine simply split and grilled in their shells with this umami seaweed butter. The butter will keep for a week in the fridge or up to 3 months in the freezer.

8 langoustines or jumbo/large
    tiger prawns, split in half
    lengthways and digestive
    tracts removed
handful of wild fennel flowers,
    to garnish (optional)

For the seaweed butter
20g dried seaweed such as
    dulse or nori
1 shallot, chopped
1 garlic clove, chopped
½ tsp fennel seeds
pinch of pink peppercorns
100g unsalted butter, at room
    temperature
¼ tsp sea salt
½ lemon, for squeezing

1. First, make the seaweed butter. Using a mini chopper or pestle and mortar, grind the seaweed until it has broken down into small flecks no more than 5mm in size. Put the shallot, garlic, fennel seeds and pink peppercorns into the bowl of a food processor with the seaweed and blitz, then add the butter, salt and a squeeze of lemon juice and blitz again until well combined. Transfer to a bowl and chill in the fridge until needed. If you're making it ahead, lay a piece of cling film out on a clean surface. Spoon the butter into the centre, then roll it up tightly into a sausage shape. Keep in the fridge until ready to use.

2. When you're ready to cook the langoustines or prawns, put them cut side up on a roasting tray and dot with the butter (about 2 teaspoons of butter on each langoustine or prawn). Grill or barbecue for 3–5 minutes, until the butter has melted and the flesh is cooked and just opaque. Serve garnished with wild fennel flowers, if you have some.

TIP: Look out for boxes of frozen langoustines at the fishmonger; they are usually a bit cheaper. You just have to thaw them in a sink of lukewarm water before you split and grill them.

Ricotta and lovage-filled ravioli
with peas and tomato

Serves 2–4

I love this method for making pretty, herbed pasta. You can use the steps below to make plain fresh pasta, leaving out the herbs, or customise the herbs you use. I use lovage because I think it's one of the most underrated herbs and I adore its slightly spicy, intense flavour, which is somewhere between curry leaf and celery. You can also double the quantity and cut some into tagliatelle, which is gorgeous with the home-smoked trout on page 136 and any leftover tomato water. Speaking of which, the real secret to this dish is the tomato water (the combination of tomato and lovage is magical) that you pour over at the last minute, adding sweetness, acidity and a hint of tomato without any actual chunks of tomato. This is a pretty swishy thing to cook for friends or loved ones. You need a pasta machine. If you want to get ahead, make and freeze the ravioli between sheets of baking parchment straight after making them.

For the tomato water
300g really ripe tomatoes,
 chopped
¼ tsp salt
¼ tsp sugar
1 tsp red wine vinegar
1 tbsp olive oil

For the pasta
215g '00' flour, plus extra for
 dusting
2 eggs plus 1 egg yolk
leaves from 4 sprigs of lovage,
 hard stems removed (or use
 a mix of parsley and chervil)
1 tbsp semolina flour

For the filling
120g ricotta or Fresh Curd
 Cheese (page 254)
1 egg yolk
grated zest of ½ unwaxed
 lemon
4 lovage leaves, very finely
 chopped
15g Parmesan, grated
nutmeg, for grating
sea salt and freshly ground
 black pepper

1. To make the tomato water, toss the tomatoes well with the salt, sugar and red wine vinegar in a bowl. Leave to sit and marinade for at least 1 hour, then strain through a fine-mesh sieve. If you are picky about the tomato seeds, line the sieve with a piece of muslin or a J-cloth (but I don't bother). Whisk the tomato juice with the olive oil and set aside.

2. Blitz the pasta ingredients in the bowl of a food processor until they clump together – if the mixture is too wet, add some more flour. Tip out the dough, roll it into a ball, wrap it in cling film and chill it in the fridge for 30 minutes.

3. While the pasta dough is resting, make the ravioli filling mixture. Combine the ricotta with the egg yolk, lemon zest, chopped lovage, Parmesan and a good grating of nutmeg in a bowl. Season to taste with plenty of salt and pepper.

4. Remove the pasta dough from the fridge, unwrap it and cut it in half. Flatten one half, dust it with a little '00' flour, then roll it out with a rolling pin until it can fit into the widest setting of a pasta machine. Feed the dough through the machine, then fold each side of the dough into the middle (similar to folding an A4 letter to fit into an envelope) and pass it through this setting again. Pass it through once more, then give it a quarter turn so it fits through and roll it through the widest setting again. Continue to run the pasta through the machine, gradually reducing the settings to the thinnest. Once you've run it through the thinnest setting, put the dough on a floured surface and repeat with the other half.

5. Once both halves are rolled out, lay them flat on the surface. Square off the ends and any ragged edges, and cut both in half so you have four lengths. Moisten one side of the lovage leaves then stick them to two of the sheets of pasta, spacing them out so you can see the leaves in their entirety. Top each of the herbed sheets with the other two plain sheets and open the setting on the pasta machine to the second thinnest.

Recipe continues over the page

To serve
20g unsalted butter
100g fresh or frozen peas
20g shaved Parmesan
handful of borage flowers or
    pea shoots/flowers

6. Run the herbed pasta sheets through the machine one more time, to seal the top layer to the bottom layer. Lay out on a floured surface.

7. You now need to space your filling out along the pasta. If you've got a ravioli mould, use that, if not, dot the filling at equal intervals, just to the left or right of the middle all the way down the length of the pasta sheet, leaving an equidistant gap of about 6cm down the length of the pasta between the fillings. You should have 15–20 dots of filling (to make 15–20 ravioli). Moisten your fingers and brush a little water around each filling, then fold the slightly wider half of the pasta sheet up and over the filling, and press it down at the edges to seal, carefully pressing down between the fillings and all the way round each filling to release any air bubbles. Use a pasta cutter or knife to cut between the filled pasta. Dust the ravioli with semolina and lay them out on a plate or tray lined with semolina-dusted greaseproof paper.

8. If you're making the pasta to cook on another day, pack it carefully into Tupperware between sheets of baking parchment and freeze immediately. If cooking later the same day, chill for a couple of hours, but not much longer as the filling can soak through the pasta and make it soggy and sticky.

9. When you're ready to make the finished dish, warm some plates in the oven and gather your tomato juice, butter, peas, Parmesan shavings and pasta. Bring a large saucepan of water to the boil and gently melt the butter over a low-medium heat in a non-stick frying pan.

10. Cook the peas in the boiling water until tender – this could take anything from 4–10 minutes, depending on the age of the peas, but frozen peas will take just a couple of minutes. Fish the peas out with a slotted spoon and set aside.

11. Now you need to salt the water to cook the pasta (we don't do this when we cook the peas as it can make the skins shrivel). A famous pasta chef called Francesco Mazzei once told me that pasta water should be as salty as the sea, so make it salty! Bring the water back up to the boil and carefully place your ravioli into the water. Reduce the heat so the water is just at a gentle boil and doesn't break the ravioli.

12. Once the ravioli float to the surface of the water – after about 2 minutes – they are ready to be fished out. Use a slotted spoon or spider to transfer them straight into the melted butter along with the peas. Season with a little salt and pepper and spoon onto plates with the butter. Give the tomato water a little whisk to emulsify the olive oil then spoon some over each serving, and garnish with Parmesan shavings and borage or pea flowers or shoots (if you have them).

Pistachio pesto linguine with brown shrimp
and runner beans

Serves 4

We fell in love with this pesto in Sicily, where pistachios have been cultivated since antiquity. They are still grown around village of Bronte, to the west of Mount Etna, whose mineral-rich volcanic soil is credited with making Sicilian pistachios the best in the world. They are longer and thinner than Middle Eastern pistachios, with vivid green flesh and purple skins. They are used extensively to service the ubiquitous Sicilian sweet tooth, in everything from gelato to ricotta-filled cannoli, and also used in savoury dishes, notably a deliciously rich pesto. Here, the pesto is combined with two very British ingredients, brown shrimp and runner beans, which work beautifully with the creamy, earthy flavour of the nuts. The dish comes together quickly, so have all your ingredients measured and laid out, and pans ready to go, before you start cooking (what chefs call 'mis en place'). You can scale the recipe down to serve two, but it's worth making the pesto to the quantities below – any leftover is great spread on bread with poached eggs, or used to dress a salad.

360g linguine
1 tbsp olive oil
4 good-quality tinned anchovy fillets
grated zest of ½ unwaxed lemon
pinch of dried chilli flakes
200g peeled brown shrimp
1 tbsp lemon juice, plus extra to serve
pinch of mace or cayenne pepper
knob of butter
160g runner beans, topped, tailed, string removed and thinly sliced lengthways
handful of raw, shelled pistachios, roughly chopped, to garnish

For the pistachio pesto
1 garlic clove, roughly chopped
85g raw pistachios, shelled
½ tsp sea salt
30g basil and mint leaves
grated zest of ½ unwaxed lemon and 2 tsp juice
30g Parmesan or pecorino
60–80ml extra-virgin olive oil
freshly ground black pepper, to taste

1. First, make the pesto. Put the garlic in a food processor or a mortar. Add the pistachios and pulse or grind with a pestle to chop and combine. Add all the other ingredients apart from the olive oil and pulse or grind to a coarse paste, then scrape out into a bowl and pour over 60ml of the olive oil. Stir vigorously to combine, until the mixture has a pesto consistency, adding more oil if you need to. Taste for seasoning. Add salt, pepper and lemon juice to taste. Pour into a sterilised jar (see page 2 for sterilising method).

2. Put four plates in a low oven to warm them up, before you start cooking.

3. Place a large, non-stick frying pan, wok or skillet on one hob and on another, bring a large saucepan of very well salted water to a vigorous rolling boil. Have tongs or a spider ready to transfer the pasta out of its cooking water and into the pan.

4. Once the water is boiling, add the pasta and set a timer for 4 minutes.

5. While the pasta is cooking, heat the olive oil in the frying pan, wok or skillet over a medium-high heat and add the anchovies, lemon zest and chilli, stirring to melt the anchovies into the oil. Cook for a minute, then add the brown shrimp, lemon juice, mace or cayenne and butter, tossing to combine. Reduce the heat to low. Add 4 tablespoons of pesto and a ladle of pasta cooking water and use a spoon to loosen the mixture to a sauce-like consistency.

6. After the pasta has been cooking for 4 minutes, add the beans to the pasta pot and cook for 2 minutes. Use the tongs or spider to transfer the pasta and beans to the pesto pan.

7. Stir, shaking the pan simultaneously, to mix everything together and release starch from the pasta to make it extra creamy. Add the rest of the pesto (8–10 tablespoons) and shake again, ladling in more pasta water to loosen if necessary. Season and serve straightaway. Finish with a little extra lemon juice and the crushed pistachios.

Seafood and fennel linguine

Serves 4

This dish captures the deliciously nuttiness of the prawns' shells by using them to infuse the pasta cooking water, and the flavourful juice from the heads in the sauce giving it an almost bisquey flavour. It relies on finding fat, fresh prawns – hit up your fishmonger. Fennel grows wild on the British coastline, in gardens and even in London's Hackney Marshes during the summer – its bright yellow flowers and the vivid anise notes of its fragrant fronds are brilliant with seafood – but you can use regular fennel too. There is a certain amount of multitasking required, so have all the ingredients prepped and ready to go.

8 large, raw shell-on king or tiger prawns
4 fresh, fat scallops (remove roe if you wish)
handful of live clams or mussels (optional)
2 tbsp olive oil, plus extra for frying the scallops
½ fennel bulb, woody base removed (keep for stock) and bulb finely chopped
1 shallot, finely chopped
1 red chilli, finely chopped
1 bay leaf
2 garlic cloves, crushed
1 large tomato, roughly chopped
125ml rosé, dry white wine or dry vermouth (I use Noilly Prat)
350g linguine
handful of samphire (optional)
2 fronds and flower heads of wild fennel, plus extra to serve (optional)
salt

To serve
handful of flat-leaf parsley, finely chopped
wild fennel or dill fronds
lemon wedges

1. Bring the seafood out of the fridge a good 20 minutes before you start cooking so that it's at room temperature.

2. First, make the base for the seafood pasta. Heat the olive oil in a large heavy-based frying pan or skillet over a medium heat, add the fennel, shallot, chilli, bay leaf and garlic with a big pinch of salt and cook for a few minutes, until fragrant and softened, but not browned. Add the tomato and cook for about 3 minutes, until it's beginning to break down into the oil, then turn up the heat a smidge and add the prawns, cooking them for a couple of minutes on each side, until the shells have changed colour and started to caramelise. Carefully transfer the prawns from the pan to a plate to cool. Don't worry if they're not totally cooked, they will finish cooking later. Deglaze the pan with the wine or vermouth, scraping up any bits that are stuck to the bottom – this is where the flavour is – and reducing the liquid by about half, then remove the pan from the heat and discard the bay leaf.

3. Meanwhile, bring a large saucepan of well salted water to the boil.

4. Once they are cool enough to handle, peel all but a couple of the prawns (I like to leave a few with shells on for presentation) and toss the shells (but not the heads) into the water. Remove the dark vein-like digestive tracts from the prawns. Take the heads and squeeze any juices from them into the fennel frying pan. This may sound odd, but bear with me: there is so much good flavour in the heads – this is where the dish's nutty richness comes from. Once squeezed, toss the heads into the water too and boil for a couple of minutes, allowing the flavour of the shells to infuse the water.

5. Remove the shells and heads from the water with a spider or slotted spoon, discard and bring the water back up to a vigorous rolling boil. Add the pasta and cook until al dente (this is usually 2 minutes less than the time stated on the packet), throwing in the samphire and wild fennel fronds (if using) to cook with the pasta for the last minute.

6. While the pasta is cooking, heat a tiny bit of olive oil in another heavy-based skillet or non-stick frying pan over a high heat, until it shimmers. Season the scallops with salt and put them into the pan. They should sizzle. Cook for a minute or two on each side, until they start to caramelise and come away from the pan easily. Transfer to a plate.

7. Place the frying pan of fennel and prawn goodness back over a medium-high heat and, using a spider or tongs, transfer the cooked pasta (and samphire and fennel, if using) from its water into the pan. Add a good ladleful of the pasta water, then add the clams to the pan (if using), cover and shake the pan to combine all the ingredients. Cook for a couple of minutes, then once the clams have opened, stir vigorously to emulsify the sauce – you need to move the pasta around so that it releases its starch and emulsifies with the water and pan sauce: it should look glossy and coat the pasta nicely. Add a slosh more pasta cooking water if you need to, but remember to keep moving the contents of the pan either by shaking it or using a spoon to agitate everything. Put the prawns and scallops in the pan and toss everything together, then use tongs to divide among plates. Garnish with chopped parsley and wild fennel or dill fronds. Serve with lemon wedges.

Wild garlic gnocchi

Serves 2–4

These green-flecked, gently allium wild garlic gnocchi make for a special supper; an elegant expression of spring that's at once comforting and reviving. Carefully fried in foaming butter until golden and crisp, the jolly little pillows of wild garlic and ricotta bob with tender poached asparagus and wilted greens in pools of warm, lemony broth. Soft herbs and grated Parmesan are scattered over at the end for a final flourish. Serve this to someone you love and watch their face light up.

good handful of rock salt
500g potatoes (Desiree, Red Skin or King Edward), skin on
20g Parmesan, grated, plus extra to serve
nutmeg, for grating
150g wild garlic leaves (or 140g spinach, 10g flat-leaf parsley, 2 crushed garlic cloves/150g watercress)
1 tbsp olive oil, plus extra for frying the gnocchi
2 tbsp fresh ricotta
2 egg yolks
150g '00' flour, plus extra for dusting
100g asparagus spears, trimmed
1 tbsp butter
300ml really good-quality chicken or vegetable stock
grated zest and juice of ½ unwaxed lemon
handful of soft herbs such as tarragon, chervil and dill
sea salt and freshly ground black pepper

1. Preheat the oven to 200°C/180°C fan/gas 6.

2. Scatter the rock salt into the base of a roasting tray and place the potatoes on top. Prick them with a fork and bake in the oven for around 1 hour, or until tender when pierced with a fork. Remove from the oven and leave until cool enough to handle but still warm, then peel. Rice the potatoes into a bowl. If you don't have a potato ricer, grate the potato into a bowl using the widest setting on a box grater. Add the Parmesan and mix lightly, then season with plenty of salt, pepper and grated nutmeg.

3. Place the wild garlic leaves in a sieve and pour a full kettle of boiling water over them. Allow to cool for a couple of minutes, then squeeze out excess moisture and blitz in a blender, with the tablespoon of olive oil, to make a smooth puree. Once cool, pour the puree into the potatoes along with the ricotta and egg yolks, then sift in the flour. Mix with your hands lightly to incorporate everything and form a dough. Divide the dough into four, roll out each piece on a floured surface into a long thin sausage and use a sharp knife to cut each sausage into little gnocchi (about 3cm wide). If you like, gently press the back of a fork against each one to create a ribbed effect. Line a baking tray with baking parchment and lightly dust it with flour. Place the gnocchi on the tray and chill for at least 30 minutes, to firm up before cooking.

4. Bring a large saucepan of well salted water to the boil. First, blanch the asparagus in the water for 3 minutes until tender, then remove with a spider or slotted spoon and cut into 4cm lengths.

5. Tip half the chilled gnocchi into the pan and boil for a couple of minutes until they float to the top. Carefully fish them out onto a plate with the spider or slotted spoon, then repeat with the remaining gnocchi.

6. Melt the butter in a frying pan with a dash of olive oil over a medium heat and pan-fry the gnocchi for about 3 minutes, until they are starting to crisp and colour, turning them to cook them evenly.

7. Meanwhile, heat the chicken or vegetable stock in a saucepan with the lemon zest and a squeeze of lemon juice to taste. Season to your liking.

8. Divide the gnocchi between bowls with the blanched asparagus and ladle over the broth. Garnish with the soft herbs and top with more Parmesan and cracked black pepper.

Spring chicken and wild garlic puff pie

Serves 4–6

I call this Spring Chicken Pie because it's a celebration of that special window at the start of spring when the brunt of winter has thawed and the ground is brought to life with green flashe s of fat wild garlic leaves. If you live in the countryside you can try and forage your own, but during the season you can also find wild garlic at farmers' markets, greengrocers and online. make the delicious pesto (page 263), wild garlic butter (page 260) and this pie. Here, I poach chicken thighs, then use the picked meat and the chickeny stock to make the pie filling, but if you don't have time you can use homemade chicken stock (page 266) or shop-bought stock with 600g poached chicken meat or leftover roast chicken. Shop-bought puff pastry works beautifully.

6 bone-in, skin-on chicken thighs
500ml homemade or good-quality shop-bought chicken stock (page 266)
100g frozen peas
100g wild garlic leaves, washed (or, if you can't find wild garlic, a mixture of 100g spinach and 4 garlic cloves), plus an extra 3 leaves to decorate the pie
1 tbsp olive oil
1 leek, washed, trimmed and cut into 1–1.5-cm slices
40g butter
60g plain flour
30ml dry white wine
1 tbsp lemon juice or white wine vinegar (optional)
2 tbsp sour cream or crème fraîche
nutmeg, for grating
a few asparagus spears, trimmed and chopped (optional)
320g rough puff or shop-bought ready-rolled puff pastry
1 egg, beaten
sea salt and freshly ground black pepper

1. Remove the chicken from the fridge 30 minutes before you start to cook.

2. Put the chicken thighs in a saucepan and pour over the chicken stock. Cover, place over a medium heat and bring to a gentle boil. Once boiling, turn the heat down and simmer gently for 20–25 minutes, until a thigh which is pierced yields no blood. Remove the thighs from the stock with a slotted spoon and set aside on a plate to cool. Once cool, remove the skin from the thighs, pick the chicken meat from the bone and place it in a bowl, discarding any skin or excess fat.

3. Turn the heat under the pan of stock up to high and boil until the stock has reduced by a third, then add the frozen peas and cook for a minute, followed by the wild garlic leaves (or spinach and garlic). Cook for 30 seconds, then remove from the heat and pour into the bowl of a food processor. Blitz until you have a green-flecked stock – this is to make your wild garlic béchamel.

4. Preheat the oven to 200°C/180°C fan/gas 6.

5. Heat the olive oil in a high-sided frying pan, add the leek with some salt and pepper and sweat for about 6 minutes, until softened and aromatic but not browning, then remove from the pan and mix into the bowl with the chicken meat. Melt the butter in the same pan, then add the flour and cook for a minute or two, stirring, until it forms a thick paste (a roux) and smells nutty.

6. Pour the wine into the pan, still stirring, and cook for a couple of minutes, then gradually add the green stock, whisking constantly. Cook for about 8 minutes, stirring until you have a silky, thickened green sauce. Remove from the heat, season to taste, and sharpen with a little lemon juice or vinegar if you think it needs it. The sauce may be a little thick, but it will loosen when you stir through the sour cream. Stir in the cream or crème fraîche and season with a little grated nutmeg. If the sauce is still a little thick, thin it slightly with a splash of water or milk – it should have the consistency of thick double cream. Stir in the chicken meat and asparagus (if using).

7. Pour the pie filling into a 23cm pie dish and allow to cool a little. Cut a circle from the puff pastry sheet a little larger than the dish and top the filling with the pastry. Use a pie bird or cut a slit in the pastry to let out steam. Crimp the edges with a fork, brush the pastry with beaten egg, top with wild garlic leaves and paint over them with egg wash. Bake for 30 minutes, until the crust is puffed and golden. Serve warm, with boiled Jersey Royal potatoes and a scattering of wild garlic flowers.

Confit chicken legs
with kimchi and broccolini udon

Serves 2

Confiting, or cooking in fat, is a game-changing way to cook chicken legs – the gently poached meat becomes meltingly tender and the skin golden, crisp and deeply flavoursome. It's a method traditionally used in France with duck legs, but I love applying it to chicken, because it enhances all of those lovely chicken flavours. Don't be put off by the quantity of oil – the chicken cooks beautifully in it but doesn't absorb it. I usually buy a whole chicken and remove the legs and wings for confiting, poaching the carcass to make stock (page 266) to use with poached breast meat for the noodle soup on page 171 – it's a fantastic way to celebrate the whole bird and get a few meals from one chicken. The udon noodles with their spicy, sour, crunchy hit of kimchi really cut through the richness.

For the confit chicken
15g flaked sea salt
grated zest of 1 unwaxed lemon, plus an extra pared strip of zest
leaves from 2 sprigs of thyme
2 organic chicken legs (if you buy a whole chicken and only use the legs, use the rest in the recipe on page 171)
2 shallots
6 garlic cloves, bruised (skin on)
1 red chilli, split lengthways
700ml olive oil, vegetable oil or duck fat

For the kimchi and broccoli udon
6 sprouting broccoli stems
150g udon noodles
2 tbsp dark soy sauce
4 tsp toasted sesame oil
1 tbsp mirin or white rice vinegar
juice of ½ lime or lemon
2 tsp honey
2 spring onions, trimmed and finely chopped (including the green tops)
150g My 'Kind Of' Kimchi (page 145), or shop-bought, drained and chopped
2 tbsp roasted, salted peanuts
2 tsp sesame seeds

1. Combine the salt, lemon zest and thyme, rub it all over the chicken legs, then chill in the fridge (uncovered) for 1 hour (or overnight). Let the legs come to room temperature 30 minutes before you cook them. Preheat the oven to 160°C/140°C fan/gas 3.

2. Wipe the chicken legs dry with kitchen paper, removing any excess salt, then place them, skin side down, in a small roasting tray (they should fit snugly) with the other confit ingredients. Pour over the oil to cover the chicken. If it's really full, place the chicken tray inside a larger roasting tray to catch any escaping oil. Cook in the oven for 1 hour, then turn the chicken skin side up and return to the oven for another hour until golden and crisp. If the skin isn't as crisp as you'd like, turn the oven up to 200°C/180°C fan/gas 6 and give it a blast of heat for 10 minutes.

3. Remove the tray from the oven and transfer the legs to a plate lined with kitchen paper to rest. Strain the oil into a bowl or jug, rescuing the chilli, zest, shallots and garlic, and squeeze the shallots and garlic from their skins to use in the noodles. Chop them together finely and set aside. Discard the thyme and store the confit oil in the fridge for future confit (or for roasting potatoes). Reduce the oven temperature to 120°C/100°C fan/gas ½.

4. When the chicken is almost ready, cook the broccoli in a large saucepan of salted boiling water for 4–5 minutes until tender, then transfer to a plate and cut into bite-size pieces. Cook the noodles in the same water for a minute less than the packet instructions state. Drain and drizzle over a teaspoon of the confit oil, separating the strands with a chopstick.

5. Whisk together the soy, sesame oil, mirin or rice vinegar, citrus juice and honey. Pop the chicken into a roasting tray and put it back in the oven to keep warm.

6. Heat 1 tablespoon of confit oil in a wok over a high heat. Add the spring onions and confit garlic, chilli, lemon zest and shallot and stir-fry for a minute, then add the kimchi and peanuts and stir-fry for another minute. Tip in the noodles and broccoli and toss, then add the soy dressing and toss again. Serve alongside the confit chicken, scattered with the sesame seeds.

Chilli and tamarind-crusted squid

Serves 4 as a starter
or snack

Sweet, creamy squid is crusted in a crunchy rice coating, quickly deep-fried until soft and yielding, and then dredged through a fiery, sticky-sour glaze of chilli and tamarind in this dish. It's a three-step process, but one that is worth the effort for the utterly addictive, finger-licking squid that results. The perfect starter for a sexy supper.

250ml rapeseed or groundnut
   oil, for frying
50g white basmati rice
2 jig-caught squid, cleaned
   and cut into 2-cm rings,
   tentacles halved at the top,
   little triangular side wings
   halved and scored

For the chilli-tamarind paste
1½ tbsp rapeseed or
   groundnut oil
1 red onion, finely chopped
2 garlic cloves
1 red chilli, sliced
5g piece of root ginger,
   finely chopped
pinch of salt
½ tsp ground white pepper
4 tbsp tamarind sauce
1 tbsp rice wine vinegar
2 tsp honey
1 tbsp water

To serve
2 spring onions, thinly sliced
handful of coriander leaves
lime wedges

1. First, make the paste. Heat the rapeseed or groundnut oil in a wok over a medium-high heat. Add the onion, garlic, chilli, ginger and salt and stir-fry for a few minutes, then add the white pepper, tamarind sauce, vinegar and honey and cook down for a couple of minutes until the sauce is caramelised and intense. Scrape the mixture out of the wok and into the bowl of a food processor. Add the water and blitz to form a thickish paste. Pour this paste back into the wok (off the heat).

2. Meanwhile, heat the oil for frying the squid in a saucepan over a medium-high heat until a piece of bread sizzles when dropped into the pan. Line a plate with kitchen paper.

3. Put the rice in the bowl of a food processor and blitz to a coarse crumb. Spread the rice crumb out on a plate. Dip the squid pieces and rings into it and toss well to coat the squid all over.

4. Now, working in batches if you need to, to avoid overcrowding the pan, fry the coated squid in the hot oil for 2 minutes. Use a spider or slotted spoon to drain the squid onto the paper-lined plate.

5. Once all the squid is fried, heat the paste in the wok over a medium heat until bubbling. Slide the squid in and toss to coat it in the paste. Transfer to a platter or bowl and serve garnished with the spring onion and coriander, and lime wedges alongside.

BBQ onglet *and kimchi sauce*

Serves 4

Onglet is a prized cut of steak that comes from the lower belly of the animal. It has a loose texture and a big, intense flavour, thanks to its proximity to the liver and kidneys, and it is technically known as offal. Its bold flavour makes it perfect for punchy sauces like this kimchi number, which can be prepared ahead of time. It's lovely with fries or crispy potatoes.

600–800g piece of onglet (hanger steak)

For the marinade
1 tbsp light soy sauce
2 tsp fish sauce
1 tsp Worcestershire sauce
1 tbsp rice wine vinegar
2 tsp toasted sesame oil

For the kimchi sauce
100g My 'Kind Of' Kimchi (page 145), or shop-bought kimchi, drained
4 tbsp mayonnaise (good-quality shop-bought, or see my recipe on page 35)
1 tsp toasted sesame oil
1 spring onion, trimmed and finely chopped
½ red chilli, finely chopped

1. First, make the kimchi sauce. Place the kimchi in a sieve and squeeze out any excess moisture. Place in the bowl of a food processor with 1 tablespoon of the mayonnaise and the sesame oil, then blitz to a paste. Transfer to a bowl and stir in the remaining mayonnaise, the spring onion and chilli and chill in the fridge until ready to serve.

2. Whisk together the marinade ingredients in a bowl. Place the onglet in a dish that will accommodate it snugly. Pour over the marinade and coat the onglet in it, then leave the meat to marinate for 30 minutes at room temperature (or in the fridge for a few hours, but let it come back to room temperature before you cook it).

3. Light the barbecue, if using, and let it burn until the coals are glowing white hot. Alternatively, heat a griddle pan over a very high heat. Cook the onglet over the glowing coals (or on the griddle) for 2–3 minutes on each side for rare or 4–6 minutes for medium. Transfer from the grill to a warm plate and leave to rest for 10–15 minutes, then slice across the grain. Drizzle with the kimchi sauce and serve.

Sunshine
Feasts

This chapter is a celebration of warm-weather cooking to share, with ideas for glorious spring and summer meals, picnics in the park or garden, beach or balcony barbecues. Plenty of the recipes let you escape the kitchen in favour of cooking outdoors; you'll find a ripe Peach, Proscuitto and Celery Leaf Panzanella (page 106) and a Whole Brined, Spatchcocked Barbecue Chicken with Charred Lemon Butter and Green Romesco Sauce (page 112), along with scallops and oysters to be barbecued in their shells with flavoured butters (page 130). Chicken, Cherries and Chicory (page 119) is a delicious but deceptively lazy summer traybake worth taking a break from sitting in the sun to prepare, and is best enjoyed with plenty of cold rosé.

Peach, prosciutto and celery leaf panzanella

Serves 4 as a side

Like the classic panzanella – a Tuscan salad made with bread and tomatoes – this relies on really ripe fruit, so only works if you can track down some exceptionally juicy peaches. It's a recipe I came up with in Italy and it's perfect for the height of summer, or for when you find yourself in a place that abounds with good peaches. I love the combination of sweet fruit, crunchy celery and its often-discarded but highly-scented leaves with the lush, salty prosciutto. Ideally, roast the bread until golden and crunchy, but it still works with ripped up crusty bread, and it's an effortless tumbled-together salad that can easily be composed al fresco.

3 slices of sourdough bread (shop-bought or see recipe on page 24)
3 tbsp olive oil
1 tbsp rosemary leaves, chopped
1 tbsp capers
juice of ½ lemon
2 tsp Dijon mustard
4–6 ripe peaches, halved and stoned
large handful of basil leaves, plus extra to serve
50g sorrel or spinach leaves
1 celery stick, strings removed and stick very finely chopped
handful of celery leaves, plus extra to serve
handful of chervil, plus extra to serve
handful of tarragon leaves, plus extra to serve
2 tbsp ricotta or Fresh Curd Cheese (page 254) (try goat's curd – homemade or shop-bought)
100g prosciutto slices
handful of toasted hazelnuts, chopped (see page 80)
1 tbsp Pink Pickled Onions (page 180)
sea salt and freshly ground black pepper

1. Preheat the oven to 200°C/180°C fan/gas 6.

2. Brush the slices of bread with 1 tablespoon of the olive oil and scatter over some sea salt and rosemary leaves. Place on a baking sheet and toast in the oven for 15 minutes, turning them over once, until crispy and golden. Remove from the oven, break up into a bowl and toss with the capers.

3. Meanwhile, whisk together the lemon juice, 2 tablespoons of the olive oil, a pinch of salt and the mustard to make a dressing, then pour half of it over the bread. Add the peach halves to the bowl with the bread, along with the basil, sorrel or spinach, celery, celery leaves, chervil and tarragon. Season with salt and pepper, add the curd, tumble everything together, then pile onto a serving platter. Top with the prosciutto, hazelnuts, pink onions and some more herbs and serve with the remaining dressing (on the side, if you like).

Asparagus and goat's curd tart

Serves 4-6

Few things are more joyful than silky green asparagus spears, and British asparagus is the best in the world. I love it so much I practically planned my wedding around the season, serving great piles of it poached and drenched in lemon butter to be eaten with greedy fingers. It's only around for a few fleeting weeks, so should be eaten with abandon. This tart makes a real fuss of it, pairing it with creamy, tangy goat's curd and pink pickled onions, inside a buttery, nutty buckwheat pastry. The asparagus cooking method was shown to me by my friend James Lowe, a brilliant chef whose obsession with British seasonality means he cooks the best asparagus around at his restaurant, Lyles.

400g asparagus spears, trimmed
½ tbsp olive oil
320g goat's curd (or 200g ricotta mixed with 120g soft, creamy goat's cheese)
grated zest of 1 unwaxed lemon and a squeeze of lemon juice
½ tsp pink peppercorns, ground
1 tbsp pesto (it's lovely with Wild Garlic Pesto, page 263)
2 tbsp Pink Pickled Onion (page 180)
sea salt and freshly ground black pepper

For the pastry
180g plain flour and 70g light spelt flour (or 250g plain flour if that's all your have) and 1 tbsp buckwheat groats
½ tsp fine sea salt
125g cold unsalted butter, cubed
1 egg yolk
1 tbsp sour cream
1–3 tbsp iced water

To garnish
1 tbsp chervil
1 tbsp tarragon
borage flowers

1. First, make the pastry. Put the flours, buckwheat and salt in a food processor and blitz for a few seconds to combine – don't worry if all the buckwheat doesn't break down, it's quite nice to leave some seeds whole. Add the butter and blitz again, until the mixture resembles coarse breadcrumbs, then add the egg yolk and sour cream and blitz until combined. Add the iced water, a tablespoon at a time, sprinkling it across the crumb and blitzing between additions until the dough clumps together (you may not need all the water). Tip the dough out and press it into a smooth ball then shape into a rectangle, wrap in greaseproof paper and chill in the fridge for at least 30 minutes.

2. Preheat the oven to 200°C/180°C fan/gas 6.

3. Roll the chilled pastry out on a lightly floured surface to a rectangle slightly bigger than a 25 x 20cm tart tin, about the thickness of a pound coin. If it's difficult to work with, roll it between two pieces of baking parchment. Line the tin with the pastry, letting it overhang, prick the base and chill for 20 minutes or so, until firm. Line the pastry shell with crumpled greaseproof paper, fill with baking beans and blind-bake for 20 minutes, then remove the paper and beans, return the pastry to the oven and bake for 10 minutes until crisp, nutty and golden. Remove and leave to cool, then remove the pastry shell from the tin.

4. Have a bowl of iced water ready. Place the asparagus in a saucepan with a tight-fitting lid, drizzle with a little olive oil – just enough to coat the spears rather than fry them – season with salt and pepper and turn on the heat to medium. Cook the asparagus, shaking the pan frequently, for about 4 minutes, until a sharp knife blade inserted into the thickest part of a spear comes out with no resistance. Remove the asparagus from the pan and plunge it immediately into iced water. Chop the stalks of half the asparagus spears into 1-cm discs, leaving the tips of the spears about 4cm long.

5. Combine the goat's curd (or ricotta and goat's cheese) with the lemon zest and juice, pink peppercorns and a large pinch of salt. Season to taste, then spread the mixture on the base of the tart shell. Dot with the pesto, then swirl the pesto into the cheese slightly. Cover with the chopped asparagus tips and spears, then arrange the long spears so they are covering the tart. Drain the onions and strew them delicately across the tart, then garnish with chervil, tarragon and borage flowers.

Slow-roast shallot, tomato and chard tart

Serves 6

Shallots are a wonder ingredient. Roasted slowly in olive oil with their papery brown skins intact, they develop into something truly magnificent: their layers lush and juicy with a caramel quality that's at once sweet and deeply savoury. Roasted shallots can be thrown into salads both warm and cold, into trays of roast potatoes, alongside roasted meats or fish, but it's great to celebrate them in a tart, too. Here they're roasted slowly with their skins on to eke out those caramel notes, then peeled and nestled in a pastry case with tomatoes and chard, and baked in a Parmesan-laced custard. This also works well with a mature English Cheddar or even a mixture of both. It's perfect for a picnic, and especially good with the fresh Cucumber, Pea Shoot, Chilli and Mint Salad on page 208 (pictured opposite).

½ tbsp olive oil
100g chard (or spinach),
    leaves and stalks separated,
    stalks chopped
3 eggs
90ml double cream
60g natural yoghurt
40g Parmesan, grated, plus
    extra to top the tart
sea salt and freshly ground
    black pepper
good-quality tinned anchovies,
    to serve (optional)

For the slow-roast filling
6 banana shallots, halved
    lengthways
50ml olive oil
200g cherry tomatoes, halved
6 sprigs of rosemary, plus
    extra to top the tart
4 garlic cloves, bashed

For the pastry
150g plain flour, plus extra
    for dusting
50g wholemeal spelt (or use
    200g plain flour if that's
    all you have)
pinch of fine sea salt
10g Parmesan, grated
½ tsp dried thyme
125g cold unsalted butter,
    diced
1 egg yolk
1–3 tbsp iced water

1. Preheat the oven to 200°C/180°C fan/gas 6.

2. First, prepare the ingredients for slow-roasting. Put the shallot halves in a roasting tray and season really well with salt and freshly ground black pepper. Pour over the olive oil and toss to make sure everything is well coated, then arrange the shallots, cut side down. Roast in the oven for 45 minutes, then remove from the oven and peel off and discard the paper skins – they should come away easily. Add the halved tomatoes, rosemary and garlic and scrape any sticky bits of shallot from the bottom of the tin, coating everything in the residual oil and seasoning again with salt. Return to the oven and roast, uncovered, for a further 30 minutes.

3. While that's roasting, make your pastry. Sift the flour(s) and salt into the bowl of a food processor and add the Parmesan and thyme. Pulse briefly to combine. Add the butter and pulse until the mixture resembles breadcrumbs, then add the egg yolk and pulse again. Add the iced water, a tablespoon at a time, sprinkling it all across the crumb and blitzing between additions until the dough clumps together. Don't add too much water here as this will make the pastry tough (you may not need it all). Tip the pastry out into a bowl and bring it together into a smooth ball with your hands, adding a smidge more flour if it's sticky. Flatten to a disc, wrap it in greaseproof paper (rather than cling film, which makes it sweat) and chill in the fridge for at least 30 minutes.

4. Remove the roasting tray from the oven but keep the oven on. Remove the rosemary, squeeze the garlic from its skins and roughly chop, then stir it through the rest of the veg. Discard any really tough bits of rosemary.

5. Remove the pastry from the fridge and unwrap it. Dust a clean surface with flour and roll the pastry out to the thickness of a pound coin (large enough to generously line a 23cm tart tin). If it's difficult to work with you can do this between two pieces of greaseproof paper. Line the tart tin with the pastry, letting it overhang to allow for shrinkage, and put the lined tin in the fridge until the pastry is firm, then prick the base with a fork and then line with crumpled greaseproof paper and fill it with baking beans. Blind-bake the pastry for 30 minutes, then lift out the beans and paper and return it to the oven it a further 10 minutes to crisp up the bottom. Remove from the oven and turn the oven down to 180°C/160°C fan/gas 4.

6. In the meantime, heat a little olive oil in a frying pan over a medium-high heat, add the chard (or spinach) leaves and stalks and gently wilt for a couple of minutes. Drain in a sieve, squeeze out any excess moisture, then roughly chop.

7. In a bowl, whisk the eggs, cream and yoghurt together with the Parmesan and a pinch of salt. Spoon a layer of the shallot mix onto the bottom of the baked tart case, followed by half the chard. Pour over half the custard, then layer on the rest of the shallot and tomato mix and the remaining chard. Pour over the rest of the custard, add a few more sprigs of rosemary to the top and a little more grated Parmesan, then drizzle over a little more olive oil or any left in the roasting tray. Bake in the oven for 25–30 minutes, or until set but still a little wobbly. Remove from the oven and allow to cool for 15 minutes or so, then serve with a sharp green salad . I love this tart with some anchovies on top, too.

Whole brined, spatchcocked barbecue chicken
with charred lemon butter and green romesco sauce

This is my go-to brine for chicken (see the next recipe for more on the advantages of brining). Use a lidded kettle barbecue or – if you only have a charcoal grill – start it on the barbecue to get the smoky flavour and finish it in the oven. If you don't have a big barbecue, break the bird down into breasts and legs on the bone and cook them separately, cooking the legs for a little longer (use the carcass for stock). Serve with the charred bean, broccoli and anchovy salad on page 202 (pictured opposite).

1 organic chicken (about 1.2kg)
1 tsp smoked sweet paprika
vegetable oil, for brushing
sea salt and freshly ground black
   pepper

For the brine
50g sea salt
25g caster sugar
1 litre water
4 bay leaves
2 garlic cloves, peeled
pared zest of 1 unwaxed lemon,
   pith scraped off
1 tsp fennel seeds or wild fennel
   head

For the charred lemon butter
50g unsalted butter
2 garlic cloves, crushed
2 tsp maple syrup or honey
1 sprig of thyme
1 tbsp tarragon leaves
½ lemon

For the green romesco
1 green pepper
2 green chillies
1 slice of stale sourdough bread
   (shop-bought or see recipe
   on page 24), soaked for
   30 minutes in 2 tbsp water
2 garlic cloves, peeled
1 tinned anchovy fillet
1 tbsp capers
30g flat-leaf parsley
leaves from 4 sprigs of tarragon
30g whole almonds (skin on or
   off) or flaked almonds

1. To make the brine, place the salt, sugar and water in a non-reactive saucepan. Bring to the boil, stirring, until the salt and sugar have dissolved, then add the other ingredients, remove from the heat and allow to cool to room temperature.

2. To spatchcock the chicken, put it on a board, breast side down, with its legs pointing towards you. Using sharp scissors or poultry shears, cut out the backbone and parson's nose in one piece (freeze to use in stock). Turn the chicken over and press on the breastbone to break and flatten. Fold the chicken in half and place it in a large Tupperware box, or a large Ziplock bag does the job nicely. Once the chicken is in a container, pour over the brine, making sure the bird is submerged. If you're using a bag, squeeze out the air to create a vaccuum before sealing. Cover and chill for at least 4 hours, preferably overnight.

3. If you're cooking on the barbecue, fill the barbecue bowl three-quarters full with charcoal and light it 20–30 minutes in advance. Remove the chicken from the brine, pat it dry with kitchen paper and let it come to room temperature, then rub the skin with smoked paprika and season. You need the coals to be glowing white for the bird, otherwise it will burn, but you can char your green pepper and chillies for the sauce while it's reaching this stage.

4. To make the romesco, cook the pepper and chillies directly over the coals (or on a griddle or under the grill), turning frequently, until charred. Transfer to a bowl, cover with cling film and cool, then rub the skins off with kitchen paper. Deseed and pulse in a food processor with the bread, garlic, anchovy, capers, herbs and almonds to a coarse paste, then add the remaining ingredients and blitz to combine. Season with salt or a little more lemon to taste.

5. For the charred lemon butter, gently melt the butter in a pan with the remaining ingredients (except the lemon, which is charred and added later).

6. Use metal tongs or a skewer to split the white coals in half and push them to either side of the barbecue, leaving a gap in the middle. Place the grill grate on the barbecue and brush it with a little oil and put the chicken, skin side down, over the gap between the coals, placing the lemon half cut side down over the coals. Cook for 6 minutes, until the lemon is caramelised and the chicken is coming away from the grate easily, then turn the chicken and remove the lemon, squeezing the juice into the butter pan. Brush the chicken with the caramelised lemon butter, cover the barbecue with a lid with the vents open and cook for another 40–50 minutes,

pinch of coriander seeds
1 tsp honey
juice of ½ lemon
100ml olive oil
pinch of salt

brushing the butter onto the bird every 10 minutes or so as it cooks. If you're roasting the chicken in the oven, cook it at 190°C/170°C fan/gas 5 for the same amount of time.

7. Use a temperature probe or meat thermometer to measure the temperature of the thickest part of the thigh and breast, and when it reads 65°C remove the chicken to rest. If it hasn't yet reached this temperature, cover again (or put it back in the oven) and cook for about 10 more minutes. Once the chicken is cooked, transfer to a board and leave to rest for at least 20 minutes while you make any side dishes.

8. Carve the chicken by taking the legs off, then the breasts, and slicing them. Serve with the sauce and some greens or potato salad on the side.

Whey-brined lamb chops

Serves 2 as a main,
4 as part of a barbecue

Whey do we brine? Well, if you'll excuse the terrible pun, there are a couple of very good reasons why brining – soaking meat, poultry or fish in a salt solution or rubbing them with a dry brine of salt and aromatics – has been practised for centuries and more recently re-embraced by restaurant kitchens the world over. Firstly, it's not that much of a faff; and secondly, it improves the cooking of most meat, fish and poultry.

Putting salt on a protein, whether in a solution or by sprinkling it straight on the flesh, means that the protein draws in the salt and plenty of extra moisture (from the salt solution or the moisture that is drawn out by the dry brine being sucked back in), so loses less liquid when cooked, keeping it juicy. The salt also works to denature the proteins and muscle fibres, allowing them to retain more moisture and also tenderises the meat. And it seasons the protein, enhancing the flavour.

You can also pimp up a brine and customise it with spices and aromatics. Whey, which adds a lactic nuttiness to the lamb in this recipe, is also great with chicken and pork. For fish and steak, I prefer a dry brine, which often simply involves seasoning the flesh really well with salt 20 minutes before cooking.

Use new season or salt marsh lamb for this recipe as it has such a special, delicate herbaceous flavour. If you don't have any whey from making labneh or ricotta or don't have enough of it, just use water mixed with a tablespoon of caster sugar and the rest of the ingredients below.

These chops are best cooked quickly on a barbecue and are lovely with a sweep of labneh and the Roast Beetroot and Buckwheat Salad on page 203 (pictured opposite).

4 lamb loin chops (about 150g each)
olive oil, for rubbing
2 tbsp Labneh (page 256) or full-fat natural yoghurt

For the brine
250ml whey (see Labneh page 256) or water
10g sea salt
1 garlic clove, chopped
1 shallot, sliced
1 tbsp finely chopped rosemary

1. Whisk the salt into the whey in a bowl until dissolved, then combine with the rest of the brine ingredients. Pour the brine into a Ziplock or other sturdy food bag or large bowl and place the chops in the brine, making sure they are covered completely with the liquid, so they brine evenly. Chill in the fridge for at least 6 hours, preferably overnight, turning them in the brine a few times.

2. Remove the chops from the fridge and the brine 30 minutes before cooking them, so they come to room temperature, and light the barbecue (if using).

3. When the coals are glowing white, rub the chops with a little olive oil and cook them for 3–4 minutes on each side. Alternatively, cook the chops on a griddle pan over a medium-high heat.

4. Transfer the chops from the barbecue or griddle pan to a plate, cover loosely with foil and leave to rest for 5 minutes before serving with salad.

Tomato galette
with lovage and broad bean salsa

Serves 4

This freeform tomato tart is one of my all-time favourite summer recipes. As they're slow-cooked, the flavour of the tomatoes concentrates, and the pastry becomes crisp and toothsome, and sturdy enough to hold in all the gorgeous tomato juices. A sharp salsa of freshly cooked broad beans mixed with the tomato juice brings it all to life upon serving. Use a whole tub of ricotta here, half in the pastry, half in the custard. If a more tender crust is preferred, leave out the rye flour and use all spelt or plain, but I personally love the crunch and texture that the rye provides.

600g tomatoes (different colours and sizes, preferably heritage), cut into 1-cm slices
½ tsp each salt and sugar
2 tsp red wine vinegar
leaves from 2 sprigs of thyme
1 tbsp olive oil

For the Broad Bean Salsa
2 tbsp olive oil
1 tbsp finely shredded lovage leaves (or a mix of flat-leaf parsley and chervil)
2 tbsp blanched and peeled broad beans (fresh or frozen) (see page 82 for blanching technique)
freshly ground black pepper

For the pastry
180g light spelt (or plain) flour and 20g wholegrain rye flour (or 200g spelt or plain flour, if that's all you have), plus extra for dusting
100g ricotta
1 tsp fine sea salt
20ml olive oil
1–3 tbsp iced water
1 egg, beaten
½ tsp fennel seeds

For the filling
1 egg yolk
100g ricotta or Fresh Curd Cheese (page 254)
pinch of salt and black pepper
2 tbsp grated Parmesan or vegetarian hard cheese
1 tbsp capers
1 tsp fennel seeds

1. First, toss the sliced tomatoes with the salt, sugar, red wine vinegar, thyme and a grind of pepper and leave them to marinate for 1 hour. Tip the tomatoes into a sieve placed over a bowl to strain off the juice, reserving the juice to use later in the dressing. Put the tomatoes back in the bowl and toss with the tablespoon of olive oil.

2. While the tomatoes are marinating, make the pastry. Put the flour(s), ricotta and salt in the bowl of a food processor and blitz until the mixture resembles breadcrumbs. Add the olive oil, then add the iced water, a tablespoon at a time, sprinkling it all across the crumb and blitzing between additions until the dough clumps together. Don't add too much water here as this will make the pastry tough (you may not need it all). Tip the dough out into a large bowl, mould it into a ball and flatten to a disc. Wrap it in greaseproof paper (rather than cling film, which makes it sweat) and put it in the fridge to rest for at least 30 minutes.

3. Preheat the oven to 200°C/180°C fan/gas 6 and line a baking sheet with baking parchment.

4. For the filling, mix together the egg yolk, ricotta, salt, pepper and Parmesan in a bowl.

5. Remove the pastry from the fridge, unwrap it and roll it out on a surface lightly dusted with flour into a dinner plate-sized circle with the thickness of a pound coin. Transfer to the lined baking sheet. Spread the custard mixture onto the pastry, leaving a 5cm border around the edge of the circle. Top the mixture with the marinated tomatoes, placing them in concentric overlapping circles. Top with the capers. Gently lift the border of the pastry up and around the filling. As you lift the dough and place it against the filling, it will pleat naturally. Be sure to patch up any tears, then brush the pastry with the beaten egg and scatter over the fennel seeds. Bake in the oven for 1 hour, until the tomatoes have shrivelled and darkened slightly, and the pastry is crisp.

6. Meanwhile, make the salsa by whisking the drained tomato juices in a bowl with the olive oil, then stir through the lovage and broad beans. When the tart is ready, remove it from the oven, leave it to settle for 10–15 minutes, then slice and serve with the lovage and broad bean salsa spooned over.

Sunshine Feasts

Chicken, cherries and chicory

Serves 4

Juicy, golden chicken thighs, caramelised bitter leaves and plump roasted cherries, married together with the anise kiss of tarragon: this dish never fails to make people happy. It's perfect for a lazy summer lunch, because once the chicken is browned it basically gets on with cooking itself, creating a beautifully balanced jus for spooning over. It's adaptable too: substitute the chicory for radicchio or whichever bitter leaf is available, and try mixing it up with apricots or plums – whatever looks most alluring at the greengrocer. If you want to make this for two people, just halve the quantities.

4 tsp sea salt flakes
2 tbsp caster sugar
½ tsp fennel seeds
8 bone-in, skin-on organic chicken pieces – preferably thighs, but a mix of thighs and drumsticks works too
2 tbsp olive oil
4 bay leaves
15g butter
4 heads of chicory (preferably red), halved lengthways
6 shallots, halved (skin on)
1 lemon, halved
150ml glass vermouth or dry white wine
300ml hot water
150g cherries (stone them if you like, but I am too lazy and think they are lovely roasted whole with the stones discarded upon eating, as you might with olives)
handful of tarragon leaves, chopped
freshly ground black pepper

1. A few hours before you cook, grind the salt, sugar and fennel seeds together using a pestle and mortar or spice grinder until the seeds are crushed into the salt, then rub the mixture on the flesh, but not the skin, of the chicken. Chill in the fridge for a few hours (you could leave it overnight) and bring out of the fridge 30 minutes before you cook. If you are short on time, just leave it in the rub while you prepare everything else for the dish.

2. Preheat the oven to 140°C/120°C fan/gas 1. Gently rinse the cure from the chicken and dry it well with kitchen paper.

3. Heat the olive oil in a non-stick frying pan or skillet over a medium heat. Working in batches, add the chicken to the pan, skin side down, and gently brown all over for 8–10 minutes, until the fat has rendered out of the skin and it's golden and crisp all over. Make sure you're wearing an apron and watch out for spitting fat! Remove with a slotted spoon and place skin side up in a large roasting tray on top of the bay leaves. Season with black pepper.

4. The chicken will have released some precious fat into the oil in the frying pan, so you're going to caramelise the chicory and shallots in it. Turn the heat down slightly, add the butter to the pan, then place the chicory, shallot and lemon halves cut side down in the pan and cook for about 5 minutes, until caramelised and softening on their cut sides. Nestle them in the roasting tray cut side up with the chicken and squeeze the lemon over the chicory, throwing the spent lemon in the tray too.

5. Turn the heat up and deglaze the pan with the vermouth or wine, scraping up any crusty bits from the bottom of the pan. Simmer until reduced by half, then pour into the tray, avoiding the chicken skin to keep it crisp.

6. Pour in the hot water, cover the tray with foil and roast in the oven for 30 minutes, then take off the foil and add the cherries and chopped tarragon. Turn the oven up to 200°C/180°C fan/gas 6, return the tray to the oven and roast for a further 30 minutes, until the chicken is cooked, the skin is golden and there is plenty of delicious juice in the tray.

7. Remove the chicken from the oven and serve with the juices spooned over, with some blanched runner or green beans and cooked pasta or rice alongside.

Barbecued bavette
with kale and pumpkin seed mojo verde

Serves 4–6

Bavette or flank steak has a slightly more toothsome texture than more expensive steaks, but its flavour is off the scale. It comes from the flank of the animal and is also known as 'skirt steak' or butcher's cut, because, like onglet, butchers are said to have kept it back for themselves, knowing the secret of its deliciousness. Source it online or from a butcher (supermarkets don't tend to sell it) and try to find some that has been dry-aged for at least 30 days as this improves flavour and tenderises it (pasture-fed beef is the way to go). The kale and pumpkin seed sauce is my version of mojo verde – a zippy green sauce from Tenerife made with coriander, garlic and cumin . It can be made ahead, but make sure it's at room temperature when the steak is served. This dish is perfect with the Asian Watermelon and Black Rice salad on page 122 and the Devilled Corn, Spring Onion and Cheddar Cornbread on page 123 (both pictured opposite).

800g bavette steak, preferably dry-aged for at least 30 days, trimmed of any excess fat and sinew
sea salt and freshly ground black pepper

For the Mojo Verde
40g pumpkin seeds
4 garlic cloves, peeled
1 tsp cumin seeds
120g coriander (leaves and stems)
40g kale, washed, tough stalks removed and leaves roughly chopped
100ml vegetable or sunflower oil
80ml extra-virgin olive oil
½ tsp ground cumin
1 tbsp sherry vinegar
grated zest and juice of 1 lime
1 tsp sea salt
1 tsp honey

1. Take the bavette out of the fridge, season it generously with salt and allow it to come to room temperature – this helps it cook evenly. If you're cooking over a barbecue (which I'd heartily recommend), light it about now.

2. To make the mojo verde, heat a dry frying pan over a medium-high heat, add the pumpkin seeds and garlic cloves and toast for a couple of minutes, stirring, until the pumpkin seeds are puffed and popping, and the garlic cloves are toasted. Add the cumin seeds and toast for a minute or so, until fragrant and slightly browned, but being careful not to let them burn. Remove from the heat and leave to cool a little, then tip everything into the bowl of a food processor or mini chopper. Pulse to a crumb, then add all the other ingredients and blitz well until you have a smooth green sauce. Taste for seasoning and sharpness: it should be earthy, sweet, sharp and savoury all at once and beautifully balanced. You might need to add a little more vinegar to help it to just pique the palate. Pour into a bowl and set aside.

3. You need the charcoal on the barbecue to be glowing white, with no visible flame. If you're cooking the steak on the hob, heat a griddle pan over a high heat until stinking hot. Once the coals are glowing, place the meat on the barbecue grill or griddle and grill for 3 minutes on each side for rare, 5–7 minutes on each side for medium rare. You can test the doneness by pressing the meat. If it's really wobbly in the middle, it will be rare. The firmer it gets, the more cooked it will be. Bear in mind though that bavette always feels a bit soft in the middle – so we're talking varying degrees of softness. Once you're satisfied (it will continue to cook while resting) transfer to a board and leave to rest uncovered for at least 15 minutes. This is crucial as the meat will relax and also retain its juices. If you cut into it straight away the juices will escape.

4. Once rested, season the meat well with black pepper and cut it against the grain into strips. Serve on warmed plates with the mojo verde and slabs of cornbread, if you like.

Watermelon and black rice salad

Serves 2

This dish is all I want from a grain salad – a vivid mixture of contrasting textures and flavours, with earthy black rice, sweet watermelon and cooling mint, fiery chilli and creamy feta. It's at once hearty and healthy, and is fantastic served on a big platter for people to share. Try it with the Barbecued Bavette on page 120, but it's also great as a lunch on its own, with barbecued chicken, fish or charred greens.

200g black rice
2 spring onions, trimmed and finely chopped
10g coriander and mint leaves, chopped, plus extra whole leaves to garnish
100g sugar snap peas, thinly sliced
30g salted peanuts, roughly chopped
300g watermelon, rind and large pips removed, flesh diced
1 tbsp crumbled feta
sea salt

For the dressing
1 tbsp white rice vinegar
juice of ½ lime
2 tsp peeled and grated root ginger
1 tbsp toasted sesame oil
1 tbsp fish sauce
2 tbsp rapeseed oil
1 tsp runny honey
2 tsp light soy sauce
1 garlic clove, crushed
½ red chilli, deseeded and finely chopped

1. Soak the black rice in cold water for a minimum of 30 minutes (up to 2 hours) before you cook it.

2. Bring a saucepan of salted water to the boil and add the rice. Cook according to packet instructions, until tender, then drain in a sieve and rinse with cold water to separate the grains.

3. Whisk all the ingredients for the dressing together.

4. Combine all the ingredients (except for the watermelon and feta) in a bowl, season with salt and dress with the dressing. Stir through the watermelon, load onto a platter and scatter with the feta and some whole mint and coriander leaves.

Devilled corn, spring onion and Cheddar cornbread

Serves 4–6

This crumbly, cheese-laden spiced cornbread is easy to make and is such a good one for picnics and barbecues. While it can't be claimed that it's authentic Southern cornbread (we're using cornmeal instead of grits because they're hard to find in the UK), it's still properly tasty. Fermented chillies cut through the sweetness and corn brings texture and chew. This can be made gluten free by swapping out the plain flour for gluten-free flour.

100g unsalted butter, plus extra for greasing
½ tsp cayenne pepper
1 tsp smoked sweet paprika
½ tsp sea salt
1 tbsp Worcestershire sauce
100g sweetcorn, preferably cut fresh from the raw cob (you can use tinned as a substitute)
250g fine cornmeal or polenta
100g plain flour
1 tsp baking powder
1 tbsp caster sugar
100g mature Cheddar cheese, grated
2 eggs
200ml buttermilk
200ml milk
2 spring onions, trimmed and finely chopped
25g Fermented Green Chillies (page 146), or shop-bought pickled green chillies
grated zest of ½ lime

1. Preheat the oven to 250°C/230°C fan/gas 9. Grease a 25 x 15cm enamel roasting tray or cake tin generously with butter and line it with baking parchment.

2. Gently melt the butter in a frying pan over a medium heat. Add the spices, salt, Worcestershire sauce and corn and cook for a couple of minutes then turn off the heat and leave to cool.

3. Sift the dry ingredients into a large bowl, add the sugar and stir through the grated cheese.

4. In a bowl or jug, beat the eggs gently with the buttermilk and milk until combined, then stir through the spring onions, fermented green chillies and lime zest. Tip the devilled corn into the egg and milk mixture and stir. Pour the wet mix into the dry mix and stir to combine, then pour into the well-buttered roasting tray or cake tin. Bake in the oven for 25 minutes, until puffed and golden and a skewer inserted comes out clean.

5. Remove from the oven, tip it out of the tin onto a board while it's still warm, then cut it into squares and serve.

Barbecued butterflied sardines

Serves 4 as a starter,
or as part of a barbecue

Packed full of flavour, these oily little fish are made for the barbecue, their skin blistering and charring, the flesh turning soft and smoky when cooked over coal. I visited Lisbon one June, during the Feast of St Anthony celebrations, when the whole city fills with smoke and its streets are lined with barbecues of grilled sardines by their thousands, which are served on crusty bread. We were only there for two days, but we became addicted to the grilled sardines. All they need is a little extra-virgin olive oil, chilli flakes and lemon, and a crusty bread roll, like they eat them in Portugal. Try to find Cornish sardines if you can, as they are more plentiful.

500g fresh sardine fillets, butterflied (ask your fishmonger to butterfly them for you)
½ lemon
2 tbsp extra-virgin olive oil, plus extra for greasing
½ tsp dried chilli flakes
sea salt

1. Light the barbecue. Once the coals are glowing, grease the grate with oil or grab a fish grilling basket or hand-held clamping grate.

2. Place the lemon cut side down over the grill. Season the fillets with sea salt then toss them with a tablespoon of the olive oil. Grill them for a few minutes on each side (directly on the grate, or contained by a fish grilling basket or clamping grate), until the flesh is just opaque and the skin is starting to char. Remove from the grill, drizzle with the remaining olive oil, scatter over the dried chilli flakes and squeeze over the lemon juice from the caramelised, grilled lemon.

Barbecued bream
with onion, sumac and runner bean salad

Serves 2

Bream cooked gently over coals, until the skin is crisp and the flesh moist and smoky, transforms it into something really special and, because the fish is usually a modest size, ideal for a diminutive beach barbecue. For the summer, it's worth investing in a couple of barbecue fish baskets – buy them online and they make cooking fish over coals much easier. The onion, sumac and runner bean salad is best made ahead and left to sit for at least an hour before serving, so that the flavours have a chance to really mingle, making it perfect for packing up and taking to the beach.

2 sea bream (about 300–400g) each, gutted and scaled
rapeseed, groundnut or vegetable oil
salt

For the onion, sumac and runner bean salad
2 red onions, thinly sliced
1 tsp salt
juice of 1 lemon
1 tbsp sumac
200g fresh, young runner beans, topped and tailed, strings removed and very thinly sliced
1 tbsp chopped flat-leaf parsley
olive oil

1. First, make the salad. Put the sliced onion in a bowl and scatter over the salt. Give it a rough scrunch with your fingers then add the lemon juice and sumac and toss to combine. Stir in the runner beans and parsley and dress with a little olive oil. Set aside.

2. Light the barbecue and let it burn until the coals are glowing white hot, then bank the coals on one side, leaving a clear space for non-direct cooking.

3. Brush the fish with groundnut or vegetable oil and season with salt. Oil the grate or place the fish in a fish basket. Barbecue the fish, turning it continuously for 15–20 minutes, until the skin is crisp and the flesh is moist and tender. Serve with the onion, sumac and runner bean salad.

Sunshine Feasts

Oysters in their shells *with smoked paprika butter*

Serves 12 as a canapé,
or 6 as starter

Cooking oysters in their shells over the barbecue is great fun. The hot shells quickly cook the molluscs, which become smoky and somehow meatier and more intensely flavoured. If you don't have a barbecue, cook the oysters under a hot grill until bubbling and cooked through.

12 rock oysters
chunks of bread, to serve
(optional)

For the smoked paprika butter
1 tsp fennel seeds
1 shallot, chopped
4 garlic cloves, crushed
100g unsalted butter, at room
temperature
large pinch of sea salt
2 tsp flat-leaf parsley leaves
80g Parmesan, grated
2 tbsp lemon juice
2 tsp Worcestershire sauce
2 tsp cayenne pepper
4 tsp smoked sweet paprika

1. First, make the smoked paprika butter. Blitz the fennel seeds in a small food processor until ground, then add the shallot and garlic and blitz to a paste. Add the butter and remaining ingredients and blitz until you have a bright red butter. Spoon the butter into the centre of a piece of cling film, then roll it up tightly into a sausage shape. Keep in the fridge.

2. Light the barbecue and let it burn until the coals are glowing white hot.

3. Now, shuck your oysters. Fold a tea towel into a strip and lie it on a chopping board (held in place underneath by some damp kitchen paper). Put the oysters on the towel, curved-side down, and wrap the tea towel over. Use a strong knife, preferably a shucking knife, to pierce the hinge, then turn it to open the oyster until you hear it pop. Work the knife around the edge of the shell, being careful not to cut into the oyster, until you can remove the top shell. Disconnect the oyster from its shell so it slides out easily.

4. Slice 12 rounds of butter, place one on top of each oyster and put the oysters on the barbecue for 5–6 minutes, or until bubbling. Serve with bread to mop up the juices.

Scallops in their shells *with green herbed butter*

Serves 12 as a canapé,
or 6 as a starter

Sweet, creamy scallops also work a treat cooked in their shells. The herbed butter melts wonderfully over the scallops. If you can't find scallops in their shells, make a little shell out of foil and follow the instructions below, or place directly on the barbecue grate or on a tray under a hot grill.

12 scallops in the shell, cleaned
rapeseed oil, for brushing
sea salt and freshly ground
black pepper

For the herbed hazelnut butter
30g whole hazelnuts
100g unsalted butter, at room
temperature
8g chervil (or 8g more parsley)
8g tarragon leaves
1 tbsp flat-leaf parsley leaves
1 shallot, finely chopped
2 tsp lemon juice

1. To make the herbed butter, preheat the oven to 200°C/180°C fan/gas 6 and roast the hazelnuts in a roasting tray for 6–8 minutes, until golden. Tip the nuts onto a tea towel and rub them to remove the skins. Pulse the nuts in a food processor to release their oils then add the butter, herbs, a large pinch of salt and pepper, shallot and lemon juice. Blitz until you have a green-flecked butter. Spoon the butter into the centre of a piece of cling film, then roll it up tightly into a sausage shape. Keep in the fridge.

2. Light the barbecue and let it burn until the coals are glowing white hot. Brush the scallops on both sides with rapeseed oil and season with salt. Place in their shells on the barbecue for 1–2 minutes, until they start to colour. Turn them over and dot each with 2 teaspoons of the butter, then return to the barbecue for 1–2 minutes, until the butter has melted.

Crab with tarragon mayonnaise

My love of crab stems from hours spent observing my dad slowly pick every last morsel of sweet white meat from its shell. The excitement and ceremony he allowed for the task taught me a reverence for the crustacean that has endured into adulthood.

I love to keep this family tradition alive. When I'm on the coast, I'll pick up some freshly cooked crab from the fishmonger and take it down to the beach with this lush, tarragon-laced mayonnaise and homemade bread. A slow beach feast for a long summer's evening.

2 whole, freshly cooked crabs from the fishmonger, cracked
sliced sourdough (shop-bought or see page 24)
lemon wedges
dried chilli flakes or crushed pink peppercorns
wild fennel fronds and flowers or ground fennel seeds, for sprinkling

For the tarragon mayonnaise
1 egg, plus 1 egg yolk, at room temperature
½ tsp salt
1 tbsp Dijon mustard
2 garlic cloves, peeled
½ lemon, for squeezing
2 tbsp extra-virgin olive oil
300ml vegetable or sunflower oil
30g tarragon, leaves picked and finely chopped

1. First, make the mayonnaise. Put the egg, egg yolk, salt, Dijon mustard, garlic and a squeeze of lemon juice in a food processor or blender and blitz until smooth. With the blades still turning, very, very slowly drip in the extra-virgin olive oil, a drop at a time, until the oil starts to emulsify and the egg mixture looks smooth and creamy. Once the olive oil is incorporated, very slowly start to drip in the vegetable or sunflower oil, blitzing the whole time, until the mayonnaise starts to thicken. Once you've added about half the oil and it's looking thick and creamy, increase the pouring of the oil to a steady stream. The adding of the oils can take anything between 10–15 minutes. If it becomes too thick and stiff at any point, just add a few drops of water or a squeeze of lemon juice and blitz again. Once the mayonnaise is plump and emulsified, add a tablespoon of cold water and blitz until creamy – this will lighten the mayo. Scrape it out into a bowl and stir through the chopped tarragon. Refrigerate for at least 3 hours to infuse (you could make it a day in advance).

2. To extract the meat from the crabs: remove the legs and claws from the cooked crabs, use nut crackers or a heavy knife to crack their shell, and use the end of a teaspoon or a crab pick to mine out the meat. To pick the meat from the cracked crab, separate the 'purse' (the bit the legs are attached to it) from the outer shell by putting the crab on its back and pushing up on the purse, it should come away quite easily, then remove and discard the 'dead man's fingers' (the inedible feathery gills attached to the purse or shell). Use a paring knife to score around the inner shell, following its natural curve, and remove it, then push the jaw down into the shell until it breaks away and remove it – the stomach sack will come away too. Scrape out the brown meat into a bowl. To get the meat from the purse, scrape all the meat from the top of it then cut it open and mine all the meat from the inside. I like mixing the white and brown meat together, but you can keep them separate if you're particular.

3. Serve the crab meat with the mayonnaise, fresh sourdough, lemon wedges, chilli or peppercorns and wild fennel fronds or flowers (or fennel seeds).

TIP: If the mayonnaise splits, do not despair. Just transfer it to a bowl, clean the bowl of the food processor then add 1 tablespoon of hot water and repeat the dripping and blitzing with the broken mixture. If this also fails, do not give up! Remove the broken mixture and clean the food processor, then try again with an extra egg yolk, blitzing and dripping the broken mixture in until it comes back together.

Cured smoked sea trout

Serves 2–4

It's easy to smoke meaty fish like sea trout or salmon in a kettle barbecue. All you need is charcoal, an egg box and wood chips. The smoked sea trout is lovely in the Salt-baked Jersey Royal Potato and Smoked Trout Salad on page 138, or with sour cream and dill on the Beetroot and Horseradish Blinis or Sour Cream Sourdough Crumpets on pages 29 and 27. Be aware that the curing and smoking process takes two days (if you have a particular occasion you want to make it for).

Try not to eat sea trout during their spawning season which runs from November until March.

1 side of wild sea trout or Norwegian Fjord trout (or salmon) (1–1.5kg)
3 handfuls of wood chips (I like applewood), plus a few extra chips which have been soaked in water for an hour or so
a couple of pieces of charcoal
1 empty tin or small foil flan dish covered loosely with foil
1 piece of foil
1 egg box

For the cure
80g sea salt flakes
80g golden caster sugar
grated zest of 1 unwaxed lemon

1. Place a piece of greaseproof paper large enough to enclose the whole fish on a plastic tray or roasting tray. Combine the cure ingredients in a bowl. Scatter a couple of tablespoons of the cure in a thin layer on the bottom of the tray. Place the fish skin side down on the layer of cure in the tray, then add the rest of the cure and coat the fish completely, then wrap it in the paper, and tightly wrap the paper in cling film. Place another, smaller tray on top and weigh it down with tins from your cupboard. Leave to cure in the fridge for at least 8 hours, or overnight.

2. The next day, rinse the excess cure from the fish and gently pat it dry. You'll notice that lots of moisture has formed in the tray as it's left the fish, and that the flesh is nice and tacky – this means that the smoke will stick to it nicely, making for a great flavour. Place the fish back in the fridge uncovered to dry out for about 10 hours.

3. Now, set up your barbecue smoker. You are going to build a small fire in your tin or foil flan dish. If you don't have a tin or foil flan dish, make a small shell or bowl out of a couple of layers of foil and place them in the bottom of the barbecue to one side. Inside, first place a few bits of torn egg box (this works well as kindling as it's uncoated), followed by a lump of coal, a bit more egg box and then the dry wood chips. Light the egg box and watch as the wood chips and coal catch. You want to let any flames burn off for a few minutes, then add the moistened wood chips on top to smoulder. Pierce some holes in the separate piece of foil and rest it on top of the tin or foil bowl. It should be producing a steady stream of smoke, but very little heat. Place your grate on the barbecue and remove the trout from the fridge. Put the trout as far away from the homemade smoker as possible, on the other side of the grill, cover the barbecue with a lid and smoke for 1–1½ hours, checking every now and then and relighting the smoker if it goes out or adding a few more wood chips if you need to. It will have changed colour to a deeper shade of coral (as pictured opposite), and the meat will be condensed, dry and no longer raw.

4. Remove the cured smoked fish from the barbecue. Let it cool, wrap it in greaseproof paper and use flaked on toast or blinis or in pasta or salads, as in the recipes on the next pages. It will keep in the fridge for up to 4 days.

Salt-baked Jersey Royal potato and smoked trout salad

Serves 2 for lunch,
or 4 as a starter or side

Salt-baking Jersey Royals concentrates the flavours of these already immensely flavourful new potatoes, taking their earthy minerality to new heights. Paired with home-smoked trout, sour cream, peppery watercress and sweet pickled radish, this is a perfect lunch or starter for spring. Use your home-smoked trout on page 136, but shop-bought also works well, and, if you can find them, use thinly sliced three-cornered leek or wild garlic instead of spring onion.

100g coarse sea salt
250g Jersey Royal potatoes, scrubbed
100g Cured Smoked Sea Trout fillet (page 136), or good-quality shop-bought smoked trout
3 tbsp sour cream
¼ tsp ground black pepper
2 spring onions, trimmed and thinly sliced
2 handfuls of watercress
handful of dill
1 tbsp salmon or lumpfish roe (optional)

For the sweet pickled radish
2 tbsp rice wine vinegar or lemon juice
2 tsp caster sugar
6 radishes (a mix of varieties works nicely and French breakfast ones look lovely), thinly sliced

1. Preheat the oven to 200°C/180°C fan/gas 6.

2. Scatter the sea salt in a thick layer on a baking tray, arrange the potatoes on top and bake in the oven for 45 minutes, or until tender.

3. While the potatoes are cooking, make the sweet pickled radish. Combine the vinegar and sugar in a non-reactive saucepan over a medium heat and whisk until the sugar has dissolved. Allow to cool then pour over the radish slices in a heatproof bowl. Leave to sit while the potatoes bake.

4. Remove the potatoes from the oven and allow to cool a little until you can handle them. Transfer the potatoes to a bowl (keep the salt in an airtight container and reuse for future salt-baking) and while they're still warm, flake half the fish over the top of them, tumbling the fish and potatoes together gently to combine. Mix the sour cream with the pepper and toss it into the potatoes along with the spring onions and two-thirds of the watercress and dill, reserving a few watercress leaves and dill fronds for garnish. Tip into a serving bowl or onto a platter and strew over the remaining smoked trout, drained pickled radishes and watercress. Top with the roe (if using) and dill fronds.

Smoked trout and radicchio salad
with beetroot and pickled gooseberries

Serves 4

Smoked trout and beetroot is a harmonious combination, and if you have any home-smoked trout (page 136) or pickled gooseberries, this healthy, hearty grain salad ticks all the boxes. There is a Nordic feeling about it, with the smoked fish, dill and pickles, and the grains and bitter leaves give it guts and heft – perfect for packing into tubs for a picnic or lunch on the go. Soaking the dry grains reduces the residue/scum which appears on the surface during cooking and helps cut down on the cooking time.

2 small or medium beetroots (use golden or candy-striped beetroots if you can find them), scrubbed

120g pearl barley, spelt or cracked freekeh, soaked in water for 2 hours (or 30 minutes if you're short on time)

2 tbsp lemon juice or raw apple cider vinegar

1 shallot, diced

3–4 tbsp extra-virgin olive oil or rapeseed oil, plus extra for drizzling

1 tsp honey

1 head radicchio (pink, castelfranco or red)

1 tbsp dill fronds, plus extra to garnish

1 tbsp flat-leaf parsley leaves, plus extra to garnish

15g Pink Peppercorn-pickled Gooseberries (page 154)

200g Cured Smoked Sea Trout (page 136)

sea salt and freshly ground black pepper

2 tbsp Savoury Granola (page 262), to serve (optional)

1. Preheat the oven to 240°C/220°C fan/gas 8 or its highest setting.

2. Place each beetroot on a piece of foil big enough to enclose it, drizzle with a little olive or rapeseed oil to coat and season with salt. Wrap the beetroots in the foil and roast in the oven on a baking tray for 1–1½ hours, until they are tender all the way through. You'll know they're done when a skewer inserted into a beetroot can be pulled out with no resistance. Remove the beetroot from the oven and leave until cool enough to handle, then rub off the skins with kitchen paper or the back of a teaspoon and cut them into wedges. You can roast the beetroot in advance.

3. Drain the grains and cook them in plenty of boiling salted water according to packet instructions, or until just tender. Drain and return to the pan.

4. Whisk the lemon juice or vinegar in a bowl with a pinch of salt and taste. If it's still unpalatably sharp, add a little more salt. Season with black pepper. Add the shallot and allow to sit for a few minutes, then whisk in the oil and honey, tasting as you go. Stop when you're happy, then pour just under half of the dressing onto the grains and stir to coat.

5. Peel any floppy or scruffy outer leaves from the radicchio and discard, then remove about eight of the nice, firm outer leaves, rip any really big ones in half, and place them in a bowl. Slice the remaining radicchio leaves and add them to the bowl. Add the herbs, beetroot wedges and pickled gooseberries and flake in the smoked fish. Lightly tumble together to combine, then dress with enough of the remaining dressing to just coat everything – be careful here as you don't want soggy salad.

6. Scatter the grains onto a platter and top with the dressed salad. Garnish with extra herbs and some savoury granola (if you like).

Fermented, Pickled and Preserved

This chapter is like a bridge between the cooking seasons: a section that explores preserving ingredients while they're at their best, through the transformative power of fermentation and pickling. Learning how simple, natural and flavour-enhancing fermentation is to do at home has been life-changing for me, and I wanted to share how fun and easy it is to harness its powers to change and improve ordinary ingredients. Use these easy recipes as a jumping off point, and soon your kitchen will be filled with lively little jars of wonderful probiotic foods.

My hope is that you'll have a go at making the sour, fiery kimchi (page 145), fizzy, funky tomatoes (page 148) and the other recipes, be astounded by how they burst with flavour, and then use them throughout your cooking to add another layer of texture and taste. Preserving with vinegar and other aromatic ingredients is another fantastic way to prolong using seasonal ingredients, and I've included some new ideas for preserving with fruit as well as veg: pink peppercorn-pickled gooseberries (page 154) are sour little flavour bombs that add zing to a smoked fish salad, while sweet, juicy pickled peaches (page 153) are made for eating with chargrilled meats.

A note on fermentation

I grew up in 1980s England, and while fermented products like wine, beer, yoghurt, cheese and olives were staples at our kitchen table, the art of fermentation as a means to preserving food wasn't something I was remotely aware of, let alone understood. Everything in a jar on our kitchen shelf had been pasteurised or pickled with vinegar (more on that later) and I wouldn't realise quite what I was missing until many years later, when I tasted my first lively mouthful of proper, palate-perking fermented sauerkraut while living in north America in my twenties.

Fermentation is the natural process that occurs when fruit or vegetables are mixed with salt and stored at room temperature in a sterile, oxygen-free environment, promoting the growth of friendly bacteria and inhibiting the presence of nasties. These obligingly heroic bacteria, along with naturally occurring wild yeasts found on the veg or fruit, have a bit of a party together, feasting on the sugars in the plant, producing lactic acid and both souring and transforming the flavour of the ingredient into something altogether more interesting.

Working as a food writer over the past decade, I would have had to have resisted pretty hard to not fall for the funky joys of fermentation. With Nordic chefs leading the charge, suddenly restaurants all over the place were re-embracing this age-old method of preservation, filling crocks with all manner of vegetables and that crucial ingredient, salt, and leaving them to magically metamorphosise for weeks at a time. I remember a formative meal at a favourite local restaurant called Raw Duck in Hackney where I tasted fermented radish (which inspired my recipe on page 147) for the first time, my mouth pleasurably puckering at the tang, my palate dazzled by the intensity of the flavours on offer. The technique has also gained traction with nutritionists and health enthusiasts who extol the gut-friendly, probiotic benefits of these foods.

But this method is not and should not just be for restaurants and health gurus, it is traditionally a home preserving technique, used by cultures the world over for millennia to preserve gluts of seasonal ingredients. Happily, it's something anyone and everyone can do at home with a little guidance and very little fuss or equipment. All you need are fresh vegetables, sterile preserving vessels, salt and some time.

The thing I love most about fermented foods is that they taste so lively, because they are, well, alive. What's amazing is that the process not only preserves the ingredient, those clever cultures transform it into something completely different to what you started with – and for home cooks and anyone interested in food, this opens up a new horizon of exciting flavours, giving your food a real edge. Start experimenting with some of the fermented recipes in this chapter and you'll see how simple it is to do, and how it can inject your cooking with heaps of character and new layers of flavour. Remember too, that a little goes a long way because veg that has been fermented tastes sour, and like a much more intense, amplified version of what you started with. Rot on.

My 'kind of' kimchi

Fills 1 x 500ml
preserving jar or
fermenting crock

Kimchi is Korea's national dish, a household staple of salted, fermented vegetables that has found its way into kitchens, restaurants and delis the world over, thanks to its incredible flavour combination of sour, fire, crunch, salt and funk. I first came across it while living out in Vancouver, where the Asian restaurant scene is phenomenal, and have been addicted to it ever since. There are more than 150 iterations of kimchi in Korea, with recipes varying according to family, region and season; I am not claiming this is authentically Korean, but it is a simple version that anyone can make at home. Shop-bought versions are widely available now, but it is worth making it yourself as it has a much fresher flavour and crunchier texture. While its flavour can initially take some getting used to, if you're anything like me, you'll want it on everything, from toasted sandwiches to fried eggs with sourdough. You can also use it in the other kimchi recipes throughout this book.

2 Chinese or napa cabbages,
halved, washed and
carefully dried
60g sea salt flakes, plus a
pinch for the jar
2 spring onions, trimmed and
finely chopped
5 radishes, cut into
matchsticks
1 large carrot, cut into
matchsticks
½ unwaxed lemon

For the paste
1 onion, chopped
8 garlic cloves, chopped
40g piece of root ginger,
peeled and chopped
1 bird's-eye chilli, chopped
2 tsp salt
2 tsp caster sugar
2 tbsp fish sauce
4 tbsp dried chilli flakes

1. Cut a 3-cm slit in the middle of the base of each half cabbage. Put in a bowl and rub the sea salt into and all over and inbetween the leaves of the cabbage without pulling the halves apart. Place the halves on top of each other and weigh them down with a bottle or tin. Keep turning the cabbage halves every hour for a few hours, until they've given up about half a cup of water and are softened, then leave them in the fridge overnight.

2. The next day, put the cabbages in a clean washing-up bowl with plenty of cold water and rinse off the excess salt, changing the water three times. Dry with kitchen paper.

3. Combine the spring onion in a bowl with the radish and carrot matchsticks.

4. In a mini chopper, food processor or NutriBullet, blitz the paste ingredients to a paste consistency. Scrape it into the bowl of radishes, carrot and spring onion and mix together. Gently rip the cabbage halves at the slit in the middle to form quarters. Now slather the paste and radish mix all over the the cabbage quarters, tucking it between the leaves.

5. Sterilise a 500ml preserving jar according to the instructions on page 2.

6. Scatter a pinch of salt in the bottom of the sterilised jar then pack the cabbage quarters into the jar, pressing them down firmly using a pestle or wooden spoon to squeeze as much liquid out of the cabbage as possible so that it will eventually entirely cover it in the jar, creating an anaerobic environment. Keep packing in the cabbage and radish mix, pressing down firmly as you go. Press down a final time, to cover the cabbage in brine (if there isn't enough brine, just mix up a little more salt brine, at a percentage of 5 per cent salt to water, and pour it over the top). Scrunch up a big ball of greaseproof paper or baking parchment and stuff it into the top of the jar to keep the cabbage in the liquid, then add the lemon half, cut side up. It usually fits neatly, like a plug. Cover with a clean muslin and seal with an elastic band.

Recipe continues over the page

7. Leave the jar in a cool, dark place for 4 days. As the days go by, the mixture will ferment and the natural yeasts and bacteria will work on the sugars, creating lactic acid which will turn it sour. Taste your kimchi after a few days. If it smells or tastes in any way bad, discard it: you want it to be crunchy and have a spicy, sour flavour. How quickly you get there will depend on the temperature of the environment, so keep checking and tasting, until you're happy with how sour it tastes. Once you're happy, keep it in the fridge. It will continue to ferment and change, but at a much slower rate, and can be kept for months in the fridge.

Fermented green chillies

Fills 1 x 450ml jar

300ml water
½ tsp caster sugar
6g salt
150g green jalapeño chillies
1 bay leaf (optional)
½ tsp coriander seeds
1 garlic clove, peeled

I've always loved adding store-bought pickled chillies to dishes, so discovering that I could easily ferment my own at home has been a game-changer. It's so easy to do and the result is tangy, fiery, savoury chillies whose flavour changes and develops with fermentation into something altogether more interesting. Try them in the Squishy Aubergine, Crispy Chickpea and Broccoli Salad (page 59), Devilled Corn, Spring Onion and Cheddar Cornbread (page 123), Waste Not, Want Not Allotment Greens Pasties (page 40), or on a Sourdough Pizza (page 62).

1. Sterilise a 450ml jar according to the instructions on page 2.

2. Bring the water to the boil in a saucepan, add the sugar and salt and stir to dissolve. Remove from the heat and allow to cool. Meanwhile, chop the chillies into 2-mm rings and with the end of a teaspoon, or wearing gloves, push out the foamy, seedy centres. Place the chillies in the sterilised jar with the bay leaf (if using), coriander seeds and garlic clove. Once the brine is cool, pour it over the chillies. Cover with a piece of muslin, securing it with an elastic band, and leave at room temperature for 3–4 days, until sour and tangy, then remove the muslin and elastic band, seal with a lid and chill. It will keep for months, but the garlic clove will start to break down into the brine. If that bothers you, just discard it.

Mixed Ferments
Turnip, beetroot and garlic
Radish, kohlrabi and red onion

Fills 1 x 250g jar

Here are a couple of ideas for mixed vegetable ferments to get you started. The method is the same, just change the ingredients. I always think both turnip and kohlrabi are an underrated veg, but they are both hard enough to stand up to a long ferment and retain good structure and crunch while taking on a really wonderful sour tang.

Combining pale, porous ingredients with beetroot (as below) also means you get a lovely pink hue on them. They're a great thing to nibble on at the start of a meal to get your juices going, but they are also wonderful used as a condiment to bring acidity and freshness to rich dishes, or layered into greens or grain salads (see the Squishy Aubergine, Crispy Chickpea and Broccoli Salad on page 59).

Basically, wherever something is quite one-note, add some finely chopped fermented veg to liven things up and bring an extra dimension. It's worth also remembering to keep the brines from your ferments, they are a brilliant pick-me-up if you're feeling a little fragile and lovely sloshed into salad dressings instead of vinegar or lemon. They will also help kick-start the next batch of ferments, if a little is added to the brine, a bit like a sourdough starter.

**For the Fermented Turnip,
Beetroot and Garlic**
6g sea salt
300ml water
pinch of fennel seeds or
2 black peppercorns
2 small turnips (250–300g in
total), peeled and cut into
thick wedges
1 beetroot, peeled and cut into
thick wedges
4 garlic cloves, peeled

**For the Fermented Radish,
Kohlrabi and Red Onion**
6g salt
300ml water
pinch of fennel seeds
½ kohlrabi (about 200g),
peeled and cut into small
wedges
2 radishes, quartered
1 red onion, quartered

1. Sterilise a 250g preserving jar according to the instructions on page 2.

2. Bring the salt, water and peppercorns or fennel seeds to the boil in a saucepan, until the salt has dissolved. Remove from the heat and allow to cool completely.

3. Pack the vegetables in the jar and pour over the cooled brine. Make sure the vegetables are all covered with liquid and no part is exposed to the air. Use a ball of scrunched up greaseproof paper to weigh any floating veg down if you need to. Cover with clean muslin, seal with an elastic band and leave in a cool, dark place for 4–6 days to ferment. Taste your ferment after a few days. If it smells or tastes in any way bad, discard it – you want a sour, slightly funky (in a good way) flavour. How quickly you get there will depend on the warmth of the environment, so keep checking and tasting, leaving it until you're happy with how sour it tastes. Once you're happy, remove the greaseproof paper, close the jar with its lid and keep it in the fridge. It will continue to get more sour in the fridge too, though this will happen at a slower rate.

Fermented tomatoes

These fermented tomatoes are fizzing with flavour and life. They explode in your mouth, showering your taste buds with their surprising, tangy, sweet, anise-spiked juices. Not only are these good for your gut, they are good for your soul, too, I think.

I first heard about fermented tomatoes from my Ukrainian friend Olia Hercules, a food writer and chef who has written extensively on the subject of fermentation and whose love of her native cuisine's heritage of preserving is truly infectious. Fermenting tomatoes not only turns them wonderfully sour (thanks to the lactic acid produced during fermentation) and amplifies their tomato flavour, but it also brings them to life as an ingredient in a new and revelatory way and also infuses them with the flavour of whatever you ferment them with.

Garlic and wild fennel are my aromatics of choice here, making these lively little toms a wonderful accompaniment to fish and seafood, whether cooked into a sauce (try some in the Seafood and Fennel Linguine on page 94), or served alongside them. In fact, they add depth and tang to any braise that calls for tomatoes. To benefit from the good bacteria and probiotics produced during their fermentation, eat them raw: as a snack, or to add another layer of flavour to salads. They are also delightful as an alternative to a bowl of olives, eaten with bread and butter at the start of a meal, taken on a picnic, or as an alternative to a normal pickle with your fish and chips!

500g small or cherry
    tomatoes, washed
2 garlic cloves, sliced
handful of fresh herbs – I
    love wild fennel but you
    could use lovage, parsley,
    tarragon or dill
10g sea salt
5ml whey (see Labneh, page
    256), or from live yoghurt
    or kimchi juice (from a
    shop-bought jar or see
    page 145) or brine from the
    ferments on previous page

1. Sterilise a 1-litre preserving jar (or 2 x 500g preserving jars) according to the instructions on page 2.

2. Prick each tomato multiple times with a skewer. Put them in the sterilised jar(s) with the garlic and herbs.

3. Put the water in a saucepan with the salt and heat, stirring, until the salt has dissolved. Remove from the heat and allow to cool. Once it has cooled completely, pour it over the tomatoes. Cover the neck of the jar with a piece of clean muslin and seal with an elastic band. Leave at room temperature for 3–4 days. As the days pass, keep tasting the tomatoes: you'll notice how the flavour changes and turns more sour and tangy. Use your judgement and preference to decide when to slow the fermentation by refrigerating – you can leave them until they go slightly fizzy (5–7 days), which I love. Once you're happy with them, remove the muslin and elastic band, seal with a lid and refrigerate. Once sealed, be sure to burp the jar every few days, by opening the lid to release any build-up of gas from fermentation. They keep for months, but I'm sure you'll use them up before then.

Fermented slaw

Fills 1 x 1-litre jar

This is slaw, and then some: sour, crunchy, funky and absolutely brilliant as a side for barbecued meat, fish or halloumi, or for topping a steaming bowl of dahl, or a rich stew. Try adding it to a cheese sandwich to take it to the next level, or mixing it with a little mayonnaise or sour cream and eating it as you would coleslaw. I've also been known to eat this on top of pizza... (apologies to any Italians reading.)

1 small red cabbage (about 800g), finely shredded using a mandoline or a really sharp knife
1 large carrot, cut into thin strips
1 white onion, thinly sliced (use a mandoline if you have one)
20g salt
1 tsp black mustard seeds
1 tsp caraway seeds
1 tbsp finely chopped flat-leaf parsley
½ lemon

1. Sterilise a 1-litre preserving jar according to the instructions on page 2.

2. Put the cabbage in a bowl with the carrot and onion and scatter over three-quarters of the salt. Use your hands to scrunch the salt into the cabbage, squeezing really firmly to start releasing the cabbage juices. Once some moisture is apparent, leave to sit at room temperature for 1 hour.

3. After this time, the veg should have released more juice. Scatter over the mustard and caraway seeds, parsley and the rest of the salt and scrunch all the veg together again, tossing to combine it and coat everything in the natural brine that's been released.

4. Now, scatter a pinch more salt on the bottom of the sterilised jar and pack the slaw mix into the jar, using your hands or a wooden spoon to push the mix down firmly so that it's covered by its brine. Cover the top of the slaw with a disc of greaseproof paper so that it's not exposed to air and then scrunch up a big ball of greaseproof or baking paper and stuff it into the top of the jar to keep the veg pressed down and under moisture, then seal the jar with half a lemon, cut half facing up: it usually fits neatly, like a plug. Leave this in a cool, dark place (a shelf in a cupboard or pantry) for 6 days at room temperature.

5. As the days go by, the mixture will ferment and the natural yeasts and bacteria present in the veg will work on the sugars, creating lactic acid which will turn it sour. Taste your fermented slaw after a few days. If it smells or tastes in any way bad, discard it – you want a sour, slightly funky (in a good way) flavour. As with the other ferments, how quickly you get there will depend on the warmth of the environment, so keep checking and tasting, leaving it until you're happy with how sour it tastes. You could leave it for a matter of weeks if you're looking for something really punchy. Once you're happy, remove the lemon and greaseproof paper, close the jar with its lid and keep it in the fridge. It will continue to get more sour in the fridge too, though this will happen at a much slower rate.

Basic kombucha

Makes 4 litres

Kombucha is a probiotic fermented tea drink which is both utterly delicious and wonderful for your gut health. I find it the ultimate non-alcoholic tipple, as it's still got the funky fermented tang I love about beer and wine. You can buy kombucha scobies online, or do what I did, and beg an obliging restaurant for one. You'll find once you get into the swing of making this you'll get addicted and start experimenting with more flavours. If you can get hold of some high-quality flavoured teas and infusions you can use those to impart different flavours – just make sure you have a base of black, green or white tea to start with. If you've never tasted kombucha before I'd recommend buying a bottle and trying it so that you know what taste you're aiming for before you start.

240g caster sugar
30g good-quality white or green loose leaf tea
1 scoby

1. Fill a large saucepan with 4 litres of water and add the sugar. Bring to the boil, stirring to dissolve the sugar, then add the tea and stir. Allow to infuse and cool to tepid, strain the tea through muslin into a sterilised crock or large glass jar (the sort of jar cafes use for communal water is perfect). Add your scoby and cover with clean muslin and secure with an elastic band. Place on a shelf and allow to ferment at room temperature for 5–7 days, tasting it frequently (depending on the time of year, it could take 7–9 days). The most important thing is that you trust your instincts. If it smells eggy or unappealing, or looks mouldy, discard it. Don't worry if there are dark patches on the scoby – this is usually just tea particle clusters – just make sure it doesn't smell off or show signs of mould. There are plenty of pictures online of what a healthy and unhealthy scoby look like, so if in doubt, check.

2. Once your kombucha has fermented to your liking – it should taste pleasingly sour and still a little sweet – it's ready to drink, just remove the scoby, putting it back in the fridge in a jar covered with a bit of the new kombucha. You can either drink it straight away or bottle it in clean reusable glass bottles and keep it in the fridge for up to 1 month. If you do this, be sure to burp the bottles every few days, by opening the cap to release any build-up of gas from fermentation. You can also have a go at flavouring and re-fermenting your kombucha to make it fizzy (see below).

TIP: Aside from its probiotic benefits, another brilliant and fun thing about kombucha is that you can flavour it in so many different ways. Start with the basic recipe above to get your head around the process, then once you've successfully made a batch, start experimenting with flavours. You can get some really excellent flavoured green teas now so you can use those for the initial fermentation, or use flavoured infusions in with the tea.

You can also use fresh or dried fruit, added after the fermentation to both flavour and carbonate your kombucha, because the yeasts and bacteria that live in the kombucha will work on the sugars in the fruit, releasing carbon dioxide to make it fizz. Try making a fresh peach purée and adding it to your bottles, or freshly crushed raspberries, poached rhubarb, or strawberries muddled with basil. The possibilities are endless!

Preserved oranges

Citrus fruit takes around 4 weeks to ferment in salt, and develop a deep, interesting flavour in the process. I fell in love with preserved lemons after discovering how easy they were to make at home, and extended the same logic to oranges, which are also beautifully preserved by packing in salt. This form of preservation takes the bitterness out of the pith, making it edible in a way we're not used to – it's great finely chopped and stirred through sauces and melted butter for fish or meat, or blitzed up with woody herbs, honey, olive oil and chilli for glazing pork, poultry or roasted veg. To make preserved lemons, follow the same method, substituting 6 organic, unwaxed lemons for the oranges and omitting the ginger and bay.

4 organic, unwaxed naval or
    blood oranges
100g sea salt flakes or coarse
    salt
35g caster sugar
10g peeled and grated root
    ginger
leaves from 2 sprigs of thyme
2 bay leaves
juice of ½ lemon

1. Sterilise two 300ml jars according to the instructions on page 2 and wash and dry the oranges.

2. In a bowl, combine the salt, sugar, grated ginger and thyme. Thinly slice the oranges. Scatter a little of the cure into the bottom of both jars, then, taking one slice of orange, dip it in the salt mix and place it in the bottom of the jar. Repeat with the rest of the slices, placing them on top of each other in the jars, and pushing down lightly to pack them in and produce the brine that needs to cover them to preserve them – there will be plenty of this. When the jars are half full, add a bay leaf to each jar and divide the lemon juice between the jars. Continue to layer up the orange until both jars are filled, then drizzle a little olive oil – enough to just cover the surface of the liquid, making sure no orange has contact with the air. Seal with a lid. Leave to ferment at room temperature for at least 4 weeks, being sure to burp (remove the lid to release any gas build-up so they don't explode) every so often before you use the oranges. The longer you leave them, the tastier they get. They will happily sit unused for years, or once opened keep for a good few months in the fridge.

151

Pickled cherries

Fills 1 x 500ml jar

These juicy little sweet pickled cherries are a brilliant and versatile way to preserve the pleasures of cherry season. They bring a pleasing sweetness and piquancy to slow-cooked meat dishes (add some thinly sliced pickled cherries to the Mulled Venison Stew on page 180) and are lovely finely chopped and scattered over the grilled scallops on page 130. They're great in fresh and grain salads, or use them instead of the dried cherries in the braised courgette dish on page 76.

150g white wine vinegar
150ml water
1 star anise
1 bay leaf
3 black peppercorns
50g caster sugar
1 tsp salt
sprig of thyme
150g cherries, halved
    and pitted

1. Sterilise a 500ml jar according to the instructions on page 2.

2. Put the vinegar, water, star anise, bay leaf, peppercorns, sugar and salt in a non-reactive saucepan with the thyme and bring to the boil, stirring. When the sugar has dissolved add the cherries and simmer for 2 minutes. Turn off the heat and pour into the sterilised jar to cool, then seal. They will keep for up to 3 months in the fridge.

Pickled peaches

Fills 1 x 750ml jar
or 2 smaller jars

350g ripe peaches (about
   6 small peaches, I love the
   flat or 'doughnut' peaches
   for this)
250g caster sugar
300ml white wine vinegar
150ml water
1 tsp salt
1 tsp fennel seeds
½ tsp pink peppercorns
1 bay leaf

I discovered the joy of pickled peaches after bagging a kilo of past-their-best peaches from my greengrocer for a steal. Some of them got eaten and made into a pie, but I had loads left so I made some into the jam on page 158 and used the rest to make this lovely pickle. Pickled fruit is underrated but it's so good in savoury meals to add a flash of sweetness and acidity. The longer these beauties are left the better – after a few months they take on an intense, almost meaty texture. The skin will wrinkle but it can be peeled off and the flesh beneath will reward with its sweet, vinegary, peachy deliciousness. These peaches are just perfect with the pork chops on page 52, eaten with a thick wedge of manchego, finely chopped on a fresh fish ceviche or in a toasted Parma ham and Taleggio sandwich.

1. Sterilise one 750ml jar, or 2 smaller jars, according to the instructions on page 2.

2. Put the fruit in the jar(s) and bring all of the rest of the ingredients gently to the boil, stirring to dissolve the sugar. Allow to cool, then pour the mixture over the peaches. Cover with a circle of greaseproof paper the same size as the neck of the jar and screw on the lid(s). Store in a cool, dark place for up to 6 months. Once opened, they will keep well in the fridge for a few months.

Pink peppercorn-pickled gooseberries

Fills 2 x 500ml jars

Get creative with the ingredients in this pickle – that is the whole joy of pickling; experiment and adapt the flavourings according to what suits. The floral notes in pink peppercorn work with the sharpness of British gooseberries, and elderflower and gooseberries are perfect bedfellows too (what grows together so often goes together), but if you can't find elderflowers, add a couple of tablespoons of elderflower cordial to the mix. Gooseberries vary in terms of tartness, so taste them before adding all the sugar, and if they are really sweet, maybe reduce the sugar quantity a little. These are perfect with oily fish such as sardines or mackerel (page 139), and lovely in spring and summer salads.

450g gooseberries, washed and any little dry brown tails pinched off
2 heads of elderflower, stems removed
250ml white wine vinegar
100g golden caster sugar
1 tsp salt
50ml gin
150ml water
½ tsp lightly crushed pink peppercorns

1. Sterilise two 500ml jars according to the instructions on page 2.

2. Divide the gooseberries between the sterilised jars with the elderflower heads (if using). Combine all the other ingredients in a non-reactive saucepan over a medium heat and heat until simmering. Simmer for a couple of minutes, then remove from the heat and allow to cool. Once cooled, pour the pickling liquid over the gooseberries, until it reaches the top of the neck of the jar. Cover with a disc of greaseproof paper or baking parchment, to protect it from the air, and seal. They will keep for a couple of months.

Fermented, Pickled and Preserved

Elderflower vinegar

Fills 2 x 300ml jars or 1 x 1-litre glass bottle

The explosion of fragrant, pale yellow elderflowers at the start of spring feels so optimistic – a harbinger of summer and the promise of longer days. We live in an area overrun with elder, and I forage bagfuls of the flowers to use for cordial, cakes, custards and this vinegar, which preserves the scent and flavour beautifully. Use it for dressings for salads, and as you would use lemon juice. It's particularly lovely with fish and seafood: I served a single oyster drizzled with a few drops of elderflower vinegar at a supper club and it went down a storm. Use it instead of lemon juice for the celebratory salad on page 35, and to dress the leaves with the Pea and Lovage Croquettes on page 42.

15–20 flowering heads of elderflower
600ml rice wine or white wine vinegar

1. Sterilise two 300ml jars or a 1-litre glass bottle according to the instructions on page 2.

2. Pick over the elderflowers to get rid of any bugs, but don't wash them as this will destroy the pollen. Snip the stems from the heads and transfer them to the sterilised glass bottle or jars. Cover with the vinegar, making sure all the elderflowers are submerged. Refrigerate for 3 weeks, then strain into another sterilised bottle or jar and keep the vinegar (in the fridge or at room temperature) for up to 3 months.

Greengage and cobnut jam

Fills 2 x 500ml jars

Greengage plums have a gorgeous sweet flavour and high acidity which make for a really special jam to go on crumpets. Kentish greengages are in season at the same time as cobnuts, a delicious seasonal hazelnut that's sold fresh in the south-east of England, rather than dry like most nuts. I like to combine them in this delicious jam, to which the cobnuts add some crunch and creaminess. This is a fairly loose jam which is lovely on homemade crumpets (page 27).

1kg greengages, halved and
  stoned
200ml water
juice of ½ lemon
550g jam sugar
100g cobnuts, shelled and
  sliced lengthways

1. Sterilise two 500ml jars according to the instructions on page 2.

2. Combine the greengages, water and lemon juice in a large saucepan or preserving pan and cook over a medium-high heat for 10 minutes, until the greengages have broken down, skimming any scum from the surface. Add the sugar and cook for 10–15 minutes, stirring so that the greengages don't stick to the bottom and burn, until it reaches setting point. Scrape down the sides of the pan frequently so the jam doesn't crystallise. If you're unsure about whether it's reached setting point, put a saucer in the freezer for a few minutes then spoon some of the jam onto it and return it to the freezer for a couple of minutes. If the surface of the jam on the cold saucer wrinkles when pushed, the jam is ready to jar. If not, cook it for a few more minutes (the temperature on a sugar thermometer should be 105°C), but be careful not to overset it – a loose jam is always better than an overset one.

3. Remove from the heat, stir in the sliced cobnuts and pour the hot jam into the warm sterilised jars, using a jam funnel, or pouring the jam into a heatproof jug and then into the jars. Top the jam with circles of greaseproof paper the same size as the neck of the jar, seal with the lids, then turn the jars upside down and allow to cool on a wire rack – this will create a vacuum and seal the jars. The jam will keep in the fridge for up to 3 months unopened, and for a couple of weeks once opened.

TIP: If you can't get hold of cobnuts you can use blanched, skinned almonds instead.

Wild autumn jelly

While 'bletted medlars' might sound like some kind of unpleasant medieval affliction, it is in fact something utterly delightful. Medlars, also known as 'cats' arseholes' because of their unusual appearance, are wonderfully eccentric little autumn fruit found at good farmers' markets, greengrocers or online from the end of September. Medlars are no use really until they've been 'bletted', which basically means they have to start to rot and break down before you can use them as before that they are too hard and acidic.

A good frost can kick-start this process, but you can also pick them and then blet them on newspaper at home (use the bottom drawer of the fridge for this) – leave them for a week or two, until the skin is dark and wrinkled and the insides are mushy. This might sound a bit of a faff, but the resulting jelly is worth it: a beautiful burnished shade of red, its flavour is redolent of stewed orchard fruit with a pleasing sourness that makes it the perfect accompaniment for cheese. If you can get hold of 1kg medlars then don't worry about the apples and quince, but these fruit add extra flavour to the mix and you can even throw some crab apples in there too.

600g medlars, bletted and halved
200g apples or crab apples, halved
200g quince, halved
2.5 litres water
650g caster or jam sugar
1 tbsp lemon juice or cider vinegar

1. Sterilise two 300ml jars according to the instructions on page 2.

2. Put the medlars, apples and quince, seeds and all, in a large saucepan or preserving pan. Cover with the water and bring to the boil. Once boiling, turn down to a simmer and cook for 1 hour, or until the fruit has softened and created a dark, brownish liquid. Line a large sieve with two layers of muslin and set it over a very deep bowl. Put the fruit and liquid in the sieve and leave for a few hours (or overnight) to naturally drip through the muslin – do not be tempted to push the fruit with a spoon as this will make for cloudy jelly. Wash and dry the pan and put a saucer in the freezer (if you don't have a sugar thermometer).

3. Once all the liquid has drained into the bowl (you should have about 1 litre), transfer it back to the pan and add the sugar and lemon juice or cider vinegar. Bring it to the boil, stirring to dissolve the sugar, then boil hard for 10–15 minutes, until the liquid has thickened and the jelly reaches setting point. You're looking for a temperature of 105°C on a sugar thermometer. If you don't have one, spoon some onto the chilled saucer and pop it back in the freezer for a few minutes. If the surface of the jelly on the cold saucer wrinkles when pushed, the jelly is ready to jar. If not, boil it for a few more minutes until it sets. Remove from the heat and pour the hot jelly into the warm sterilised jars, using a jam funnel, or pouring the jelly into a heatproof jug and then into the jars.

4. Top the jelly with circles of greaseproof paper the same size as the neck of the jar, seal with the lids, then turn the jars upside down and allow to cool on a wire rack – this will create a vacuum and seal the jars. The jelly will keep in the fridge for up to 6 months unopened, and for a couple of weeks once opened.

Peach, raspberry and rose water jam

Fills 5 x 300ml jars

This jam is great for the end of the summer when the greengrocers are selling peaches cheaply; I once got a kilogram of past their best peaches for 75p. The raspberries bring acidity and a gorgeous pink blush to the jam, while the rose water infuses it with a hint of Turkish delight. This jam is also wonderful on the Sour Cream Sourdough Crumpets on page 27.

1kg ripe, overripe and nearly-gone peaches (skin on) – I prefer the flat doughnut ones – washed, halved, stoned and finely chopped
100g golden caster sugar
juice of ½ lemon
550g jam sugar
160g raspberries
1 tsp good-quality rose water

1. Sterilise 5 x 300ml jars according to the instructions on page 2.

2. Toss the chopped the peaches in a bowl with the golden caster sugar and lemon juice and leave to macerate for a few hours at room temperature (or overnight in the fridge) – this will encourage them to give up their juices and make them easier to jam. Once macerated, tip the peaches into a large saucepan or preserving pan with the jam sugar and cook over a medium-high heat for 20 minutes, stirring so that nothing sticks and burns. Skim any foamy scum from the surface, and, if there are still visible lumps of peach, mash them down into the liquid with a potato masher or the back of a wooden spoon.

3. Add the raspberries and rose water and cook for a further 15–20 minutes, until thick and gloopy, and most of the peaches have been incorporated into the jam. If you're unsure about whether it's reached setting point, put a saucer in the freezer for a few minutes then spoon some of the jam onto it and return it to the freezer for a couple of minutes. If the surface of the jam on the cold saucer wrinkles when pushed, the jam is ready to jar. If not, cook it for a few more minutes (the temperature on a sugar thermometer should be 105°C), but be careful not to overset it – a loose jam is always better than an overset one.

4. Pour the hot jam into the warm sterilised jars, using a jam funnel, or pouring the jam into a heatproof jug and then into the jars. Top the jam with circles of greaseproof paper the same size as the neck of the jar, seal with lids, then turn the jars upside down and allow to cool on a wire rack – this will create a vacuum and seal the jars. Keep your jam in the fridge and give spares to friends and family. It should keep for up to 3 months unopened, and for a couple of weeks once opened.

Cherry vodka

Makes 1.5 litres

Kent, where I grew up, is known as the garden of England, and it's famous for its orchards and especially its bountiful summer harvests of cherries. I spent a lot of time when I was young clambering up fruit trees, picking cherries from the highest branches and inventing a new sport that my parents fortunately knew nothing about, called 'tree surfing'. It involved bouncing with both feet on one flimsy, flexible tree branch, preferably as far off the ground as possible, while holding onto a higher branch for dear life.

This vodka is a rather more grown-up ode to my love of cherries, and is something I developed after drinking Ginjinha in Lisbon – a local speciality cherry liquor which is made with local sour cherries and served in little hole-in-walls across the city. This version uses ripe summer cherries and warming spices, and is perfect for the cocktails opposite, which were kindly contributed by my good friend Joe McCanta, an amazing mixologist and vodka expert. This vodka makes for a really lovely gift and if made in summer it will be ready in time for Christmas.

450g cherries, halved and pitted
170g caster sugar
4 green cardamom pods, bashed
1 cinnamon stick
70cl (700ml) bottle of good-quality vodka

1. Sterilise a 1.5-litre glass jar according to the instructions on page 2.

2. Put the cherries and sugar in the sterilised jar, toss the cherries with the sugar and leave for 10 minutes, to allow the sugar the draw out the cherry juice. Add the bashed cardamom pods and cinnamon stick and pour over the vodka. Seal, shake the jar gently and keep in a cool, dark place for a couple of months, shaking the jar every day for the first week and then a couple of times every week. After 2 months, taste the vodka. If you're happy with the flavour, strain the vodka into sterilised bottles, discard the spices and keep the cherries in a jar or airtight container in the fridge for use in cocktails or desserts. If you think it needs more time, leave it for a further few weeks to a month. The cherries are perfect for the Chocolate and Cherry Pavlova on page 240.

Joe McCanta's …
Cherry vodka sour

Makes 2 cocktails

100ml cherry vodka
50ml fresh lemon juice
20ml maple syrup
1 egg white
8–10 ice cubes
vodka-soaked cherries or maraschino cherries, to decorate

1. Chill two martini or coupe glasses by filling them with ice.

2. Pour all the ingredients into a cocktail shaker and dry shake for 20 seconds without ice. Add the ice and shake again for 30 seconds, until nice and frothy. Strain into the chilled glasses and serve with a boozy vodka-soaked cherry or maraschino cherry.

Spiced cherry espresso martini

Makes 2 cocktails

100ml cherry vodka
60ml rich fresh espresso
30ml pomegranate molasses
pinch of sea salt
8–10 ice cubes
tonka bean, for grating

1. Chill two martini or coupe glasses by filling them with ice.

2. Pour all the ingredients into a cocktail shaker along with the ice and shake for 45 seconds, then strain into the cooled glasses. Grate over some tonka bean and serve.

Damson gin

Makes 1 litre

The fleeting season of deep purple damsons is happily extended by simply getting them very drunk. Soaking these tart little plum-like fruits in gin with sugar, and allowing time to do their thing, rewards with a punchy crimson liqueur that warms the cockles and soothes the soul. Snap damsons up as soon as they ripen at the end of August and throughout September, infuse some gin and then bottle it up for Christmas presents for people who will share it with you. Don't give it all away though, you can drink a nip while you use it to poach the pears for the galette on page 251. You can use this recipe to make sloe gin too, if you can get your hands on some.

450g damsons or sloes
300g caster sugar
70cl (700ml) bottle of gin

1. Wash the damsons or sloes and pick them over to remove any stalks or leaves then prick them each a few times. Place them in a large clean jar, or divide between two smaller jars, and pour over the sugar. Close the lid and shake the jar to cover the fruit in the sugar, then pour over the gin, shake again and seal. Leave the jar in a cool, dark place for 8 weeks, shaking the jar whenever you remember.

2. After 2 months the gin will be a lovely deep purple colour and will have taken on all the flavour from the damsons or sloes. To filter your gin, strain it through a sieve lined with clean muslin, then use a funnel to pour it into clean glass bottles.

3. If you like, you can make the gin-soaked damsons into liqueur chocolates. Just melt some dark chocolate in a heatproof bowl over a pan of simmering water (making sure the bottom of the bowl isn't in contact with the water). Destone the damsons and line a baking tray with baking parchment. Use a toothpick to dip the boozy damsons in the melted chocolate until coated, then leave to set on the lined baking tray.

Rhubarb gin

Makes 1 litre

Few things are as jolly-making as rhubarb gin, particularly when made with bright pink stems of forced rhubarb from Yorkshire. This is so easy to make, it's rather dangerous. Shake it with leftover rhubarb poaching liquor from making the Rhubarb and White Chocolate Blondies on page 248 or the poached rhubarb on page 237, or add it to a cocktail, using Joe Mccanta's cherry sour recipe on page 161 as a guide.

800g forced rhubarb stalks, cleaned and cut into 4-cm lengths
350g caster sugar
thumb-sized strip of pared lemon zest
½ vanilla pod, split
70cl (700ml) bottle of gin

1. In a large glass jar, combine the rhubarb with the sugar, lemon zest and vanilla pod. Close the lid and give it a good shake to coat the lengths in the sugar. Leave overnight – in which time some of the bright pink juices will have escaped from the rhubarb.

2. Pour over the gin, close the lid and give it another shake, then leave somewhere cool and not in direct sunlight for about 4 weeks, shaking every now and then when you remember.

3. After this time it will be ready to bottle and drink. Strain it through a muslin-lined sieve and pour into a sterilised glass bottle. You could keep the boozy rhubarb to purée and mix into cocktails (try topping with prosecco for rhubarb bellinis). The longer you leave your gin once infused, the paler pink it will get – still delicious, but not as beautiful, so perhaps plan something with friends when your batch is ready.

Fermented, Pickled and Preserved

Comfort Cooking

My kitchen is naturally somewhere I want to spend more time in the colder months, pouring myself coffee (or wine), and getting stuck into a leisurely cooking session, slowly rolling out rich walnut pastry for the Squash, Mushroom and Sage Tart (page 175). This is food for those chilly days when your cockles need warming with bowl of Restorative Ginger Chicken Soba Noodle Soup (page 171) and feasts like the sumptuous Slow-cooked Spiced Lamb Shoulder (page 166) are the perfect weekend cooking project. Fragrant with warming spices and brightened with pink pickles, it's the sort of thing worth gathering the troops for. Warm and wow them with the pull-apart lamb along with the golden Coconut Milk and Turmeric Potato Gratin (page 168), or the magnificent, meat-free Sheepless Shepherd's Pie (page 179), which even the most vehement carnivore will approve of.

Slow-cooked spiced lamb shoulder

Serves 4–6

This is ideal for feeding a crowd. The lamb shoulder is coated in a fragrant roasted spice oil with fresh chillies and curry leaves and cooked gently for hours until it just falls off the bone. Serve it with its insanely flavourful roasting oil spooned over and sweet, pink pickled onions to cut through the richness. It's fantastic with the Coconut Milk and Turmeric Potato Gratin on page 168 as an alternative to a classic British Sunday roast. Seek out tender salt marsh lamb for this recipe, if you can.

lamb shoulder (about 1.5kg)
1 tsp sea salt
½ tsp brown sugar
100g coconut oil
2 tsp black mustard seeds
4 tsp dried curry leaves (or
     2 tsp fresh curry leaves)
6 green cardamom pods,
     bashed
3 tsp Kashmiri chilli powder
1 ½ tbsp Roasted Curry
     Powder (below) or Korma
     curry powder
50ml rapeseed oil
6 garlic cloves, peeled
3 red chillies, split in half
     lengthways
grated zest of 1 unwaxed
     lemon
1-cm piece of root ginger,
     peeled and roughly chopped

**For the roasted curry powder
(makes about 130g)**
20g basmati rice
40g coriander seeds
30g cumin seeds
20g black peppercorns
10g fenugreek seeds
1 heaped tsp cloves
seeds from 1 tsp green
     cardamom pods

For the pickled red onion
1 red onion, thinly sliced
juice of 2 limes
1 tsp salt
2 tsp caster sugar

1. First, make the roasted curry powder. Heat a dry frying pan over a medium heat. Add the rice and toast it, stirring, until it's starting to brown, then add all the other spices and toast for 3–5 minutes, until darkish brown but not burned. Transfer the spices to a spice grinder or pestle and mortar and blitz or grind to a powder, then pass through a sieve. Store in a sealed jar. It will keep well for a few months, but is best used fresh.

2. Trim any excess hard fat from the shoulder, stab it all over with a knife then rub it with the salt and sugar. If there's time, leave to sit overnight in the fridge, or for at least an hour, removing it from the fridge an hour before you want to cook it.

3. Heat 1 tablespoon of the coconut oil in a frying pan over a high heat. Add the mustard seeds and once they are crackling, add the curry leaves and cardamom pods. Cook until sizzling, then remove from the heat, allow to cool for a minute or two then stir in chilli powder and curry powder and remaining oils. Leave to cool completely.

4. Preheat the oven to 180°C/160°C fan/gas 4. Wipe any moisture from the lamb with kitchen paper. Put the lamb in a roasting tray and coat it in the curry oil, then spoon or pour over the rest of the oil. Top with the garlic, chillies, lemon zest and ginger. Cover with foil and roast for 4–4½ hours, basting every hour or so, until the meat comes away from the bones easily and is pull-apart tender.

5. While it's roasting, pickle the onion. Put the sliced onion in a heatproof bowl, just cover with boiling water and let it sit for 15 minutes. Drain off the water, whisk the lime juice with the salt and sugar and pour it over the onion. Leave to steep while the lamb cooks.

6. When the lamb is done, remove it from the oven and leave it to rest, covered loosely with foil, for at least 30 minutes. Drain the excess confit fat from the tray into a bowl, jug or Tupperware (to use in the Coconut Milk and Turmeric Potato Gratin, page 168, or curries). Pull the meat off the bones, discard the bones and toss the meat in the residual flavoured oil and any tasty crusty bits that have formed on the bottom of the roasting tray.

7. Serve the lamb with the pink pickled onions spooned over, with crunchy red cabbage and carrot slaw and the coconut milk gratin (page 168).

TIP: The roasted curry powder can also be used in the Sri Lankan-style Beetroot Curry (page 56) and Tomato, Coconut and Spinach Dahl (page 57).

Coconut milk and turmeric potato gratin

Serves 4–6

I wouldn't dare call this dauphinoise, but the principle is the same, except the potato is cooked in creamy coconut milk spiked with the golden goodness of turmeric and ginger, freshened with thinly sliced spring onion. It's rich and warming but surprisingly delicate. If you ignore the serving suggestion of using fat from the slow-cooked lamb, it's also vegan.

300ml coconut milk
2 tsp ground turmeric
ground seeds from 4 green cardamom pods
1-cm piece of root ginger, peeled and grated, plus extra to taste
3 spring onions, trimmed and thinly sliced
3 tbsp confit lamb fat (page 166) or coconut oil, melted, plus extra to top the gratin
600g waxy potatoes such as King Edward, Desiree or Maris Piper, peeled and thinly sliced
sea salt and freshly ground black pepper

1. Preheat the oven to 200°C/180°C fan/gas 6 (if you're not cooking the potatoes at the same time as the lamb).

2. Stir together the coconut milk, turmeric, cardamom seeds, ginger and half the sliced spring onions in a large bowl with 1 teaspoon of salt. Add the fat and potato slices and toss it all together and season with salt and pepper, then layer the potatoes in a 24 x 18cm rectangular roasting tray, gratin dish or roasting tray, topping the potatoes with any residual mixture from the bowl. Scatter the gratin with half of the remaining spring onions and a little more grated ginger. Dot with a bit more lamb confit fat or coconut oil and roast on the top shelf of the oven for 1½ hours (if you're cooking it with the lamb, cook it at 180°C/160°C fan/gas 4 for 1 hour, then increase the temperature to 200°C/180°C fan/gas 6 for the final 30 minutes).

3. Remove from the oven and scatter with the rest of the spring onion.

Red cabbage and carrot slaw

Serves 4–6 as a side

This bright, crunchy winter slaw is wonderfully fresh and zippy, a perfect accompaniment to rich meat dishes.

½ red cabbage, finely shredded
1 carrot, cut into fine matchsticks or peeled with a julienne peeler
2 spring onions, trimmed and thinly sliced
1 tsp salt
1 tsp caster sugar
1 red jalapeño chilli, thinly sliced or 1 tbsp Fermented Green Chillies (page 146)
juice of 1 lime
handful of mint, leaves picked
handful of coriander, leaves picked
handful of dry-roasted peanuts, chopped

1. Combine the cabbage, carrot, spring onions, salt and sugar in a bowl and give everything a good scrunch together with your hands to incorporate.

2. Leave to sit for 5 minutes, then add in the chilli. Dress with the lime juice and toss through the herbs and peanuts.

169

Comfort Cooking

Restorative ginger chicken soba noodle soup
with corn, sweetheart cabbage and chilli oil

Serves 2

Chicken noodle soup is one of the most homely and nourishing things you can make: few things warm the spirit more than wrapping your hands around a bowl of fragrant, steaming broth and slurping until it's all gone. Inevitably there's some chicken stock in the freezer, noodles in the cupboard and random veg in the fridge that can be married together into something sating and delicious. The ginger gives such warmth and life; the cabbage and corn make it a perfectly balanced meal in a bowl, and the chilli oil adds oomph and indulgence. Japanese soba noodles are made with buckwheat and have a soft texture and slightly nutty flavour, but use whichever noodles you have. Any confit chicken oil left over from the Confit Chicken Legs on page 100 will make this taste even more chickeny and delicious.

200g soba noodles
400ml All-purpose Chicken Broth (page 266)
25g piece of root ginger, thickly sliced
1 spring onion, trimmed and finely chopped
1 tbsp fish sauce
1 tsp honey or brown sugar
light soy sauce, to taste
lemon juice, to taste
sweetcorn cut from 1 fresh corn cob (or 100g frozen)
½ sweetheart cabbage, hard core removed and leaves shredded (or 100g roughly chopped kale leaves, tough stalks removed)
250g cooked chicken breast or leg meat (page 266), shredded
freshly ground black pepper

For the chilli oil
4 tbsp confit chicken oil (page 100), groundnut, coconut or rapeseed oil
1 red chilli, halved lengthways, deseeded and finely chopped
2-cm piece of root ginger, finely chopped
1 garlic clove, finely chopped
1 tbsp light soy sauce or tamari
1 tsp toasted sesame oil
2 tsp toasted sesame seeds
½ tsp dried chilli flakes (I love Urfa chilli flakes for this)

1. First, make the chilli oil. Place the oil, chilli, ginger and garlic in a frying pan. Turn the heat on to medium and gently bring up the temperature of the oil. Cook for a few minutes, until the garlic begins to sizzle and turn golden (being careful not to take it too far), then quickly pour the oil into a heatproof glass or ceramic bowl and stir in the soy sauce, toasted sesame oil, sesame seeds and chilli flakes while the oil is still hot. Whisk to combine, taste to make sure the flavours are balanced, adding a little more soy sauce or chilli if you think it needs it, then set aside.

2. Warm two bowls in a low oven and bring a large saucepan of well salted water to the boil.

3. Cook the soba noodles in the boiling water until al dente (for about 2 minutes less than the time stated on the packet), then drain and toss with a teaspoon of the chilli oil.

4. Pour the chicken broth into a saucepan and add the ginger, half the spring onion, the fish sauce and honey or sugar. Bring to a very gentle boil, then turn the heat down to a simmer. Taste and season with soy sauce and lemon, then slide in the corn and cabbage and cook for 4–5 minutes until both are tender. Discard the ginger.

5. Put the shredded chicken in the warm bowls and season with black pepper. Divide the noodles between the bowls and spoon the cabbage and corn on top. Pour over the hot stock and garnish with the remaining chopped spring onion. Drizzle with the chilli oil and serve.

Slow-cooked pork belly with apples
and rhubarb ketchup

Serves 6

This dish has a real feeling of autumn about it, and was something I came up with during our first year on the allotment, after inheriting a productive rhubarb crown and apple tree. I had a supper club coming up, and this dish became the main course: meltingly tender slow-cooked pork belly with the crackliest crackling, served with a sherbety, pink rhubarb ketchup with soft, pork-seasoned apples and roasting tray veg. It's a really good dish for feeding a crowd. If you can, salt the pork the day before you cook it to really bring out its flavour and tenderise the meat. Try it with crushed boiled potatoes tossed with a little oil, salt and pepper and chopped lovage, and buttered chopped carrots lifted with a few drops of cider vinegar.

2kg high-welfare pork belly, ribs in, skin scored
1 apple, cored and sliced
1 fennel bulb, sliced
2 celery sticks, strings removed and sticks sliced
1 carrot, halved
2 white onions or 4 shallots, halved (skin on)
3 bay leaves
500ml chicken stock (shop-bought or see page 266)
125ml dry cider or white wine
1 tbsp plain flour

For the cure
1 tsp fennel seeds
1 tsp dried chilli flakes
1 tsp thyme leaves

For the rhubarb ketchup
500g trimmed pink forced rhubarb, cut into 3–4-cm slices
2 shallots, peeled and halved
thumb-sized piece of root ginger, sliced
100g caster sugar
120ml cider vinegar
grated zest and juice of 1 orange
seeds from 4 green cardamom pods
2 black peppercorns
1 tsp ground cinnamon
2 star anise
2 bay leaves

1. Grind the cure ingredients in a pestle and mortar or spice grinder. Use a knife to stab some slashes in the underside of the pork then rub the salt mix all over it (but not on the skin). Leave it to cure skin side up in the fridge, uncovered, for at least 3 hours, preferably overnight.

2. Remove the pork from the fridge an hour or so before you cook it so it can come up to room temperature. Pat it dry with kitchen paper and preheat the oven to 140°C/120°C fan/gas 1.

3. Place the apple (skin on), fennel, celery, carrot, onions or shallots and bay leaves in a large roasting tray. Place the pork on top, skin side up, and roast in the oven for 5 hours. After 5 hours, remove the pork from the oven, turn the heat up to 220°C/200°C fan/gas 7 and pour the chicken stock and cider or wine into the tray around the pork, without letting it get on the pork's skin (you need it dry for nice crunchy crackling).

4. For the rhubarb ketchup, line a roasting tray with greaseproof paper. Place the rhubarb, shallots and ginger in the tray and cover with the sugar. Pour over the vinegar and orange juice, add the orange zest, spices and bay leaves. Cover with foil and place in the oven, along with the pork. Roast both trays for a further hour (the pork on the top rack, the rhubarb beneath), in which time the pork skin should crackle and the rhubarb will cook down until tender.

5. Remove both trays from the oven and place the pork on a platter to rest. Make the rhubarb ketchup by removing the star anise, bay leaves and peppercorns from the rhubarb tray, then blitzing the contents, along with the apple and celery from the pork tray, in a food processor, until smooth. Season with salt and pepper to taste. It should be sharp, sweet and fruity, and a pretty soft pink colour (if you've used forced rhubarb).

6. To make the gravy, place the pork roasting tray over a medium heat, drain any juices from the resting pork into the tray and scatter over the flour. Mash the veg in the tray with the back of a wooden spoon and stir and cook until thickened, adding some boiling water to thin the gravy down. Taste for seasoning then strain through a sieve into a warmed jug.

7. Once the pork has rested, turn it upside down and cut it into squares with a sharp knife. Serve the pork with a dollop or swoop of rhubarb ketchup and blanched purple sprouting broccoli.

Squash, mushroom and sage tart

Serves 6

This decidedly autumnal tart brings together three great pals: mushrooms, squash and sage — the savoury, sweet and aromatic – all of which sit merrily together in a short, golden walnut pastry with the creamy tang of Comté for company. You could add bacon, if you're that way inclined, but otherwise this is a meat-free meal that will sate and delight.

350g peeled, deseeded butternut or acorn squash, sliced into 2–2.5-cm half-moons
1 tbsp olive oil, plus a drizzle for frying
250ml double cream
3 eggs
dried chilli flakes, to taste
nutmeg, for grating
small bunch of fresh sage, leaves picked
100g Comté or other hard cheese, grated
knob of butter, plus a little extra for frying
200g mushrooms (preferably wild), sliced
sea salt and freshly ground black pepper

For the pastry
50g whole, skin-on walnuts
150g plain flour, plus extra for dusting
pinch of fine sea salt
120g cold unsalted butter, diced
1 egg yolk
1–3 tbsp iced water

1. Preheat the oven to 220°C/200°C fan/gas 7.

2. First, make the pastry. Blitz the walnuts in a food processor to breadcrumb consistency. Add the flour and salt and pulse briefly to combine, then tip in the butter and pulse until you have a crumb consistency again. Add the egg yolk and pulse again. Add the iced water, a tablespoon at a time, sprinkling it across the crumb and blitzing between additions until the dough clumps together (you may not need all the water). Tip the dough into a large bowl and squish it into a smooth ball, adding a little more water or flour if required. Flatten to a disc, wrap in greaseproof paper and chill in the fridge for at least 30 minutes.

3. While the pastry is chilling, toss the squash with the tablespoon of olive oil, season with salt and pepper and roast in the oven for 12 minutes, until softened and browning. Remove from the oven and set aside.

4. Remove the pastry from the fridge and unwrap it. Dust a clean surface with flour and roll the pastry out to the thickness of a pound coin (large enough to generously line a 23cm tart tin). If it's difficult to work with you can do this between two pieces of greaseproof paper. Line the tart tin with the pastry, letting it overhang to allow for shrinkage. Chill the pastry until firm, then turn the oven down to 200°C/180°C fan/gas 6. Prick the pastry with a fork, line it with crumpled greaseproof paper, fill it with baking beans and blind-bake for 15 minutes. Remove from the oven, lift out the beans and paper then return it to the oven for a further 12 minutes, until the base is crisp and golden. Remove from the oven.

5. Whisk the cream and eggs in a bowl, then season with salt, pepper, chilli flakes and a good grating of nutmeg. Roughly chop half the sage and add it with the grated cheese.

6. Heat a knob of butter and dash of olive oil in a frying pan over a medium-high heat, add 4 sage leaves and fry for a minute to infuse the oil with their flavour, then add the mushrooms, season with salt and pepper and fry for about 5 minutes, until they have browned and given up their moisture.

7. Pour enough of the custard into the pastry case to coat the base thinly, then layer up the squash and mushrooms, pouring a little custard between the layers. Top with the rest of the custard, fry the few remaining sage leaves in a bit more butter and pour over the top of the tart. Bake the tart in the oven for 25–30 minutes, until deeply golden and just set. Remove from the oven and leave it to settle for 20–30 minutes, then slice and devour.

Spiced, slow-cooked brisket and beets

Serves 4–6

Beef brisket has so much flavour, and is wonderful when cooked slowly until it pulls apart. Cover it in this aromatic spice rub and combine it with the earthy flavour of beetroots prepared two ways. This is comfort food for crisp, chilly days, and it does take some time, so can be cooked the day before then reheated until piping hot just before serving. This is great with homemade ferments like the fermented turnips, beetroots and slaw (pages 147 and 149).

1 tbsp sea salt
1 tbsp dark muscovado sugar
1.5kg boned, rolled beef brisket
1½ tbsp olive oil, plus extra for browning the meat
2 red onions, thinly sliced
2 raw beetroots, peeled and cut into 1.5-cm slices
2 garlic cloves, crushed
pinch of coriander seeds
2 sprigs of thyme
500ml chicken or beef stock
2 tbsp Worcestershire sauce
3 tbsp red wine vinegar
salt

For the spice rub
2 tsp ground cumin
1 tbsp smoked sweet paprika, plus extra 2 tsp for the shredded meat
2 tsp caraway seeds

To serve
Pink Pickled Onions (page 180)
1 tbsp sliced cucumber
1 tbsp dill fronds
Pickled Beetroots (page 60)
sour cream

1. Combine the salt and sugar in a bowl or tray big enough to hold the brisket, then add the meat and cover it with the mixture, rubbing it all over. If there's time, leave to sit overnight in the fridge, or for at least an hour, removing it from the fridge an hour before you want to cook it. In a small bowl, combine the spice rub ingredients. Wipe away the moisture that has come out of the meat and then rub it all over with the spices. Preheat the oven to 160°C/140°C fan/gas 3.

2. Heat the olive oil in a heavy-based frying pan or skillet over a medium-high heat. Slide in the onions, beetroot, garlic, coriander seeds and a good pinch of salt and cook, stirring, for 6-8 minutes, or until the onion has softened and is smelling fragrant.

3. Scrape the the mixture into an ovenproof casserole dish that's big enough to hold the brisket (if you don't have one, you can use a roasting tray and some foil). Heat a little more oil in the frying pan or skillet, add the brisket and sear it all over for a minute or so, being careful not to burn the spices. Transfer the meat to the casserole or roasting tray, on top of the onions and beets, and throw in the thyme. Pour in the stock, Worcestershire sauce and vinegar and cover with a lid (or foil tightly if using a roasting tray). Roast in the oven for 4–5 hours, basting and turning the meat every hour or so. Keep checking how the meat is feeling, it needs to be pull-apart tender, and because ovens and briskets vary, it's not an exact science; it might be done after 4 hours, it could take longer. Keep going until the meat is shreddable at the edges, and add more moisture if it looks dry.

4. Remove the brisket from the oven, transfer to a plate or tray and leave to rest for 45 minutes to 1 hour. While that's happening, turn the oven up to 200°C/180°C fan/gas 6 and return the casserole to the oven, uncovered, for 15 minutes to reduce the liquid. If you've been using a roasting tray more of the liquid may have escaped and it may already be reduced enough. Remove from the oven and skim some, but not all, of the fat from the surface of the sauce; you want there to still be some in there to lubricate the meat.

5. Once rested, remove the string from the brisket, shred the meat and toss it into the casserole. Combine with the juices, beetroots, onions (add a splash more water if it needs it) and the extra 2 teaspoons of smoked paprika and warm through. Taste for seasoning. Serve immediately or, if you're doing this ahead, leave to cool and refrigerate, then warm through in a low oven for 10–15 minutes, or until piping hot.

6. To serve, combine the pink pickled onions with the cucumber and dill and serve along with the pickled beets and sour cream. The brisket is great on warmed up tacos, flatbreads, jacket potatoes or piles of buttered mash.

Comfort Cooking

Sheepless shepherd's pie

Serves 6–8

This vegetarian feast of a dish has all the warmth, comfort and complex flavours of shepherd's pie, but rather than using lamb, the rich, deeply umami ragu is made with braised lentils, mushrooms and vegetables. The secret ingredient here is pickled walnuts, which lend a dark nuttiness and piquancy that enlivens every mouthful. The whole lot is topped off with a caramelised celeriac, brown butter and crispy sage topping. Cheese lovers can further enrich the filling with melty Taleggio or brie.

200g green or puy lentils, soaked in cold water for 30 minutes, drained
3 bay leaves
2 tbsp olive oil
1 onion, diced
2 celery sticks, trimmed and finely chopped
1 carrot, diced
2 garlic cloves, crushed
pinch of dried chilli flakes
2 large plum tomatoes, chopped (or ½ x 400g tin chopped tomatoes)
30g butter, plus a knob for frying sage and greasing
6 sage leaves, plus 3 for pie topping
400g field or chestnut mushrooms, sliced
500ml vegetable stock
1 tsp honey
80g pickled walnuts, chopped, plus 1 tbsp of the vinegar
100g brie, Taleggio or semi-soft (washed-rind) cheese of choice, sliced (optional)

For the celeriac topping
100ml whole milk
1 celeriac (400–500g), peeled and cut into 10-cm chunks
50ml double cream
30g butter
nutmeg, for grating
10g Parmesan, grated
sea salt and freshly ground black pepper

1. Bring a large saucepan of salted water to the boil and add the lentils and a bay leaf. Cook for 15 minutes, or until tender, skimming any scum from the surface. Drain and set aside.

2. Heat the olive oil in a heavy-based non-stick frying pan or skillet over a medium heat, add another bay leaf, the onion, celery, carrot, garlic and chilli flakes with a large pinch of salt and fry for 8–10 minutes, until the onions are softened and starting to brown. Add the chopped tomatoes and cook for 5 minutes, until the tomatoes are breaking down into the sauce. Remove from the heat and set aside while you fry the mushrooms.

3. Melt the butter in another frying pan over a medium-high heat and stir in the 6 sage leaves. Add the mushrooms and a good pinch of salt and fry for 6–8 minutes, until they are deeply coloured, have given up their moisture and are smelling nutty. Slide the mushrooms into the tomato pan, add the lentils and pour over the vegetable stock. Return this pan to a medium heat, stir and cook for 5–8 minutes, until the stock has reduced. Season with pepper, stir in the honey, pickled walnuts and vinegar and the cheese, if using, and remove from the heat.

4. Preheat the oven to 200°C/180°C fan/gas 6.

5. Now, cook the topping. Pour the milk into a non-stick saucepan, add the remaining bay leaf, the celeriac and another good pinch of salt. Cover and turn the heat to low-medium. You're going to caramelise the celeriac: as the milk evaporates and the solids and celeriac that are in contact with the pan start to colour and deepen in flavour, the rest of the celeriac steams until tender. To ensure it caramelises rather than burns, gently shake the pan every few minutes to dislodge the celeriac, adding a splash of milk if it gets dry. Cook for 12–15 minutes, until tender. Add about a tablespoon of boiling water and give it a good stir, scraping up the bits from the bottom. If it's not quite ready, cook for a couple more minutes, adding a bit more hot water if it's looking dry.

6. Put the celeriac in a food processor, add the cream, butter, a good grating of nutmeg, the Parmesan and some more salt and pepper and blitz until smooth and creamy – it should be a lovely deep golden colour. Taste to make sure you're happy.

7. Pile the ragu into a buttered pie dish or roasting tray and top with the celeriac, spreading it into swirls with the back of a spoon. For added luxury, melt the remaining knob of butter in a frying pan until slightly browned and smelling nutty, toss in the remaining sage leaves and fry until crisp. Pour this over the top of the pie and bake in the oven for 25–30 minutes, until hot through, golden and crusty. Serve with blanched chard or cime di rapa.

Mulled venison stew

Serves 6

I'm not the biggest fan of mulled wine (give me a mulled cider any day though) but love using the warming flavours of it for this rib-sticking venison stew. This also works a treat with beef shin, but venison has such a special, complex flavour that lends itself particularly well to the robust spices at play here. I've served this at many a Christmas party – it's easy to scale up and pre-cook, then serve warm in a big pot over the stove along with rice or piles of sour cream mash. Let everyone dive in and help themselves while you rock around the Christmas tree.

1 dried chipotle chilli (or 1 tbsp chipotle chilli paste)
200ml boiling water
1kg venison shoulder (or beef shin), cut into 2–3-cm chunks
4 tbsp plain flour
1½ tbsp olive oil
100g smoked pancetta lardons
1 onion, finely chopped
2 celery sticks, strings removed and sticks finely chopped
1 large carrot, finely chopped
1 bay leaf
2 sprigs of thyme
2 tbsp chopped flat-leaf parsley, plus extra to garnish
1 cinnamon stick
pinch of cumin seeds
1 star anise
1 tbsp tomato purée
400ml spicy red wine (Malbec or similar)
grated zest and juice of ½ orange
250ml chicken or beef stock
sea salt and freshly ground black pepper

For the pink pickled onions
1 small red onion, thinly sliced
3 black peppercorns
1 clove
1 tsp caster sugar
½ tsp salt
4 tbsp cider vinegar

1. Put the dried chilli in a heatproof bowl, cover it with the boiling water and leave to soak for at least 20 minutes. Drain, keeping the soaking liquor, and roughly chop the chilli. Dry the venison chunks well with kitchen paper, season the flour with salt and pepper and toss the meat in the seasoned flour.

2. Heat the oil in a large ovenproof casserole dish over a medium-high heat, add the pancetta lardons and fry for 4–5 minutes, until they are lightly coloured, are starting to caramelise and some of the fat has been rendered out. Transfer the lardons to a bowl with a slotted spoon and set aside, removing any burnt bits from the pan. Now, working in batches, brown the venison in the fat in the pan for a few minutes on each side, patiently turning the meat so it has a good colour all over. Add the browned meat to the pancetta.

3. Slide the vegetables and bay leaf into the pancetta fat along with the chopped chilli, herbs and spices. Cook over a low-medium heat for 10–15 minutes, adding a little extra oil if necessary, then stir in the tomato purée. Cook for a minute then pour over the red wine and orange juice and zest and turn up the heat, giving the pan a good stir to release any bits stuck to the bottom.

4. Preheat the oven to 200°C/180°C fan/gas 6.

5. Return the venison and pancetta to the casserole dish. Add the chilli soaking liquor and bring to the boil. Cover with a lid or foil and roast in the oven for 1½–2 hours, until the venison is meltingly tender and the sauce is thick and rich. Taste for seasoning and adjust accordingly.

6. While the venison is cooking, make the pink pickled onions. Place the sliced onion in a heatproof bowl, cover with boiling water and leave for 1 minute. Drain off the water, then add the spices, sugar, salt and cider vinegar to the bowl and stir to combine. When you're ready to serve, drain on some kitchen paper, to get rid of some of the brine.

7. Serve the venison with the pink pickled onions and some chopped parsley to garnish. I love it on piles of mash, cut through with sour cream.

Sausage, apple and radicchio traybake

Serves 2–3

When we were kids we'd get really good sausages from the local butcher as a special treat. My dad would slowly roast the sausages in the oven with halved and well seasoned tomatoes. We'd eat the sausages with the soft, sharp tomatoes, different mustards (Dijon, English and wholegrain) and, best of all, slices of white bread that had been dredged in the roasting tray, picking up the caramelised tomato juices and sausage dripping. This version doesn't use tomatoes, but instead assembles some of the most delicious winter ingredients, including radicchio, that most meaty of leaves, which brings a wonderful bitterness and texture, nutty, creamy celeriac and sweet acidic apples. I like to roast chunks of bread in the tray with the sausages so they soak up the juices and crisp up in the roasting tray too. It's lovely served with some freshly boiled gnocchi, smothered with butter or sour cream and a teaspoon of wholegrain mustard, or the Lifesaver Lentils on page 198.

1 head of radicchio
½ leek, washed, trimmed and cut into 3-cm slices
about 8 sage leaves
2 banana shallots, held together at the root and split into quarters
1 English apple (preferably cox), cored and cut into wedges (skin on)
½ celeriac (about 300g), peeled and cut into bite-size pieces
2 slices of sourdough, torn into bite-size pieces
3 tbsp olive oil
1 tbsp cider vinegar (I love the raw, live, unfiltered kind which smells like an apple farm)
1 tbsp wholegrain mustard
1 tsp honey
6–8 very good-quality sausages (Italian or Cumberland), halved lengthways
sea salt and freshly ground black pepper

1. Discard any scruffy outer leaves from the radicchio, split it down the middle in half and cut out the hard base. Cut the radicchio into quarters, then the quarters in half again (8 wedges of radicchio in total) and set aside.

2. Preheat the oven to 200°C/180°C fan/gas 6 and find the biggest roasting tray you own. You might need to use two smaller trays if you don't have a large one – you don't want to overcrowd the ingredients and inhibit all that irresistible caramelisation and crunchy crust formation.

3. Put the leek, sage, shallots, apple, celeriac and sourdough in the tray and drizzle with 1 tablespoon of the olive oil. Season with black pepper and a little salt (bearing in mind the sausages will be fairly salty) and get your hands in there and give it all a good toss about.

4. Whisk together the remaining olive oil with the vinegar, mustard and honey. Add the sausages to the tray, drizzle over the dressing with a spoon and toss with your hands to thoroughly combine – everything needs to be kissed by this dressing. Roast in the oven for 45 minutes, tossing and basting everything in the juices halfway through to ensure it cooks evenly. After 45 minutes, add the radicchio, toss everything again (don't worry if the sausages break up, they will still taste delightful) and roast for a further 15–20 minutes, until the sausages and celeriac are nicely coloured and the shallots have caramelised. Remove from the oven and serve with your choice of accompaniments.

Two ways with celeriac 'pappardelle'
... with sage butter, chard and hazelnuts

Serves 2

I'd love to tell you that making this celeriac 'pappardelle' (in giant inverted commas!) is easier than cooking the true pasta version, but I can't. The truth is, peeling and then shaving this bulbous root into the fine lengths you'll need for this dish is a pain. But it's worth the faff, I promise! And if you can't get the pappardelle-style ribbons, then shaving it into thin, irregular slices that will carry the sauce works just as well. The nutty, almost truffle flavour of celeriac with browned sage butter, earthy wilted greens and toasted hazelnuts, all lifted with a bit of lemon, is such a treat, and a nutritious meat-free dinner.

2 tbsp skinned hazelnuts
juice of 1 lemon
1 small celeriac, peeled (roughly 1kg unpeeled weight)
1 small bunch of chard or cime di rapa, leaves and stalks separated and roughly chopped
80g unsalted butter
2 small handfuls of sage, leaves picked
½ tbsp olive oil, plus extra for drizzling
20g Parmesan, grana padano or vegetarian alternative, grated, plus extra to serve if you like
sea salt and freshly ground black pepper
dried chilli flakes, to serve (optional)

1. Preheat the oven to 190°C/170°C fan/gas 5.

2. Put the hazelnuts in a roasting tray and roast them in the oven for 6 minutes, until golden and toasted, then remove from the oven and roughly chop.

3. Fill a bowl with water and add a little of the lemon juice. Using a good vegetable peeler, cut long, wide strips (about the width of pappardelle) around the circumference of the celeriac, into the water, until you have lots of ribbons. They may look quite ragged and non-uniform, which is fine, but if you're a neat freak and it's important to you that it really looks like pappardelle, you can stack them up on top of each other and straighten the edges by cutting them down in a straight line with a knife. Allow for slightly more per person than you would if using pasta.

4. Bring a large pan of salted water to the boil and have a spider or slotted spoon at the ready. Drain the celeriac, add it to the pan and cook for 1 minute, then scoop it out into a sieve and leave it to steam for a minute or two, then put it in a bowl with a squeeze of lemon tossed into it and set aside. Add the stalks of the chard of cime di rapa to the pan and cook for a minute or so until tender (this will depend on their thickness), then add the leaves and cook for another minute. Drain the whole lot in the sieve, reserving a cup of the cooking water (I find the easiest way to do this is to place a cup under the sieve or colander when I drain the greens), then thoroughly squeeze any excess water out of the greens – you don't want them making the dish watery – and chop.

5. In a large, high-sided non-stick frying pan over a medium heat, heat the butter and sage leaves together until the butter is just starting to brown and smell nutty. Add a squeeze of lemon juice, the olive oil and 2 tablespoons of the greens cooking water to the butter, whisking to emulsify, then add the hazelnuts, greens and celeriac and season with a little salt, pepper and lemon juice. Toss everything together to coat it well in the butter, then add the cheese, and, if it needs it, a slosh more of the cooking water to loosen. Shake the pan to combine everything, until it's looking glossy. Divide between warm bowls and drizzle with a little olive oil, extra cheese and chilli flakes if you like.

... with slow-cooked pork and saffron ragu

Serves 4

The day I realised that you could shave celeriac into thin ribbons and treat it like pasta was a game-changer. I came back from a friend's wedding in Tuscany where I'd eaten a luxurious version of the famous local wild boar ragu and set about recreating it, but felt its richness called for something lighter than pasta.

It is lovely with pasta, but the celeriac's nutty earthiness brings another layer of flavour that just knocks the pasta option out of the park here. And I don't say this lightly – I love pasta. I served this at my residency at Carousel in Marylebone, which was a bit nerve-wracking for this home cook but worth it to see a restaurant of people enjoying my food. Suffice to say this dish was a hit with those guests, and it will be with yours too.

2 tbsp olive oil
1 bay leaf
leaves from 2 sprigs of thyme
pinch of fennel seeds
pinch of dried chilli flakes
1 onion, finely chopped
1 celery stick, strings removed
    and stick finely chopped
1 carrot, finely chopped
1 garlic clove, crushed
200g tinned chopped
    tomatoes or 2 nice plum
    tomatoes, chopped
pinch of saffron threads
500g pork shoulder or wild
    boar, cubed,
glass of dry vermouth (I use
    Noilly Prat) or white wine
500ml chicken or veal stock
Parmesan, for grating, plus
    rind for the ragu
1 tbsp double cream
1 tsp caster sugar
1 cox apple
1 tbsp finely chopped flat-leaf
    parsley
sea salt and freshly ground
    black pepper

For the celeriac
½ lemon, for squeezing
1 large celeriac (about 400g),
    peeled

1. Preheat the oven to 170°C/150°C fan/gas 4.

2. Heat 1 tablespoon of the oil in a large, ovenproof casserole dish over a medium-high heat, add the bay leaf, thyme, fennel seeds and chilli flakes. Stir, then add the onion, celery, carrot, garlic and a good pinch of salt and cook for about 8 minutes, until the onion is softened. Tip in the tomatoes and cook for a few minutes until they are incorporated into the sauce.

3. Put the saffron into a heatproof dish and cover with 1 tablespoon of boiling water. Set aside.

4. In a separate heavy-based frying pan, heat the remaining olive oil over a medium-high heat. Add the meat and fry (in two batches if necessary) until well browned all over. Transfer to a plate, then deglaze the pan with the vermouth or wine, scraping up any crusty bits from the bottom of the pan. Pour the deglaze liquid into the casserole dish and add the browned meat, followed by the stock, a cup of water and the Parmesan rind. Stir, taste and season with salt and pepper. Cover the casserole and cook in the oven for 1½–2 hours, or until the meat is just falling apart, stirring so it doesn't stick and adding more water if needed.

5. While the ragu is in the oven, fill a bowl with water and squeeze in some lemon juice. Using a good vegetable peeler, cut long, wide strips (about the width of pappardelle) around the circumference of the celeriac, into the water, until you have lots of ribbons. They may look quite ragged and non-uniform, which is fine, but if it's important to you that it really looks like pappardelle, stack them on top of each other and straighten the edges by cutting them down in a straight line. Allow for slightly more per person than you would if using pasta.

6. When you're happy with the ragu, fork through the meat to meld any chunks into the sauce and pour in the cream, sugar, saffron and its water. Grate the apple (no need to peel it) into the ragu, stir and taste for seasoning. Cover and keep warm while you cook the celeriac.

7. Bring a large saucepan of salted water to the boil. Drain the celeriac, add it to the pan and cook for 1 minute, then scoop it out with a spider, slotted spoon or tongs and add it to the ragu. Stir it in, along with the chopped parsley, and warm through for a couple of minutes, adding a splash of the celeriac cooking water to loosen if needed. Divide among warm bowls and top with grated Parmesan.

Mushroom, squash and halloumi stroganoff
with crispy sage

Serves 4

This makes for a hearty, indulgent autumnal veggie feast. Try and seek out something more interesting than butternut squash for this – kabocha, acorn or, if you can find it, crown prince squash, which has an almost toffee-sweet flesh. I love to serve this with nutty black rice, but long-grain basmati or wild rice also works well.

300g wild or black rice
300g acorn, butternut, kabocha or crown prince squash, scrubbed (only peel if skin is really tough), seeds removed and cut into 1.5–2-cm slices
2 tbsp extra-virgin olive oil, plus an extra drizzle for the squash
30g butter, plus a knob for frying the sage
small bunch of sage leaves, plus 2 leaves thinly sliced
250g halloumi, cut into 1-cm slices
leaves from 2 sprigs of thyme
2 onions, sliced
1 garlic clove, crushed
300g mushrooms (I love a mixture of wild mushrooms such as field mushrooms, winter girolles and ceps, but chestnut and oyster mushrooms work really well too), small kept whole, larger roughly sliced
glass of white wine
250g sour cream
1 tbsp Dijon mustard
50g cavolo nero (or purple or green kale), stalks removed and leaves roughly chopped
sea salt and freshly ground black pepper

1. Soak the black rice in cold water for a minimum of 30 minutes (and up to 2 hours) before you cook it.

2. Preheat the oven to 220°C/200°C fan/gas 7.

3. Toss the sliced squash with a drizzle of olive oil – just enough to coat it all over – and season with salt and plenty of black pepper. Spread it out on a baking sheet or roasting tray, making sure the slices are well spaced. If you need to, use two trays. Roast in the oven for 30–35 minutes, until softened and colouring, but not falling apart. Remove from the oven and set aside.

4. While the squash is roasting, heat the olive oil in a large, heavy-based frying pan or skillet over a medium heat, then add the knob of butter and once that's melted, add the whole sage leaves and fry for no more than 30 seconds until crispy, being careful not to burn them. Use a slotted spoon to transfer to a plate lined with kitchen paper, then season with sea salt flakes.

5. Add the halloumi to the pan and fry for a couple of minutes on each side, until crispy and golden. Transfer the halloumi to a plate and set to one side with the sage.

6. Cook the rice according to packet instructions, fork through and keep warm.

7. Add the 30g butter and the thyme to the pan, along with the onions, and fry for about 10–15 minutes, until sweet and softened. Add the garlic, mushrooms and sliced sage leaves and cook for about another 6 minutes, until the mushrooms are coloured and have released their moisture. Pour in the white wine and cook until it has mostly evaporated, then stir in the sour cream and Dijon mustard. Once it's bubbling add the cavolo nero leaves, and cook for 3–5 minutes, until the sauce has thickened and the cavolo nero is cooked, adding a slosh of water if the sauce needs it. Stir through the roasted squash and halloumi. Serve on piles of warm rice, with the crispy sage leaves scattered on top.

Whole roast cauliflower
with saffron-baked chickpea orzo and crispy capers

Serves 4

There is good reason why this method for cooking cauliflower has caught on. Roasted whole until deeply golden, charred and crisp on the outside, and buttery tender within, cauli's flavour is coaxed from coyly whispering 'oh hey, I'm a side dish kind of veg' to dancing on the table, high kicking and shouting, 'I'm more than the sum of my florets!'. Served up with a bowlful of silky, saffron-laced orzo shot through with crunchy chickpeas, this bulbous brassica becomes a centrepiece-worthy vegetarian feast.

1 cauliflower (about 500g) or 2 smaller ones
2 garlic cloves, crushed to a paste
pinch of dried chilli flakes
4 tbsp olive oil, plus extra for drizzling
40g golden sultanas
2 tbsp lemon juice
large pinch of saffron threads
3 tbsp capers
knob of butter
6 shallots, thinly sliced
leaves from 2 sprigs of thyme
leaves from 2 sprigs of rosemary, roughly chopped
½ tsp sugar
200g orzo
150ml white wine or vermouth
1 x 400g tin chickpeas, drained
80g pecorino, Parmesan or veggie cheese, grated, plus extra to serve
2 slices of Preserved Orange (or lemon) (page 151), cut in half, or grated zest of 1 unwaxed lemon
350ml boiling water
30ml double cream
sea salt and freshly ground black pepper
handful of flat-leaf parsley, to garnish

1. Preheat the oven to 200°C/180°C fan/gas 6.

2. Put the cauliflower, leaves and all, in a roasting tray stem side down.

3. In a bowl, mix the crushed garlic and chilli flakes with half the olive oil and rub it all over the cauliflower. Season it well with salt and pepper and roast in the oven for 1 hour – 1 hour 20 minutes.

4. Meanwhile, put the sultanas in a bowl with the lemon juice and leave to soak.

5. Place a large ovenproof, heavy-based frying pan or skillet over a medium heat, add the saffron and dry-toast for under a minute, just until just colouring, then tip it onto a chopping board or into a mortar and chop or bash it to a powder. Heat the remaining olive oil in the frying pan over a medium-high heat until shimmering and slide in the capers. Fry for 2 minutes, until puffed and crisp but not burned, then transfer to a plate lined with kitchen paper using a slotted spoon, keeping the pan on the heat. Set the capers aside for later.

6. Turn the heat under the pan down a smidge and add a knob of butter to the caper pan, along with a few good grinds of black pepper, then add the sliced shallots, thyme and rosemary with a large pinch of salt and the sugar. Cook for 10–12 minutes, stirring, until the shallots are softened and sweet and just starting to brown, then add the ground saffron and stir well. Add the orzo and drained sultanas and cook for a few more minutes, toasting the orzo, then deglaze with the wine or vermouth. Cook for another couple of minutes until the liquid has evaporated, then stir through the chickpeas, most of the cheese, ¼ teaspoon of salt and the preserved orange or lemon (or lemon zest). Season again and pour over the boiling water and cream. Stir well to combine and remove from the heat. If you don't have an ovenproof frying pan, at this stage transfer this mixture to a roasting tray.

7. Once the cauliflower has just 15–20 minutes of roasting time left, transfer the orzo frying pan, skillet or tray to the oven, sprinkle the remaining grated Parmesan or veggie cheese over the cauliflower and roast everything for the final 15 minutes. After this time check the cauliflower. It should be golden and caramelised all over and tender. Check it by sticking a

knife deep into the base and giving it a wiggle – it should cut through really easily with very little resistance. If it needs more time, take out the orzo and continue to roast the cauliflower until tender – you can reheat the orzo in the oven before you serve.

8. When the cauliflower is done, tip the orzo mix onto a serving platter, garnish with the crispy capers, season with salt and pepper, scatter over the chopped parsley and serve alongside the nutty roasted cauliflower, for everyone to cut into. Alternatively, chop up the cauliflower and toss it through the orzo. Drizzle over some more extra-virgin olive oil and serve with a rocket or radicchio salad and extra cheese grated over.

Sides

There are some lovely sides scattered throughout the book, but here you'll find some extra ideas and favourites of mine, including creamy Celeriac Remoulade (page 201, a must for any picnic or barbecue) and my Lifesaver Lentils (page 198), a hero dish in its own right if you're looking for a last-minute fridge and storecupboard forage dinner. Thinking of making the Rhubarb Poaching Liquor Glazed Parsnips (page 197) as a side to a special meal? Proceed with caution, as they might just steal the show...

Rhubarb poaching liquor roast parsnips

Serves 4 as a side

It might seem like an unusual combination, but something rather magical happens when parsnips and rhubarb get together. In fact, they have a bit of a love-in, as I discovered when I found myself in possession of some leftover rhubarb poaching syrup. The sweet pink syrup, which is infused with orange zest and sherbety rhubarb, adds a sweet, tangy charisma to the root. Both rhubarb and parsnips share an earthiness which harmonises in this dish, and adding a dash of beetroot pickling liquor emphasises this. The syrup reduces and caramelises on the outside of the parsnip, coating them in a sweet, sour glaze that gives way to the nutty, soft parsnip underneath when you bite into it. This is particularly good with the Slow-cooked Pork Belly with Apples and Rhubarb Ketchup on page 172.

400g parsnips, peeled and halved lengthways
1 tbsp rapeseed oil
100ml Rhubarb Poaching Liquor (page 237) and any bits of poached rhubarb and orange zest
50ml Beetroot Pickling Liquor (page 60) (optional)
3 sprigs of thyme
sea salt

1. Preheat the oven to 220°C/200°C fan/gas 7.

2. Put the parsnips in a saucepan with a teaspoon of salt and cover with water. Bring to the boil, turn down to a simmer and cook for 4 minutes, then drain, give them a shake to fluff them up a little, and toss them into a roasting tray with the rapeseed oil, the rhubarb poaching liquor and beetroot pickle liquor. Season with sea salt and throw the thyme on top. Roast in the oven for 20 minutes, turning them halfway through, or until the parsnips are sticky and glazed.

3. Remove from the oven and serve.

Lifesaver lentils

Serves 4

If there are lentils in the cupboard and a few floppy vegetables in the fridge, there's a meal in the making. These miraculously nourishing and tasty legumes are endlessly versatile – they are great for the Sheepless Shepherd's Pie on page 179, and in this recipe, so filling and delicious. This is great with the Sausage, Apple and Radicchio Traybake on page 183 and perfect with any leftover cold cuts, or even with crispy fried halloumi or an egg on top.

200g puy or green lentils
1½ tbsp extra-virgin olive oil
2 bay leaves
handful of flat-leaf parsley
 (leaves and stems),
 finely chopped
1 leek, washed, trimmed and
 thinly sliced
1 celery stick, strings removed
 and stick diced
1 small onion, diced
2 garlic cloves, crushed
1 small carrot, diced
glass of white or red wine
500ml water, or chicken or
 vegetable stock
1 tbsp wholegrain or Dijon
 mustard
sea salt and freshly ground
 black pepper

Optional
100g smoked bacon or
 chorizo, finely chopped
handful of mushrooms, sliced

1. If you have time, soak the lentils in a bowl of cold water for up to 2 hours before you cook them. Rinse and drain.

2. Heat the olive oil in a large, heavy-based frying pan or skillet over a medium-high heat. Add the bay leaves, parsley stems, leek, celery, onion, garlic, carrot and chorizo/bacon/mushrooms (if using) and a large pinch of salt. Season with black pepper and cook, stirring, for 8–10 minutes, until the onion has softened and all the vegetables are fragrant and tender.

3. Add the lentils and coat with the mixture, then pour in the wine and cook until it has almost evaporated. Add the water or stock and ½ teaspoon of salt, bring to the boil, then turn down to a simmer and cook uncovered, stirring, for 40–45 minutes, until the lentils are tender and cooked through. Stir through the mustard and parsley leaves and serve.

Shredded savoy cabbage
with pickled walnuts

Serves 2

This salad makes a wonderful autumnal accompaniment to rich meat dishes or as a great starter. It also works well with shredded Brussels sprouts in the place of the savoy cabbage, and if you happen to have celeriac lurking about, it's a lovely addition too, raw and thinly sliced or grated. Pickled walnuts are one of my store cupboard favourites; they offer so much sweet acidity, texture and depth. If you're opening a jar for this recipe, bear in mind they can also be used in the salad dressing below, or in the Sheepless Shepherd's Pie on page 179.

½ savoy cabbage, tough core removed and leaves very finely shredded
1 shallot, peeled and thinly sliced
2 pickled walnuts, finely chopped, plus 1 tbsp pickled walnut vinegar from the jar
½ sharp apple such as cox, cored and thinly sliced or cut into thin strips (use a mandoline if you have one)
handful of walnuts, roasted and roughly chopped, or toasted pumpkin seeds
handful of flat-leaf parsley leaves, finely chopped
½ tsp grated root ginger (optional)
pinch of caraway seeds
1½ tbsp walnut oil, groundnut oil or extra-virgin olive oil
sea salt and freshly ground black pepper

Put the cabbage and shallot in a large bowl and scatter over ¼ teaspoon of salt. Now use your hands to briefly (but thoroughly) rub the salt into the cabbage and shallot, scrunching it with your hands. Don't be gentle here: you want the salt to penetrate the leaves and start to break them down and tenderise them. Leave the cabbage to sit for about 20 minutes, then pour off any excess moisture and add the tablespoon of vinegar from the walnut jar and stir to combine. Add the apple, pickled walnuts, roasted walnuts or pumpkin seeds, parsley, ginger (if using) and caraway seeds. Toss everything together then dress with the oil. Season to taste with salt and pepper and serve.

Pickled walnut dressing for radicchio or chicory

You can also make a wonderful dressing for bitter leaves such as radicchio or chicory with pickled walnuts.

Blitz 1 pickled walnut with 1 tablespoon of its vinegar in a food processor with a pinch of salt, 1 tablespoon of chopped roasted walnuts, 1 tsp of Dijon mustard and 1 garlic clove, then pour in 2 tablespoons walnut or groundnut oil and 1 tablespoon of water and blitz to a dressing.

Grilled radicchio salad with pickled walnut dressing

I love this dressing drizzled onto grilled radicchio – something about the sweet astringency just works so well with the bitter leaves.

Simply cut a head of radicchio into 8 wedges, toss with a little rapeseed oil and salt and pepper and grill until tender and slightly charred. Serve on a platter drizzled with the dressing, or even better, on warmed cannellini bean purée. Garnish with chopped flat-leaf parsley.

Gorgeous greens fregola salad

Serves 4 as a side,
2 as a starter

Fregola is a wonderful toasted spherical Sardinian pasta, and one of the smallest pasta shapes. It's perfect for satisfying salads and soaking up sauces and marinades, but if you can't find it use giant couscous, or failing that, orzo. I've got a thing for raw sugar snaps: thinly sliced, they add brightness, sweetness and crunch to salads. The griddled, marinated courgettes in this recipe are fantastic for using in salads like this, but are also lovely in sandwiches or served with grilled meat and fish. This salad is great with the Tahini Roast Salmon (page 75) as an alternative to the gremolata.

1 head of broccoli, broken into
    florets, stalk peeled and
    diced
200g fregola
1 red chilli, deseeded and
    finely chopped
100g sugar snap peas,
    thinly sliced
2 spring onions, trimmed
    and thinly sliced
1 green apple, cored and
    diced (skin on)
1 tbsp capers
1 tbsp toasted pumpkin seeds
handful of dill fronds,
    roughly chopped
handful of mint leaves,
    roughly chopped
sea salt and freshly ground
    black pepper

For the marinated courgette
1 courgette, cut lengthways
    into strips, thicker than
    ribbons
2 tbsp extra-virgin olive oil
leaves from 1 sprig of thyme
grated zest and juice of
    ½ unwaxed lemon

For the dressing
grated zest and juice of
    ½ unwaxed lemon
1 tbsp olive oil
1 tsp honey
½ garlic clove, finely grated

1. First, grill and marinate the courgette. Heat a griddle pan over a high heat and scatter it with a large pinch of sea salt. Grill the courgette strips in batches for a few minutes on each side, turning them over once charred and softened. Place the courgette in a bowl. Whisk together the olive oil, a pinch of salt, the thyme and the lemon juice and zest. Pour this mixture over the courgette and leave it to sit for 30 minutes.

2. Bring a large saucepan of well salted water to a vigorous rolling boil. Add the broccoli stalks and cook for 1 minute, then add the florets and boil for another 3 minutes. Remove with a slotted spoon, cut into bite-size pieces and place in the bowl with the griddled courgette. In the same water, cook the fregola for about 8 minutes until al dente (about 2 minutes less than the time stated on the packet). Drain well, then plunge the fregola into a bowl of cold water to stop it cooking. Drain again and place in a bowl. Fork it through to make sure it's not stuck together, then toss in the courgettes and broccoli and the marinade. Add all of the remaining salad ingredients into the bowl, then whisk together and season the dressing ingredients, pour over the salad and serve, or pack into a tub if making in advance, for a picnic. It will keep well made a day ahead, too.

Celeriac remoulade

Serves 2–4

Celeriac is a marvel. While it looks a bit gnarly on the outside and can be a brute to peel, once you get past that bulbous exterior, its pearly flesh is one of the most versatile vegetables we have: it has an unusually sweet, nutty and utterly addictive flavour, and I use it in a fair few recipes throughout this book.

A close relation of leaf celery, it's a special variety grown for its delectable root, and is low in carbohydrate and very high in dietary fibre, so you can feel pretty good about eating it, but bear in mind it's also a fantastic vehicle for inordinate amounts of creamy additions. Keep an eye out at the greengrocer for celeriac roots that still have their green shoots of celery attached, as it's a good sign of freshness and smaller-scale production.

The first time I ever tried it was as a child, in a remoulade just like this one, on a French camping holiday. My mum brought out a plastic packet of the finely julienned, mayonnaise-cloaked vegetable she'd picked up at a local shop, and we ate it on crusty French bread with juicy rotisserie chicken. This may have been one of the first times it really dawned on me that vegetables could be just as enjoyable as their less worthy plate-fellows. A bowl of this remoulade always goes down well on the table at dinner parties, you can add a drop or two of truffle oil if you're feeling fancy, and it's brilliant packed into tubs for picnics or spooned into crisp chicory leaves for an easy canapé. Try it with the Confit Chicken Legs on page 100 as an alternative to the kimchi noodles.

½ celeriac (about 300g), peeled, cut into thin strips or coarsely grated
2 tsp lemon juice
½ tsp sea salt
5 tbsp good-quality mayonnaise (or homemade – see page 35 or 135)
1 tbsp natural yoghurt or crème fraîche
2 tsp Dijon mustard
2 tsp finely chopped tarragon leaves (optional)
1 tbsp finely chopped flat-leaf parsley or chervil leaves (optional)
pinch of saffron threads, softened in 1 tsp warm water (optional)
freshly ground black pepper

Toss the celeriac in a bowl with the lemon juice and season well with salt and a good grinding of black pepper. Allow to sit for a few minutes, then stir through the mayonnaise and natural yoghurt or crème fraîche, mustard and herbs (leave out the tarragon if you're using tarragon mayo). Taste and adjust the seasoning accordingly. For something a bit different, add the optional saffron and its water, stir thoroughly and allow to infuse for an hour or two before serving.

Charred broccoli and runner beans
with anchovy dressing

Serves 4 as a side

This charred greens dish makes a beautiful accompaniment for any grilled or barbecued meat or fish, particularly my Spatchcock Barbecue Chicken (page 112) and Chicken, Cherries and Chicory (page 119). Play around with it seasonally, using different greens from kale or cavolo nero to purple sprouting broccoli and green beans. The charring element of this adds a lovely smoky depth to the dish and is fun if there's a barbecue on the go for one of the other barbecue dishes. If not, leave out the charring and get the blanched greens straight into the anchovy dressing. Runner beans can yellow once blanched, so prepare a bowl of iced water to plunge them into once cooked, to set the chlorophyll so it stays lovely and green.

30g good-quality tinned anchovy fillets in oil
grated zest and juice of ½ unwaxed lemon
1 tsp Dijon mustard
pinch of dried chilli flakes
50ml olive oil
200g runner beans
200g sprouting broccoli or Tenderstem broccoli
sea salt and freshly ground black pepper

1. Roughly chop the anchovy fillets on a board, mushing some of them up into a paste but keeping some as tangible chunks. Put them in a bowl and add the lemon juice and zest, Dijon mustard, chilli flakes and olive oil. Whisk together, season with salt and pepper and check that you're happy with how it tastes. It should be punchy – don't forget it's a dressing for the bitter and sweet of the beans and broccoli.

2. Bring large saucepan of salted water to the boil. When I say salted, I mean salted – add a good tablespoon or so of salt. Have a spider or slotted spoon, a large plate lined with kitchen paper and a bowl of iced water ready by your side. While it's coming to a vigorous rolling boil, top and tail the runner beans and trim any really woody bits from the broccoli stalks. Blanch the broccoli for 3–4 minutes, until tender (a sharp knife inserted into the stalk should slide out easily). Remove from the water with a spider or slotted spoon and put straight onto the paper-lined plate. Slide the runner beans into the still vigorously boiling water and blanch for 4–6 minutes, until tender (there is a trend for undercooked runner beans, but I like them either completely raw or cooked until tender). Remove from the water using the spider or slotted spoon, and put them straight into the iced water to set the chlorophyll, then drain. If you're not charring the greens and beans, leave this part out and toss both straight in the anchovy dressing.

3. If you are charring the greens on a barbecue, toss them straight onto the grate. Cook, turning with tongs, until the leaves of the broccoli are crisping up and charring, and the beans are visibly charring too. Once suitably charred, remove them from the barbecue and dress thoroughly while warm in the anchovy dressing.

4. I like to let the greens sit and absorb the flavours of the dressing for about 10 minutes. This dish is best served at room temperature.

Roast beetroot and buckwheat salad

Serves 4 as a side

I had the great pleasure of experiencing a Polish wedding when our friends got married in the bride's homeland, just outside Warsaw. They told us beforehand that vodka is drunk rather than wine at the reception and I was worried. I shouldn't have been, because as much as Polish weddings are about vodka and dancing, they are also about food. Course after course of delicious Polish fare graced the table during the seven-hour party, each course punctuated by enthusiastic cries of *goszko goszko!*, at which point the bride and groom had to stand up and kiss. It was raucous fun, and while I don't remember every dish, some stayed with me – the meal started with chicken broth, ended with the most restorative borscht and in a course between these we ate beetroots fried with buckwheat and onions. The irresistible, unusual combination of earthy beetroot, nutty buckwheat and sweet onions inspired this salad. This is great with the Whey-brined Lamb Chops on page 115.

4–6 medium beetroots (about 500g)
3 tbsp olive oil, plus extra for drizzling
1 tsp dried oregano or thyme
4 small red or tropea onions (or Roscoff onions), sliced
leaves from 1 sprig of thyme
1 bay leaf
150g buckwheat
300ml water
1 tbsp toasted pumpkin seeds
salt

For the dressing
1 garlic clove, grated
2 tbsp dill fronds, roughly chopped, plus 1 tbsp for scattering
2 tbsp tarragon leaves, roughly chopped, plus extra for scattering
1 tbsp cider vinegar
1 tsp honey
2 tbsp olive oil
1 tbsp water
pinch of salt
pinch of freshly ground black pepper

1. Preheat the oven to 240°C/220°C fan/gas 8. Put each beetroot on a piece of foil, drizzle with a little olive oil to coat and season with salt and a pinch of dried thyme or oregano. Wrap the beetroot in their individual sheets of foil, place on a baking tray and roast for 1–1½ hours, until a skewer inserted into a beetroot can be pulled out with no resistance. You can roast the beetroot in advance.

2. While they're roasting, fry the onions. Heat 2 tablespoons of the olive oil in a heavy-based frying pan or skillet over a medium heat, add the onions, 1 teaspoon of salt and the thyme leaves and cook, stirring, for 20–30 minutes, until softened, sweet and caramelised.

3. Remove the beetroot from the oven and leave until cool enough to handle, then rub off the skins with kitchen paper or the back of a teaspoon and cut them into wedges.

4. Heat the remaining tablespoon of olive oil in a saucepan with a tight-fitting lid (but with the lid off for now) over a medium heat, add the bay leaf and buckwheat and fry for a few minutes, stirring, until the buckwheat is toasted. Add the water and ½ teaspoon of salt and bring to the boil, then reduce the heat and simmer for 10 minutes. Turn off the heat, cover with the lid and allow to stand until all the water is absorbed and the buckwheat is puffed up.

5. Whisk the dressing ingredients together in a cup or jug and taste for seasoning. Stir the onions and pumpkin seeds into the buckwheat and dress with half the dressing while the buckwheat is still warm. Place the buckwheat and onion mix on a platter and top with the beetroot wedges and some more dressing. Garnish with the extra herbs and serve.

TIP: Make the Labneh on page 256 and add a swoop of it on the platter under the salad.

Raw courgette, Parmesan and artichoke heart salad

Serves 2–4 as a side

This salad is great served on repeat in the humid heights of summer because it's so quick and easy to throw together. The nuttiness of the raw courgettes with the crumbly Parmesan and creamy, piquant artichokes is a winning combo, all lifted by fresh basil and sprightly lemon zest. It takes no time to throw together but feels premium (read: good enough to make for friends).

2 medium courgettes (a mix of yellow and green is nice), peeled into ribbons
80g jarred artichoke hearts, sliced and ½ tbsp oil from the jar
handful of basil leaves
handful of mint leaves
½ red chilli, deseeded and diced
grated zest and juice of ½ unwaxed lemon
10g shaved Parmesan (or use vegetarian parmesan or hard cheese)
½ tsp pink peppercorns
1½ tbsp extra-virgin olive oil
sea salt and freshly ground black pepper

Toss all of the ingredients, apart from the olive oil, together in a salad bowl and leave to sit for 5 minutes. Season with salt and pepper and dress with the extra-virgin olive oil just before serving.

Orzo and summer vegetable salad

Serves 6

Orzo salads are always an easy win. They are a picnic staple for me because they last well, and in fact improve in flavour if the ingredients have had a few hours to mingle. This one is packed with an array of colourful summer veg, with sweet roast tomatoes, griddled, marinated courgettes and silky broad beans. Saffron, pine nuts and Nocellara olives bring an edge of luxury to the salad, too.

200g cherry tomatoes (it's nice to use a combination of yellow and red), halved
extra-virgin olive oil, for drizzling
leaves from 4 sprigs of thyme
large pinch of saffron threads
100g broad beans (shelled weight)
2 tbsp pine nuts
2 spring onions, trimmed and thinly sliced
¼ fennel bulb, tough outer layer and woody base removed (keep for stock), tender bulb finely chopped
1 red chilli, deseeded and finely chopped
300g orzo
2 tbsp green olives, pitted and torn in half (I love Nocellara)
100g marinated green and yellow courgettes (page 200)
handful of flat-leaf parsley leaves, finely chopped
handful of dill fronds, finely chopped
juice of ½ lemon
sea salt and freshly ground black pepper

1. Preheat the oven to 180°C/160°C fan/gas 4.

2. Put the tomato halves in a bowl, coat with a little olive oil and season well with salt and pepper. Lay them out on a baking sheet and scatter over the thyme leaves. Roast in the oven for 45 minutes–1 hour, until softened, shrivelled and concentrated. Meanwhile, soak the saffron in ½ tablespoon of boiling water to release its colour and flavour.

3. Bring a large saucepan of well salted water to a vigorous rolling boil. Blanch the broad beans for 3–5 minutes (how long they take to will depend on the beans' size and age). Transfer the beans to a bowl of iced water, then peel away their skins by gently piercing the white skin with a nail and carefully squeezing out the vivid little green beans into a bowl.

4. Toast the pine nuts in a dry frying pan until golden and nutty – keep a close eye on them, because they can burn when left unattended.

5. Heat a tablespoon of olive oil in a frying pan over a medium heat, add the spring onions, fennel and chilli with a pinch of salt and pepper and fry for about 5 minutes, until softened, sweet and starting to caramelise, and the fennel is taking on some colour. Remove from the heat and set aside.

6. Cook the orzo in plenty of boiling salted water according to packet instructions, or until al dente, then drain and rinse under cold water. Transfer the orzo to a bowl and, once cool, pour over a glug of olive oil and the saffron and its soaking liquid, forking through to separate the grains. Stir in the roasted tomatoes, toasted pine nuts, olives, broad beans, marinated courgettes, herbs and the fennel mixture.

7. Add the lemon juice and taste to check the seasoning. Add a glug of extra-virgin olive oil for good measure and serve, or pack into a tub for a picnic. It will keep well and can even be made a day ahead.

Raw chopped carrot and beetroot salad
with roasted almonds

Serves 6

This bright, crunchy raw salad – earthy, sweet and fresh with a zip of onion – is a moreish, satisfying meal that is cleansing and comforting all at once. It's great for a midweek lunch as it's quick to rustle up, and there's usually a beetroot and carrot or two lurking in the bottom of the fridge. It holds up to being made ahead and packed into a lunchbox and works just as well as a sharing dish in the middle of the table.

2 tbsp raisins
1 tbsp cider vinegar or lemon juice
200g whole, skin-on almonds
extra-virgin rapeseed oil
1 tsp smoked sweet paprika
½ tsp sea salt
400g raw beetroots, peeled and roughly chopped
400g raw carrots, peeled
½ red onion or 2 shallots, chopped
handful of dill fronds, roughly chopped
handful of flat-leaf parsley leaves, roughly chopped
1 tsp runny honey

1. Preheat the oven to 200°C/180°C fan/gas 6.

2. Soak the raisins in the vinegar or lemon juice for at least 30 minutes.

3. Put the almonds in a roasting tray, drizzle them with a little rapeseed oil, add the smoked paprika and salt and toss to coat. Roast in the oven for 8 minutes, until crisp. Remove and allow to cool.

4. Place the chopped beetroot, carrot and onion or shallot in the bowl of a powerful food processor and pulse until well chopped (to the size of pearl barley). If you don't have a powerful food processor you can grate them or finely chop them by hand. Transfer to a bowl and stir through the chopped herbs and roasted almonds.

5. Whisk 2 tablespoons of rapeseed oil with the raisins, vinegar or lemon juice and honey and pour enough over the salad to sufficiently dress it. Stir to thoroughly coat, taste for seasoning and adjust accordingly, then serve.

Cucumber, pea shoot, chilli and mint salad

Serves 2–4

Like all really good friends, cucumber and mint bring out the best in each other, and I love contrasting their fresh, cooling qualities with sweet pea shoots, fiery chillies and crunchy smoked paprika-roast almonds in this simple dish. This is the sort of salad you'll want to eat repeatedly in the heat of high summer, preferably packed into a tub and taken down to the park or beach. It sits well on the side of any barbecued meat, fish or veg, and is particularly lovely with the Slow-roast Shallot, Tomato and Chard Tart on page 110.

50g whole, skin-on almonds
rapeseed oil, for drizzling
½ tsp smoked sweet paprika
1 large cucumber, shaved into
    ribbons with a vegetable
    peeler or mandoline
4 radishes, thinly sliced or
    shaved with a mandoline
handful of pea shoots
1 red chilli, halved, deseeded
    and thinly sliced
grated zest of 1 unwaxed
    lemon and juice of ½
large handful of mint, leaves
    picked, large leaves thinly
    sliced
a few dill fronds, leaves picked
sea salt and freshly ground
    black pepper

1. Preheat the oven to 180°C/160°C fan/gas 4.

2. Put the almonds in a roasting tray, drizzle with a little rapeseed oil, add the smoked paprika and a pinch of salt and toss to coat. Roast in the oven for 8 minutes, until crisp, then remove from the oven and leave to cool.

3. Put the cucumber, radishes, pea shoots and chilli in a bowl and season with the lemon zest and some salt and pepper.

4. Add the mint, dill and almonds, squeeze over the lemon juice and drizzle with a little rapeseed oil. You don't want it greasy or over-dressed, so be light with the oil, but taste until it's dressed and seasoned to your liking. Serve straight away, or pack into a tub if making in advance for a picnic. It will keep well for a couple of hours.

Shaved fennel, radish and pickled peach salad

Serves 4 as a side

In the warmer months I crave cooling salads of finely shaved veg – they are just so refreshing and bright. This one is a favourite: peppery radish, crunchy fennel and sweet, piquant pickled peaches, along with plenty of lemon juice and crisp, paprika-roasted almonds. Save the dill-like fronds from the fennel bulb to throw into the mix as they have a lovely intense anise flavour. It's worth using a mandoline to slice the veg if you can: it will get it thinner than slicing by hand (unless you have mad knife skills, which I certainly don't). If you haven't made the pickled peaches on page 153, use ordinary peaches briefly marinated in a little cider vinegar sweetened with honey.

50g whole, skin-on almonds
rapeseed oil, for drizzling
½ tsp smoked sweet paprika
2 fennel bulbs, tough outer
layer and woody base
removed (keep for stock),
tender layers thinly sliced
or shaved on a mandoline
4 radishes, thinly sliced (use a
mandoline if you have one)
juice of 1 lemon
1 tsp fennel seeds
2 Pickled Peaches (page 153),
peeled, halved, stoned
and roughly chopped, or
2 quick-marinated peaches
(see intro)
handful of mint leaves, torn
handful of basil leaves, torn
2 tbsp olive oil
sea salt and freshly ground
black pepper

1. Preheat the oven to 180°C/160°C fan/gas 4.

2. Put the almonds in a roasting tray, drizzle them with a little rapeseed oil, add the smoked paprika and a pinch of salt and toss to coat. Roast the almonds in the oven for 8 minutes, until crisp. Remove from the oven and leave to cool.

3. Put the shaved fennel and radishes in a bowl and dress with the lemon juice and a large pinch of salt. Allow to sit for a few minutes, then stir through the fennel seeds, peaches, herbs and olive oil. Season to taste with salt and pepper, scatter with the roasted almonds and serve straight away.

Sweet Things

The excitable, greedy little girl, climbing fruit trees in Kent to fill her cheeks and show the squirrels who's boss, is still alive and well in this chapter, where you'll notice an abundance of desserts based around my favourite seasonal fruits, from Strawberry and Elderflower Tarts (page 220) encased in brown butter pastry, to fudgy Fig Leaf and Cherry Clafoutis (page 231). And what could be more joyful than ripe, juicy fruit harnessed right in its prime? Possibly homemade doughnuts (page 245), freshly fried and filled with bay leaf custard, to be drizzled with sharp hedgerow jam.

Rhubarb and elderflower cake

Serves 8-10

Rhubarb and elderflower yoghurt cake was one of the first things I baked when I returned from living in Vancouver. I was so excited to be back and able to get hold of local rhubarb and elderflowers. Poaching rhubarb in elderflower cordial lends a lovely floral note to the vegetable, and folding tangy natural yoghurt into the cream filling cuts through the sweetness of the sponge. This cake should be moist, messy and abundant: it's all about the flavours with this one.

For the roasted rhubarb
400g trimmed rhubarb, cut into 8-mm slices
110g caster sugar
grated zest and juice of ½ unwaxed lemon
2 tbsp elderflower cordial

For the cake
95g whole, skin-on almonds (or use blanched or ground almonds)
115g unsalted butter, at room temperature, plus extra for greasing
200g golden caster sugar
grated zest of 1 unwaxed lemon
2 eggs, plus 1 egg white
1 tsp vanilla extract
1 tbsp elderflower cordial, plus extra for brushing
100g plain flour
1 tsp baking powder
½ tsp bicarbonate of soda
pinch of salt
130g full-fat natural yoghurt
elderflowers, to garnish (or rose, lilac, geranium or peony flowers or petals)

For the filling
300ml double cream
2 tbsp elderflower cordial
100g full-fat natural yoghurt

1. Preheat the oven to 200°C/180°C fan/gas 6. Grease the sides of two 20cm round cake tins with butter and line the bases with baking parchment.

2. First, roast the rhubarb. Line a high-sided roasting tray with baking parchment, add the rhubarb, top with the sugar, lemon juice and zest, and elderflower cordial. Cover the tin tightly with foil and roast in the oven for 25 minutes, until soft. Remove from the oven and reduce the oven temperature to 195°C/175°C fan/gas 5. Strain the rhubarb from the poaching liquor, reserving the pink syrup.

3. Put the almonds in the bowl of a food processor and blitz until ground (if using whole almonds), but still retaining some texture.

4. Put the butter in the bowl of a stand mixer fitted with a whisk attachment (or using an electric hand-held whisk) and cream it on medium speed for 2 minutes, then, using a rubber spatula, scrape down the butter from the sides of the bowl and add the sugar and lemon zest. Turn up the mixer speed slightly and continue whisking for 5 minutes until light and fluffy. Turn the mixer speed down slightly, add the eggs, egg white, vanilla extract and elderflower cordial and mix together. Combine the flour, almonds, baking powder, bicarbonate of soda and salt. Scrape the butter mixture down from the sides of the bowl, turn the mixer to low speed – so it's just stirring – then spoon in the flour and almond mixture in four batches, alternating with spoonfuls of the yoghurt, and finishing with the flour and almonds. Mix until just combined, with no streaks remaining, then add half the roasted rhubarb and 1 tablespoon of its syrup to the batter and fold it in.

5. Divide the batter evenly between the cake tins and bake in the oven for 20–25 minutes, until a skewer inserted into each cake comes out clean. Remove the cakes from the oven, leave them to cool in their tins on a wire rack, then carefully remove the cakes from the tins.

6. Whip the cream to soft peaks in a bowl and fold in three-quarters of the remaining roasted rhubarb, along with the elderflower cordial and yoghurt.

7. Place one of the cakes flat side down on a cake stand or plate, prick it all over with a skewer, and use a pastry brush to brush the cake with a little more elderflower cordial. Spoon on half the cream mixture, top with the other cake, and brush that cake with cordial, too. Spoon over the remaining cream mixture, top with the remaining rhubarb and spoon over some of the poaching syrup. Garnish with elderflowers or seasonal flowers.

Sweet Things

Elderflower fritters
with preserved lemon posset

Serves 4

Discovering salty, concentrated preserved lemons (page 151) and the way they elevate your cooking is a life-changing moment for most home cooks, and experimenting with them in desserts is also a revelation, especially when you pair them with something incredibly sweet. Here, they are used to infuse lemon posset: golden, silken and rich, it's sort of like a citrussy salted caramel, and just the thing for dipping impossibly light, crisp, elderflower fritters into. The whole thing explodes in your mouth with pollen, citrus and summer. Delightful.

sunflower or vegetable oil, for
    deep-frying
60g '00' flour
40g cornflour
150–200ml iced elderflower
    pressé, prosecco or
    sparkling water mixed with
    2 tbsp elderflower cordial
6 heads of elderflower, broken
    into smaller clumps, plus
    extra elderflowers to
    garnish
1 tbsp caster sugar

**For the preserved lemon
posset**
300ml double cream
140g golden caster sugar
4 slices of preserved lemon
    (about 50g), deseeded
    (shop-bought or see recipe
    on page 151)
grated zest and juice of
    ½ unwaxed lemon

1. First, make the posset. Put the cream and sugar in a heavy-based saucepan over a low-medium heat and heat gently, stirring to dissolve the sugar. Once the sugar has dissolved and the mixture is on the cusp of boiling, add the preserved lemon slices and lemon juice and simmer for 2 minutes, stirring with a spatula. Remove from the heat and taste the mixture (be careful not to burn your tongue) – it should be sharp but pleasingly piqued by the salt. It will depend on the preserved lemons you're using, but if you think it needs it, add just a pinch more of salt to bring out the flavour (rather than make it salty). Leave to infuse for 5–10 minutes, then strain through a sieve, stir in the zest and pour into shallow serving dishes. It is incredibly rich, so there will be just enough to dip the fritters into. Chill in the fridge for at least 1 hour.

2. Fill a small saucepan with enough oil for deep-frying – about 500ml – and place over a medium-high heat. Test the oil is hot enough by dropping in a small piece of bread: if it sizzles and turns golden the oil is ready. Line a plate with a few layers of kitchen paper and place it next to the pan of oil, and find a slotted spoon or spider.

3. To make the batter, combine the flours in a bowl and gradually add in the iced pressé or other chilled liquid, whisking. You want it the consistency of double cream and not much thicker. Holding an elderflower bunch by the stem, dip the flowers into the batter, covering the flowers and the lower part of the stem. Shake off some excess batter and drop it into the hot oil. Fry for a minute or so, until puffed and slightly golden, then remove with a slotted spoon or spider and drain on the paper-lined plate. Dust immediately with some of the caster sugar and repeat with the rest of the elderflower heads.

4. Serve the elderflower fritters with the posset, for dipping.

Peach and basil Eton mess

This dessert is a celebration of summer. Use flat or 'doughnut' peaches – they have an intense perfume and sweeter flavour with notes of almond – but if you can't find them normal peaches will do. They just need to be ripe, so ripe that when you touch the skin you can feel the flesh squish underneath. If you end up with under-ripe peaches, roast them in a hot oven for 15 minutes or so to bring out their sugars and soften them up a bit. The meringue and basil cream can be made up to a day in advance.

6 ripe and fragrant flat
  peaches (or regular
  peaches)
1 tbsp caster sugar
100g white currants or
  raspberries, to garnish

For the hazelnut meringue
4 egg whites, at room
  temperature
250g caster sugar
3–4 drops vanilla extract
50g whole, skin-on hazelnuts,
  chopped

For the basil cream
300ml double cream
50g golden caster sugar
70g basil leaves, plus extra for
  the peaches

1. Place the cream and golden caster sugar for the basil cream in a saucepan and gently bring to the boil, stirring to dissolve the sugar. Once dissolved, remove from the heat and place over a bowl of iced water to cool down. Tear in the basil leaves, swirl them into the cream and allow to cool. Once cool, cover and leave to infuse in the fridge for 3 hours, or preferably overnight.

2. Preheat the oven to 170°C/150°C fan/gas 4.

3. Whisk the egg whites in a spotlessly clean bowl with an electric hand-held whisk or in a stand mixer fitted with the whisk attachment until soft peaks form, then gradually add the sugar, a tablespoon at a time, whisking until the mixture is thick and glossy, and all the sugar has dissolved – there should be no grains left. This could take 10–15 minutes. Whisk in the vanilla extract and gently fold in the chopped nuts.

4. Use a little of the meringue mix to stick some baking parchment to a flat baking sheet, then – bearing in mind that height is the key to fluffy meringue – spoon the mixture onto the paper and lightly spread it out to a rough circle, keeping away from the edges (you don't want to smooth it down too much). Bake in the oven for 35–40 minutes, until it is puffed and crisp and allow to cool completely in the oven. Don't worry if the top cracks, it will still taste delightful, and you're going to break it up anyway. This is a quick-cook meringue which will be fluffy and marshmallow-like in the middle, so perfect for Eton mess.

5. Once the meringue is baked, risen and crisp on top, remove it from the oven and carefully lift it (and the parchment) away from the baking tray and onto a wire rack to rest until it's cool.

6. Strain the infused cream into a bowl and whip to soft peaks, until it's soft and cloud-like. At this point you can chill the cream and place the meringue in an airtight container if you're making ahead. If you are ready, get six dishes or bowls: I like to use glass dishes for this to show off all that cream and beautiful pink peach skin.

7. Halve and stone the peaches, then tear them up into a bowl. I say tear rather than chop, because they should be soft enough to tear. But of course you could chop them if you like. Take one or two pieces and squeeze them to release their juice, then toss the peaches in that juice and add the tablespoon of sugar, which encourages the peaches to release more juice. Tear up a couple of basil leaves and toss them through with the peaches for good measure.

8. Break your meringue up into the bowls, top with a generous spoonful of the cream and some peach pieces, and repeat. Garnish with sweet little basil leaves. Devour.

Strawberry and elderflower tarts
with brown butter pastry

These joyful little tarts are summer in a pastry case. When strawberries and elderflowers hang out together, something delicious happens: the sweet, fragrant pollen from the flowers melds with the strawberry juices, making a sort of floral dressing. The pastry for this recipe was a happy accident, thanks to a kitchen mishap: I blind-baked at too high a temperature for too long (I bake with music on and didn't hear my oven timer), which caramelised the butter in the pastry, making for a deeply nutty flavour. This complements the creamy neutrality of the ricotta and sweetness of strawberry and elderflower.

200g strawberries, hulled and halved
1 tbsp caster sugar
1 tbsp elderflower cordial
2 heads of elderflower, flowers picked
120g ricotta or Fresh Curd Cheese (page 254)
1 tbsp icing sugar
2 tbsp good-quality flower or acacia blossom honey (set or runny) (preferably unpasteurised and unfiltered)

For the pastry
200g '00' flour, plus extra for dusting
large pinch of fine sea salt
1 tbsp caster sugar
100g cold unsalted butter, diced
2 tbsp sour cream

1. First, make the pastry. Combine the flour, salt and sugar in a bowl and stir. Add the butter and rub it in, lightly squeezing it with the flour between your fingers and thumb and fanning, a bit like you're dealing cards. You want mostly fine flakes of butter, with some large flakes remaining (to caramelise in the pastry). Stir in the sour cream and use your hands to squish the mix together, kneading it in the bowl until you have a solid, smooth lump of dough. Tip it out onto a clean surface dusted with flour and give it a brief knead to bring it together – it might be a little fragile so work gently. Mould it into a ball and flatten to a disc. Wrap it in greaseproof paper (rather than cling film, which makes it sweat) and chill in the fridge for at least 30 minutes.

2. Preheat the oven to 200°C/180°C fan/gas 6.

3. Remove the pastry from the fridge and unwrap it. Dust a clean surface lightly with flour and roll the pastry to about the thickness of a pound coin. If it's difficult to work with you can do this between two pieces of baking parchment. Line 6 x 10cm tart tins with the pastry, letting it overhang to allow for shrinkage, then line the tart shells with crumpled greaseproof paper and fill with baking beans. Blind-bake in the oven for 30–40 minutes, until golden and flecked with dark spots where the butter has caramelised. The tart shell should be a deep honey colour but not too dark brown. Remove from the oven, remove the paper and beans and leave to cool.

4. Toss the strawberries in a bowl with the sugar, cordial and half the elderflowers. Allow to macerate at room temperature for 1–1½ hours, stirring occasionally and being careful not to smush the strawberries. If you're using shop-bought ricotta, line a sieve or bowl with a few sheets of kitchen paper and strain off some of the moisture (shop-bought ricotta tends to be quite wet), then place the cheese in a bowl and sift in the icing sugar, using a whisk or fork to get rid of any lumps.

5. If you're using set honey, warm it gently in a little frying pan until it's pourable. Fill the tart cases with a teaspoon each of honey on the bottom, followed by the sweetened ricotta and top with the strawberries. Scatter with the remaining elderflowers and serve.

Summer gooseberry and raspberry upside-down cake
with clouds of rose water cream

Serves 4–6
(depending on greed)

This juicy upside-down cake is reminiscent of macaroons and Turkish delight, with rose water-laced clouds of whipped cream, baked summer fruit and almond and coconut sponge. Pairing tart gooseberries with raspberries gives it a sweet, sour and textural contrast with pockets of moist fruit keeping every mouthful interesting. The sponge can easily be made ahead and topped with the cream and flower petals just before serving.

butter, for greasing
50g flaked almonds
250g raspberries
250g gooseberries, washed
  and any little dry brown
  tails pinched off
100g plain flour
2 tsp baking powder
pinch of fine salt
100g ground almonds
100g desiccated coconut
4 eggs
120g golden caster sugar
100ml whole milk
1 tsp vanilla extract
1 tbsp olive oil
rose petals or other edible
  flowers, to serve

For the rose water cream
400ml double cream
1 tbsp golden caster sugar
3 tsp rose water

1. Preheat the oven to 200°C/180°C fan/gas 6, grease a round 22cm cake tin and line it with baking parchment.

2. Scatter half the flaked almonds over the base of the cake tin, followed by the berries and the rest of the almonds.

3. Sift the flour, baking powder, salt and ground almonds into a bowl, add the desiccated coconut and stir to combine.

4. Put the eggs and sugar in the bowl of a stand mixer fitted with the whisk attachment and whisk on medium speed for a few minutes until frothy, then whisk in the milk, vanilla extract and olive oil. Alternatively, use a bowl and an electric hand-held whisk. Fold the frothy egg mix into the dry ingredients to make a thick but wet batter. Pour this over the berries and bake in the oven for 35–40 minutes, until a skewer inserted into the cake comes out clean. Remove from the oven and allow to cool in the cake tin, then turn it out onto a plate, with the gooseberries on top.

5. Using a balloon whisk and elbow grease, or very gingerly with a stand mixer, whip the cream with the caster sugar until it reaches soft, floppy peaks (keeping a close eye on it so that you don't over-whip it). When it's almost at the perfect soft consistency, add the rose water and mix it through. Pile the rose water cream on top of the cake and scatter with rose petals or other edible flowers.

Apricot, buttermilk and hazelnut tart

The pastry for this tart is almost like a hazelnut biscuit; it's so crumbly and buttery against the soft, honeyed flesh of poached apricots. If you don't have skin-on hazelnuts you can use skin-on almonds instead, but the flavour of hazelnuts with the apricots is just divine. The perky buttermilk custard is sharp and creamy all at once, with a hint of molasses from the muscovado sugar, and a seductive wobble. I love garnishing this tart with lavender flowers, whose fragrance, combined with the apricots and sweet cream, brings to mind soporific summers in Provence or Sicily.

2 egg yolks
75ml buttermilk
150ml double cream
pinch of salt
grated zest of ½ unwaxed lemon
140g light muscovado sugar
6 Rosé and Lavender Poached Apricots (page 238), halved and stoned
handful of whole, skin-on almonds, thickly sliced
lavender flowers, to decorate
crème fraîche, to serve

For the pastry
50g skin-on hazelnuts
200g plain flour
125g cold unsalted butter, diced
1 egg yolk
pinch of fine sea salt
1 tbsp caster sugar
2 tbsp iced water

1. First, make the pastry. Put the hazelnuts in the bowl of a food processor or blender and blitz to a coarse crumb. Add the flour, butter, egg yolk, salt and sugar and blitz again, to breadcrumb consistency. Add the iced water, a tablespoon at a time, sprinkling it scross the crumb and blitzing between additions until the dough clumps together. Tip the dough out into a bowl and squish it into a ball, adding a dash more water if it needs it, or a dusting of flour if it's a little sticky. Mould it into a ball and flatten to a disc. Wrap it in greaseproof paper (rather than cling film, which makes it sweat) and leave it to rest in the fridge for at least 30 minutes.

2. To make the filling, whisk the egg yolks, buttermilk, double cream, salt, lemon zest and muscovado sugar together in a bowl to make a smooth custard. Set aside.

3. Preheat the oven to 200°C/180°C fan/gas 6.

4. Remove the pastry from the fridge, unwrap it (leaving it sitting on the greasproof paper) and place another piece of paper on top. Roll it out between the sheets of paper to the thickness of a pound coin (large enough to line a 23cm tart tin). Line the tart tin with the pastry, letting it overhang to allow for shrinkage, and put the lined tin in the fridge until the pastry is firm. Prick the base with a fork, line the pastry with the crumpled greaseproof paper and fill with baking beans. Blind-bake the pastry for 25 minutes, then lift out the beans and paper and return it to the oven for a further 5–8 minutes, until golden and crisp. Remove from the oven and turn it down to 170°C/150°C fan/gas 4.

5. Allow the pastry shell to cool for a couple of minutes then fill it with the custard. Place the apricot halves cut side down in the custard and scatter over the almonds. Bake the tart in the oven for 45 minutes, until the custard is puffed and golden. Carefully remove it from the oven – it will still be quite wobbly but don't panic, it will set once cooled. Allow it to cool then place in the fridge to set for an hour or so. Remove it from the fridge a good hour before you want to serve it so it's at room temperature. Garnish with lavender and serve with crème fraîche.

TIP: If you can't get hold of fresh apricots, this also works well with tinned.

Roast fig tarts
with fig leaf custard

These crisp little almond pastry tart shells are brimming with silken custard, rich with the almost coconut flavour of furry fig leaves, and topped with jammy roasted figs.

I feel incredibly lucky to have some amazing bakers in my life who have changed the way I look at dessert. Henrietta Inman is a pastry chef with a reputation for making some of the tastiest tarts in London, and Claire Ptak of Violet Bakery is someone I admire for her sensational cakes and commitment to seasonality. Henrietta's little fig and lemon curd tarts inspired this recipe, and it was Claire that taught me that fig leaves could be used to infuse custard. So these two brilliant women are also to thank for what will be a new favourite recipe.

10g butter, plus extra
    for greasing
9 ripe figs (I like green ones)
1 tbsp runny orange
    blossom honey
2 sprigs of thyme,
    leaves picked

For the pastry
50g almonds (preferably skin-
    on, but skinless or ground
    will work too)
200g plain flour
110g cold unsalted butter,
    cubed
15g crème fraîche
1 egg yolk
pinch of fine sea salt
1 tbsp caster sugar
2 tbsp iced water

For fig leaf custard
150ml double cream
450ml whole milk
80g golden caster sugar
6 fresh fig leaves
3 large egg yolks
30g cornflour
pinch of salt

1. To make the fig leaf custard, put the cream, milk and half the sugar in a saucepan over a medium heat and stir gently until the sugar has dissolved, the mixture has just reached boiling point and there are little bubbles popping to the surface. At this point, remove it from the heat and add the fig leaves, scrunching and tearing them a little to release the oils in the leaves, submerging them in the liquid with a wooden spoon. Plunge the pan immediately into a basin of very cold water and allow to cool and infuse for 1–2 hours (overnight is even better).

2. Once the custard has infused, whisk the egg yolks with the remaining golden caster sugar and the cornflour and salt in a large bowl until frothy and pale. Strain the cooled infused cream into the egg yolk mixture and whisk it until well combined.

3. Wash and dry the saucepan and prepare another basin of very cold water. Return the mixture to the pan and heat over a low-medium heat, bringing it slowly to the boil and stirring continuously with a whisk for 5–8 minutes, paying particular attention to the bottom and edges of the pan and whisking out any lumps. You should feel the mixture thickening significantly – you will need to whisk vigorously to get rid of any lumps, cooking the mixture until the cornflour is cooked out. Keep tasting it and if it feels mealy in the mouth, it's not there yet. Remove from the heat, and if you're concerned that it's a little lumpy, add a splash of milk and whisk it in until smooth. Cool by placing the pan in the basin of cold water as you did before. Once cool, cover with cling film and chill for at least 2 hours.

4. To make the pastry, put the almonds in the bowl of a food processor and blitz to a coarse crumb. Add the flour, butter, crème fraîche, egg yolk, salt and sugar and blitz again until the mixture resembles breadcrumbs. Take off the lid and sprinkle the iced water over the crumb a tablespoon at a time, blitzing between additions until the dough clumps together. Tip the dough out into a bowl and squish it into a ball, adding a dash more water if it needs

it, or a dusting of flour if it's a little sticky. Mould it into a ball and flatten to a disc. Wrap it in greaseproof paper (rather than cling film, which makes it sweat) and leave it to rest in the fridge for at least 30 minutes. Preheat the oven to 200°C/180°C fan/gas 6.

5. Remove the pastry from the fridge, unwrap it (leaving it sitting on the greaseproof paper) and place another piece of paper on top. Roll it out between the sheets of paper to the thickness of a pound coin. Take one 8cm individual tart tin (you will need 6), place it top down on the pastry and cut out 6 circles using it as a guide, then line the tins with the pastry, pushing the pastry into the shape of the tins. Line each case with greaseproof paper and fill with baking beans, place them on a baking sheet and blind-bake for 20 minutes. Lift out the beans and paper and return the tins to the oven (on the baking sheet) for 5 minutes, until the pastry is crisp and golden. Remove from the oven and allow to cool completely. Turn the oven down to 180°C/160°C fan/gas 4.

6. Take the custard out of the fridge and use a whisk to loosen it and beat out any lumps, adding a dash of cold milk if it's too solid. You want it to be a spoonable custard. If it's lumpy do not despair – quickly blitz it in a food processor or with a stick blender until smooth. Grease a roasting tray or ovenproof dish with butter. Split all the figs in half, place in the tray and drizzle with a little of the runny honey and scatter with the thyme leaves. Dot with the butter and place skin side down in the buttered roasting tray or ovenproof dish. Bake in the oven for 10 minutes, until softened. Take 3 of the figs (6 halves) and finely chop. Divide these between the pastry cases, then spoon over enough of the custard to fill the pastry, smoothing it with the back of a spoon. Top with the remaining fig halves and serve.

Fig leaf and cherry clafoutis

Serves 4

Clafoutis is a classic French dessert of baked, thickened batter, usually dotted with plump ripe cherries and baked until set. It's simple, adaptable and indulgent. In this version, the cream is infused with the gentle flavour of green fig leaves, resulting in an incredible, fudge-like custard. The French bake the cherries whole, but I prefer to pit them and let the juices bleed into the batter a little. This is the ultimate portable dessert as it is just as nice eaten at room temperature as it is warm, making it ideal for park or beach picnics. Serve it with fresh cherries on top, and a dollop of sharp crème fraîche or clotted cream.

125ml whole milk
125ml double cream
100g caster sugar
4–6 young furry fig leaves
50g butter, melted, plus extra
   for greasing
2 tbsp demerara sugar
100g plain flour
pinch of salt
2 eggs, beaten
350g ripe cherries, pitted
crème fraîche, to serve

1. Put the milk, cream and half the caster sugar in a saucepan over a medium heat and gently bring to the boil, stirring until the sugar has dissolved. Remove from the heat, then rip and scrunch up the fig leaves to release their oils and submerge them in the milk and cream mix with a wooden spoon. Plunge the pan immediately into a basin of very cold water (ensuring that no water gets into the pan) and leave to cool and infuse for at least 2 hours, preferably overnight (in the fridge).

2. Preheat the oven to 180°C/160°C fan/gas 4 and grease a Pyrex baking dish or flan dish just wide enough to hold the cherries in one layer with butter. Scatter over the demerara sugar and rotate the dish to distribute the sugar evenly across it.

3. Sift the flour into a bowl and add the remaining sugar and the pinch of salt. Add the eggs, beating them until smooth, then mix in the melted butter. Strain the cream, milk and fig leaf mix then gradually add it to the batter mix, whisking until there are no lumps (strain through a sieve if necessary). Leave to rest for 10 minutes.

4. Put the cherries in the dish in a single layer and gently pour over the batter. Bake in the oven for 30–35 minutes, until golden and just set but still wobbly. Remove from the oven and leave the clafoutis to settle for 10–15 minutes then serve, warm, with cool crème fraîche.

Muscovado pavlova
with caramelised oranges and cardamom custard

In this winter pavlova recipe, orange slices are soaked through with a deep, dark caramel, sat atop clouds of whipped cream and cardamom-flecked custard, among layers of marshmallow-soft muscovado meringue. Warming spice, vivid citrus and deep notes of molasses from the muscovado make this dessert an absolute showstopper.

300ml double cream
3 tbsp kefir or buttermilk

For the cardamom custard
150ml double cream
150ml whole milk
40g golden caster sugar
10 green cardamom pods,
    lightly bashed in a pestle
    and mortar
3 egg yolks
15g cornflour
pinch of salt

For the meringue
175g golden caster sugar
75g light muscovado sugar
½ tsp cream of tartar
pinch of salt
4 egg whites (keep the yolks
    for the custard)
½ tsp vanilla extract

For the caramelised oranges
3 oranges (navel or blood are
    best), peeled of skin and
    pith and sliced into thin
    rounds
70g golden caster sugar
30g dark muscovado sugar
pinch of salt
grated zest and juice of
    1 orange
2 sprigs of rosemary

1. To make the custard, pour the cream, milk and half the sugar into a saucepan and gently bring to the boil over a medium heat, stirring until the sugar has dissolved, the mixture has just reached boiling point and there are little bubbles popping to the surface. Remove it from the heat and stir in the cardamom pods. Plunge the pan immediately into a basin of very cold water and allow to cool and infuse for 1–2 hours (overnight is even better).

2. Once the custard has infused, whisk the egg yolks with the remaining golden caster sugar, the cornflour and the salt in a bowl until frothy and pale. Strain the cooled, infused cream into the egg mixture and whisk briefly to combine, then wash and dry the saucepan and prepare a basin of very cold (or iced) water. Return the mixture to the pan and heat over a low-medium heat, bringing it slowly to the boil and stirring continuously with a whisk for a few minutes until the cornflour is cooked out and the mixture thickens. Remove from the heat and cool by placing the pan in the basin of iced water. Once cool, cover the surface of the custard with cling film to avoid a skin developing, then chill for 2 hours.

3. Preheat the oven to 170°C/150°C fan/gas 4 and line two baking sheets with baking parchment.

4. Make sure the bowl you're going to whisk the egg whites in is spotlessly clean (squeeze a drop of lemon juice into the bowl and rub it over the bowl with a piece of kitchen paper).

5. Combine both the sugars, cream of tartar and salt in a bowl and rub out any lumps of muscovado with your fingers (if it's really lumpy, blitz it in a food processor to a fine powder). Put the egg whites in the clean bowl and whisk, using a stand mixer fitted with the whisk attachment or a hand-held electric whisk at its highest setting, until stiff peaks form. Now, whisking constantly, add the sugar in three batches, allowing each addition to incorporate into the egg whites before adding the next. Add the vanilla and keep whisking for 5–6 minutes, until any visible lumps of sugar have dissolved. The mixture should be glossy, smooth and fluffy.

6. When you remove the whisk from the mixture, use a bit of the mix stuck to the whisk to stick the baking parchment to the baking sheets. Now, using a metal spoon, divide the meringue mixture between the two lined baking sheets, dolloping it on and spreading it out into circles the size of small dinner plates (20–25cm in diameter), using the back and edges of the spoon, or a skewer to create cloud-like whisps and peaks which will make your pavlova look really appetising. Bake in the oven for 35–40 minutes. This is a quick-cook pavlova that results in gloriously soft, marshmallow-like meringue, so don't worry if it cracks, it will still taste delicious. Turn the heat off and allow the meringue to cool completely in the oven. Don't make the mistake of forgetting it's in there and turning the oven on full blast to heat it up for something else – a word of warning from experience!

7. To make the caramelised oranges, place the orange slices in a heatproof bowl. Combine the sugars and salt in a non-stick frying pan with the orange juice and zest and place over a low-medium heat, stirring and cooking gently until all the sugar has melted. Add the rosemary sprigs and stir with a wooden spoon until you have a dark caramel the shade of treacle. Add a tablespoon of water if it needs thinning as the consistency will depend on your orange – it should be as thin as orange juice. Pour the caramel onto the oranges, discarding the rosemary sprigs, and allow them to sit while you prepare the rest of the pavlova.

8. Once cool, carefully peel the parchment from the meringue discs and lift one onto a serving platter or cake stand.

9. Whip the double cream in a bowl to soft peaks and remove the custard from the fridge. Lightly fold a tablespoon of the orange caramel syrup, the kefir and then all of the custard through the cream, until just rippled.

10. Spread most of the cream and custard mixture onto the base meringue, saving some to cover the top layer, top with half the caramelised orange slices, and sandwich with the other meringue. Pile the remaining cream and custard mix onto the top meringue and cover with the remaining orange. Drizzle with a little more syrup and serve.

VARIATION   Rhubarb and Custard Pavlova
Adapt the recipe above to make a beautiful rhubarb and custard pavlova. It's best made from January to March, when bright pink forced rhubarb from the Yorkshire triangle is in season.

Poach the rhubarb according to the instructions on page 248 and use 250g golden caster sugar instead of muscovado, folding 125g of chopped hazelnuts through the meringue before you bake it. The cardamom custard will work a treat!

Go-to crumble topping

Makes about 500g

This topping is warming and comforting as every crumble should be, but it's also nourishing thanks to the oats, nuts and seeds. It's sort of a mix between a crumble and granola and there is much more texture in this than in a bog-standard crumble topping – I like to vary the ingredients through the year, adding warming spices for winter and swapping out hazelnuts for flaked almonds in summer because they are particularly good with stone fruit like peaches and apricots.

120g spelt flour
50g desiccated coconut
140g light muscovado sugar
100g jumbo oats
50g pumpkin seeds
40g flaked almonds (summer)
40g skinless, blanched
    hazelnuts, chopped (winter)
½ tsp ground cardamom
½ tsp ground ginger (winter)
½ tsp ground cinnamon
    (winter)
pinch of salt
150g butter, melted

Optional extras
50g buckwheat groats (lovely
    with peaches, plums or
    apricots)
20g cacao nibs (great with
    rhubarb or cherries)

1. Combine all of the dry ingredients in a bowl and pour over the melted butter. Mix thoroughly with a spoon until a crumble forms. If you want to roast it to keep in a jar and scatter over poached fruit for an instant crumble, or as a topping for yoghurt or ice cream, preheat the oven to 200°C/180°C fan/gas 6. Spread the mixture out on a baking sheet and roast in the oven for 30 minutes. Alternatively, keep the raw crumble in a Tupperware in the fridge until you plan on using it – it will keep for a few days.

2. To make the crumble, grease a pie or crumble dish with butter and fill it with poached fruit (suggestions on the following pages). It's up to you how much poaching syrup you want to keep in there. I usually drain away and reserve about half the syrup so it's not too wet, but there's just enough to keep it nice and moist. Top with the raw crumble and bake at 200°C/180°C fan/gas 6 for 20–30 minutes, until the crumble topping is crisp and golden and the filing is bubbling at the sides. Serve with cream.

Poached rhubarb for crumble

You can use outdoor rhubarb for this (I often make it with allotment rhubarb), but I like to make it between January and March when vivid bright pink forced rhubarb from Yorkshire's rhubarb triangle is available. These sherbet pink stems are one of winter's brightest kitchen highlights and they have a particularly sweet flavour, thanks to the way they are grown in dark sheds, forcing the rhubarb to grow quickly in search of light. You can use this poached rhubarb for crumble, or as a topping for porridge or yoghurt. Remember to save your rhubarb poaching liquor for the glazed parsnips on page 197. It's also great for shaking with your rhubarb gin and an egg white to make a rhubarb sour cocktail.

400g trimmed rhubarb (preferably the bright pink, forced rhubarb), sliced into 2–3cm lengths
100g caster sugar
grated zest and juice of ½ unwaxed lemon or blood orange
1 vanilla pod, split lengthways

Optional extras
bay leaves
green cardamom pods
star anise
sliced fresh ginger

1. Preheat the oven to 200°C/180°C fan/gas 6 and line a roasting tray with baking parchment.

2. Arrange the rhubarb neatly, tightly packed and side by side, in the roasting tray. Top with the sugar, citrus zest and juice and scrape the seeds from the vanilla pod in there too, throwing the spent pod on top. Add any optional extra aromatics, cover the tray tightly with foil and roast in the oven for 15–20 minutes, until tender but still holding its shape. Remove from the oven. You can either wait for it to cool and then keep in a jar or container in the fridge covered with the syrup ready for use or make it into a crumble immeditaely, using the crumble topping opposite.

Sweet Things

Rosé and lavender poached apricots

Serves 6

I adore apricots but usually the ones we get in the UK need a little sweetening up and cooking them in syrup works a treat. Something magical happens when poached with lavender: the floral herbaceous notes of the purple flower gives a gorgeous edge to the yellow stone fruit. Leave the stones in when poaching them because they add another layer of flavour and help keep their shape. They are perfect for the Apricot, Buttermilk and Hazelnut Tart recipe on page 224, with yoghurt, or topped with my go-to crumble recipe on page 236 and baked.

300ml rosé wine
300ml water
100g golden caster sugar
15g honey
3 flowering, fragrant lavender
    sprigs
strip of pared unwaxed lemon
    zest
6 whole apricots

1. Combine the rosé, water, sugar, honey, lavender and lemon zest in a non-reactive pan and bring to a gentle boil so that little bubbles are forming around the edge of the pan (don't let it boil more vigorously than that), stirring to dissolve the sugar.

2. Slide in the apricots and cover with a cartouche – a circular piece of greaseproof paper the same diameter as the pan with a hole cut in the middle to let out steam. Very gently poach the fruit for 10–25 minutes. How long it takes will depend on how ripe the apricots are: keep an eye on them and turn them once, as you don't want them to go mushy. They should retain their shape and integrity but be tender and sweet. When you're happy with them, remove the pan from the heat and scoop the apricots out with a slotted spoon. Allow to cool on a lipped tray, reserving the syrup. Once cool, put the apricots in a jar or Tupperware and pour over enough of the poaching liquor to cover. Using straight away (they are lovely with the crumble topping on page 236), or keep in a sterilised jar or Tupperware, covered with the syrup, in the fridge for up to 2 days.

Chocolate and cherry pavlova

This chocolate and cherry pavlova is inspired by the flavours of one of my favourite retro desserts; black forest gateau. It's even better the day after it has been made, so feel free to make it ahead of time and chill in the fridge until ready to serve.

100g dark chocolate, broken into squares
4 egg whites
220g caster sugar
½ tsp white wine vinegar
100g blanched, skinless hazelnuts, roughly chopped

For the filling and topping
500g cherries, pitted
glass of marsala or cherry liqueur
350ml double cream
10g dark chocolate, for grating

1. First, macerate the cherries. Place them in a bowl, pour over the marsala and toss them through the wine until they are thoroughly coated. Set aside.

2. To melt the chocolate, heat 2.5cm of water in a saucepan over a medium heat. Place a heatproof glass or metal bowl on top and put the chocolate squares in the bowl. Stir slowly with a wooden spoon or silicone spatula to melt, then remove from the heat.

3. Preheat the oven to 130°C/110°C fan/gas ¾ and line two baking sheets with baking parchment.

4. Whisk the egg whites in a spotlessly clean bowl or stand mixer until stiff peaks form. Then, with the whisk still turning, gradually add the sugar, in three batches, whisking constantly for 4–6 minutes until the mixture is thick and glossy. Whisk in the vinegar. Remove the bowl from the stand mixer (if using). Pour the melted chocolate down the sides of the bowl, turning the bowl to distribute it evenly, then add the nuts and fold them through lightly with a metal spoon until the meringue is marbled with chocolate.

5. When you remove the whisk from the mixture, use a bit of the mix stuck to the whisk to stick the baking parchment to the baking sheets. Spread a circle of the chocolate and hazelnut meringue (20–25cm in diameter) on each baking sheet. Bake in the oven for 2 hours, or until they peel away easily from the parchment (don't worry if it cracks; it will still taste delicious). Remove from the oven and carefully lift the meringues and parchment onto wire racks to cool. Peel the parchment from the meringues, then, using a wide palette knife, carefully lift them one of them onto a serving platter or cake stand.

6. Whip the cream in a bowl until it just reaches soft peaks – be very careful not to over-whip it. Drain the marsala from the macerating cherries into the cream and fold it through, along with half of the cherries. Spread slightly more than half of the mix on the bottom layer of meringue, top with the other disc of meringue, the remaining cream mix and then the remaining cherries. Grate over the dark chocolate and serve.

Rummy raisin bread and butter pudding

Serves 6–8

It's a strange thing when I stop to think that my dad, who adored food so vociferously and was such a huge part of my culinary education, will never know that I've made his passion my life. I often cook dishes with him in mind though, and rather than being maudlin or melancholic, it's a happy way to celebrate and remember a man with a boundless appetite for food and life. He won't ever taste this, but I know he would have loved it, such was his penchant for rum and raisin ice cream on our French camping holidays, and his love of bread and butter pudding, or 'B and BP', as he used to call it with an excited twitch of the shoulders. This version fuses the two, soaking the raisins in rum then stirring it into the custard to coat the bread, which is cooked until bubbling, golden and utterly delicious. Do as my dad would do and douse your helping with too much double cream.

20g raisins
85ml rum, plus 1 tbsp rum
40g salted butter, plus extra for greasing
350g good-quality rustic, crusty bread (or four large oval slices, each sliced in half)
3 eggs, beaten
60g caster sugar
pinch of salt
350 whole milk
100ml double cream, plus extra for pouring
grated zest of 1 unwaxed lemon
grated zest of ½ orange, plus extra for topping the pudding
nutmeg, for grating
60g grapes (golden muscat work well)
30g demerara sugar

1. Soak the raisins in the tablespoon of rum for a couple of hours.

2. Preheat the oven to 180°C/160°C fan/gas 4 and grease a 20–25cm ovenproof dish or roasting tray with butter.

3. Spread the bread with butter on one side and arrange it in the buttered ovenproof dish or roasting tray.

4. In a jug or bowl, whisk together the eggs, sugar and salt until frothy, then pour in the milk, cream, 85ml rum, raisins and their rum, citrus zests and a good grating of nutmeg and whisk until well combined.

5. Scatter the grapes among the bread slices then pour over the custard. Grate over a little more zest and a little more nutmeg then scatter over the demerara sugar. Bake in the oven for 25–30 minutes, until the pudding is crisp and golden and the custard is set. Serve piping hot with extra cream poured over.

Spiced apple cake
with cardamom butterscotch and tahini buttercream

Serves 8–10

'It's got to be worth the calories.' These wise words were spoken to me down a crackly phone line from Glastonbury by Claire Ptak, owner of the Violet Bakery in Hackney – and baker of *that* royal wedding cake – back when her business was just gaining momentum. I interviewed Claire for a piece on an exciting new generation of bakers, and her matter-of-fact assertion that, given cake's not unsubstantial calorie content, it should always deliver tenfold in the pleasure stakes, is a sentiment I share. If you're going to go to the trouble of baking, having sticky fingers, pulverising perfectly good butter into too much sugar for icing, and making lots of washing up, the results must make you, and everyone you share your cake with, silent in happy delight with the first mouthful, and then greedily reach for more. This cake is definitely worth the calories. Spiced, honeyed apple purée makes for a tangy, moist crumb shot through with walnuts for bite, while nutty, tahini-laced Italian meringue buttercream imparts a silken creaminess to each mouthful. Cardamom-spiked salted butterscotch adds an addictive spice and sharpness.

1 tbsp butter, plus extra for greasing
500g cooking apples, peeled, cored and roughly chopped
juice of ½ lemon
3 tsp ground cinnamon
5 tbsp runny honey
100g natural yoghurt
100g walnuts, roughly chopped
350g plain flour
½ tsp ground cardamom
2 tsp ground ginger
1 tsp freshly grated nutmeg
½ tsp fine sea salt
2 tsp baking powder
4 eggs
200g golden caster sugar
150g light brown muscovado sugar, sifted
150ml rapeseed or vegetable oil, plus extra for greasing

1. Preheat the oven to 220°C/200°C fan/gas 7. Grease three 20cm cake tins with butter and line the base and sides with baking parchment.

2. Put the chopped cooking apples in an oiled roasting tray, along with lemon juice and 1 teaspoon of the cinnamon and toss, then dot with the butter. Drizzle with the honey, cover the tray with foil and roast for 30 minutes, or until the apple is soft enough to purée.

3. Transfer the apple to the bowl of a food processor and blitz to a smooth purée, then transfer to a bowl and clean out the food processor bowl. Once cool, stir 175g of the purée into the yoghurt and set aside. Keep the remaining purée for the sponge and butterscotch.

4. Turn the oven down to 190°C/175°C fan/gas 5.

5. Put 50g of the walnuts in the bowl of a food processor, blitz to a flour, then sift it into a large bowl with the flour, remaining cinnamon, spices, salt and baking powder and stir.

6. In the bowl of a stand mixer (or using another bowl and an electric hand-held whisk), whisk the eggs and sugars vigorously until thick and frothy, then slowly pour in the oil, until well combined. Take the bowl out of the mixer, and sift in a third of the flour mix, folding to incorporate. Now add half the apple-yoghurt mix, fold that in, followed by another third of the flour, then the rest of the yoghurt and chopped walnuts, and finally the rest of the flour.

Recipe continues over the page

For the salted cardamom butterscotch
30g unsalted butter, diced
130ml double cream
145g light brown muscovado sugar
generous pinch of sea salt
seeds from 4 green cardamom pods, ground

For the tahini buttercream
3 egg whites
250g golden caster sugar
300g unsalted butter, at room temperature
2 tbsp tahini
1 tbsp vanilla bean paste (or 2 tsp vanilla extract)
pinch of salt
dehydrated apple slices and blackberries, to decorate

7. Divide the batter evenly among the prepared tins and bake for 25–30 minutes, or until a skewer inserted into the middle of each cake comes out dry. Remove from the oven and allow to cool for 12–15 minutes on a wire rack, then remove the cakes from their tins. If they have domed during baking, level out the sponges by carefully using a serrated knife held parallel to the surface to cut off the dome and form a flat surface.

8. To make the salted cardamom butterscotch, put the butter, cream, sugar, salt, cardamom seeds and 2 tablespoons of the apple purée in a medium non-stick pan and bring to the boil, stirring continuously (although it may look super-tempting, don't swipe your finger over the spoon: caramel can give a nasty burn). Turn down to a simmer and cook the sauce for 10 minutes, stirring occasionally, until smooth, thick and glossy. Remove from the heat and set to one side. If, when it's cooler, the mixture is too stiff, warm it up over the heat with a splash of milk to loosen it; you want it still warm and runny enough so that you can pour it over the cake (the consistency of thick paint). Fill a squeezy bottle if you have one, to make things easier.

9. To make the tahini buttercream, put the egg whites and sugar in the bowl of a stand mixer fitted with the whisk attachment. Place the bowl over a pan of boiling water, making sure the bottom of the bowl isn't touching the water, then whisk by hand until the sugar dissolves and the mixture is no longer gritty. Put the bowl in the mixer, then whisk until soft peaks form and the bowl returns to room temperature. Switch to the paddle attachment, add the butter, one spoonful at a time, until well combined, then add the tahini, vanilla and a pinch of salt. Beat to a light, fluffy icing then transfer half the buttercream to a piping bag fitted with a 2–3-cm round nozzle.

10. Place the sturdiest layer of sponge on a platter or cake stand and pipe a ring of the buttercream around the edge of the sponge to form a barrier which will keep the purée in. Spoon a little of the apple purée onto the cake and spread it out with the back of your spoon, then pipe a zigzag of buttercream across the purée and top with the middle sponge. Repeat the same thing on this sponge, then top with the final layer.

11. To ice the cake, spoon half the remaining buttercream on top of the cake, and use a stepped palette knife to spread it out over the top, then put some more on your palette knife and ice around the sides of the cake as a crumb coating. Chill the cake in the fridge for 20 minutes, then use the remaining icing to cover everything evenly. Chill for another 15–20 minutes, until the icing feels cool, then dot some of the butterscotch around the very edge of the top of the cake, allowing it to partially drip down the sides, creating a lovely drip effect. Cover the top of the cake evenly with as much butterscotch as you like, then decorate the cake with dehydrated apples and blackberries.

Bay leaf custard and bramble jam doughnuts

Makes 8–10

As kids, we would get dragged out of bed at an unfriendly hour to traipse around boot fairs before 'the dealers' got to all the best swag, because my mum had a good eye and furnished our house with second-hand finds. For some reason, it was always freezing cold when my parents took us bargain hunting.

The only thing that could stop us whinging about the weather was the freshly fried doughnuts from our favourite food vendor who would unflinchingly pipe rings of thick dough into bubbling hot fat. They would bob there for a matter of seconds, then, once golden, he'd fish them out with a long fork and toss them straight into mounds of caster sugar before scooping them into paper bags and hoisting them into our greedily outstretched hands.

Pulling open the greasy paper bag and inhaling the sweet, yeasty scent of the warm doughnuts mingling with the frosty morning air, was almost as delicious as the first bite of crisp, buttery dough. There are few things that bring as much joy as a freshly made doughnut, and these homemade versions are filled with creamy bay leaf-infused custard and topped with a tart hedgerow jam, a nod to the autumnal memories of those chilly boot-fair mornings.

150ml whole milk
1 tbsp fast-action dried yeast
1 tbsp golden caster sugar, plus 4 tbsp extra to coat the doughnuts
50g unsalted butter
300g strong white bread flour, plus extra for dusting
½ tsp fine sea salt
1 egg, lightly beaten
vegetable oil, for greasing the tins and for deep-frying

For the bay leaf custard
150ml double cream
450ml whole milk
70g golden caster sugar
6 fresh bay leaves
3 large egg yolks
pinch of salt
20g cornflour

1. To make the bay leaf custard, put the cream, milk and half the sugar in a saucepan over a medium heat and stir gently until the sugar has dissolved, the mixture has just reached boiling point and there are little bubbles popping to the surface. At this point, remove it from the heat and add the bay leaves, scrunching and tearing them a little to release the oils in the leaves and submerging them in the liquid with a wooden spoon. Plunge the pan immediately into a basin of very cold water and allow to cool and infuse for 1–2 hours (overnight is even better).

2. In a large bowl, whisk the egg yolks and salt with the remaining sugar and the cornflour until frothy and pale. Strain the cooled infused cream into the egg yolk mixture and whisk it until well combined.

3. Wash and dry the saucepan and prepare another basin of very cold (or iced) water. Pour the mixture into the clean pan and heat over a low-medium heat, bringing it slowly to the boil and stirring continuously with a whisk for a few minutes, cooking until the cornflour is cooked out and the mixture thickens. Whisk vigorously to smooth out any lumps. Remove from the heat and cool by placing the pan in the basin of cold water. Once cool, transfer to a piping bag and keep in a jug in the fridge for at least 2 hours, or preferably overnight.

4. To make the doughnuts, gently warm the milk in another saucepan. Mix the yeast in a bowl with 1 teaspoon of the sugar and 40ml of the warm milk, and set aside for 15 minutes. Melt the butter in a saucepan over a low heat.

Recipe continues over the page

For the bramble jam
250g jam sugar
400g blackberries
100g elderberries
juice of ½ lemon

5. Sift the flour and salt into a bowl and stir in the rest of the tablespoon of sugar. Pour in the yeast mixture, the remaining 110ml milk (reheat it slightly if you need to, but make sure it's not too hot – it should be comfortable to hold a finger in), the melted butter and the egg, then mix into a dough. Tip out onto a lightly floured surface and knead for 5–10 minutes until smooth. If you have a stand mixer, fit it with a dough hook attachment and knead it in there for 5 minutes. Once your dough is kneaded, put it in a bowl, cover the bowl with cling film, then leave somewhere warm for 45 minutes –1 hour, or until doubled in size.

6. Meanwhile, make the jam. Put a saucer in the freezer (if you don't have a sugar thermometer). Warm the sugar over a low heat in a saucepan for a few minutes, being careful not to burn it. Add the blackberries and elderberries and cook for a few minutes until they release their juice, then add the lemon juice, turn up the heat and bring to the boil, stirring gently. Skim off any surface scum and boil for about 8 minutes, until it reaches setting point (you're looking for a temperature of 105°C on a sugar thermometer, but if you don't have one, proceed with the saucer test). Spoon a little jam onto the cold saucer. Put it back in the freezer for a few minutes and if the surface of the jam on the cold saucer wrinkles when pushed, the jam is ready. If it isn't ready yet, keep cooking and testing the jam. This is supposed to be quite a loose, spoonable jam, so don't boil it for too long. Once you're happy with the consistency, remove the pan from the heat and leave it to cool slightly while you finish making the doughnuts.

7. Knock the air back from the dough for a minute or so, then divide and shape the dough into 8–10 equal balls, cupping your hand loosely over each one and lightly moving your hand in a circular motion – as if drawing circles. Grease two baking sheets with oil and transfer the balls to the oiled sheets. Leave to prove at room temperature for a further 30 minutes.

8. Heat the oil in a deep-fat fryer, or fill a saucepan one-third full of oil and heat until it reaches 180°C (a piece of bread dropped into the oil should turn golden in a few seconds). Put some golden caster sugar on a large plate. Fry the doughnuts in batches of 2 or 3 for 1 minute, then turn them in the oil and fry for a further minute until golden all over. Remove with a slotted spoon, drain on kitchen paper and roll immediately in the sugar.

9. Use the tip of a long, sharp knife (a paring knife works well) to make a deep incision into the top or side of the doughnut, then insert the nozzle of the piping bag inside the incision and gently pipe in custard, until it's coming out of the hole. Repeat this until every doughnut is full and serve them with the jam.

Rhubarb and white chocolate blondies

Makes 12 blondies

I've always found blondies a bit one-note sickly sweet, until I played around with adding sherbety sour poached rhubarb to the equation. The bright pink tang of the melty rhubarb breaks up the sweetness of these blondies and is SO GOOD against the creaminess of the white chocolate and cobnuts. If you can't get hold of cobnuts, blanched almonds or hazelnuts work nicely, too.

100g unsalted butter, plus extra for greasing
120g plain flour
¼ tsp fine salt
175g light brown muscovado sugar
1 large egg
100g white chocolate, roughly chopped
60g shelled cobnuts (or almonds), thickly sliced

For the rhubarb
250g trimmed rhubarb, chopped into 3-cm lengths
100g caster sugar
1 vanilla pod, split
grated zest and juice of 1 orange

1. Preheat the oven to 200°C/180°C fan/gas 6 and line a baking tray with baking parchment. Grease a 20 x 25cm brownie tin with butter and line the base and sides with baking parchment.

2. Place the rhubarb in the baking tray in a neat layer and scatter over the caster sugar and vanilla pod. Pour over the orange juice and sprinkle over the zest. Cover the tray tightly with foil and bake in the oven for 12–14 minutes, until the rhubarb is just soft. Remove from the oven, remove the foil and set aside to cool. Once cool, drain the rhubarb from its syrup, reserving the syrup in a jar for later use in another dish (see page 197).

3. Put the flour and salt in a bowl and mix to combine. Melt the butter gently in a pan.

4. Place the muscovado sugar in a separate bowl and stir in the melted butter, until well combined and free from lumps. Add the egg and stir vigorously until smooth. Sift in the flour and fold it in lightly, until no streaks remain. Add the chopped chocolate and half the cobnuts and stir to combine.

5. Spoon most of the batter into the prepared brownie tin, reserving a few spoonfuls for the top, and smooth it out using the back of a spoon. Top with the poached rhubarb, spoon over the remaining batter so it's partly covering the rhubarb and scatter over the remaining cobnuts. Bake in the oven for 30–35 minutes, until a skewer inserted into the brownie mixture comes out with some crumbs on it and is a little moist, but not coated with raw mixture. Remove from the oven and leave to cool completely in the tin, then cut into 12 squares.

Damson gin-poached pear and elderberry galette

Serves 6-8

This rustic, freeform tart is a celebration of autumn. Pears are poached in deep crimson damson gin and then layered atop elderberries, glazed with the reduced gin and elderberry syrup and baked inside a buttery spelt crumb. It's a comforting sweet that evokes autumnal walks and hedgerows of childhood, and the boozy damson gin nips of being a grown-up. It's best served with whipped double cream with a tablespoon of buttermilk folded in to sharpen it.

200ml Damson Gin
(page 162)
200ml water
40g golden caster sugar
400g firm pears, peeled,
cored and thinly sliced
1 vanilla pod, split
80g elderberries (or
blackberries)

For the pastry
200g spelt flour, plus extra
for dusting
pinch of fine sea salt
1 tbsp caster sugar, plus extra
for sprinkling
120g cold unsalted butter,
diced
1–3 tbsp iced water
1 egg, beaten

1. First, make the pastry. Sift the flour into a large bowl. Tip in the salt and sugar and stir. Now slide in the butter and lightly rub it into the flour, squeezing the butter between your fingers and thumb and fanning, a bit like you're dealing cards. You want nice fine flakes of butter (don't worry about taking it as far as breadcrumbs). Once it's all pretty much rubbed in, gingerly pour in 1 tablespoon of the iced water, being sure to sprinkle it all over the mixture. Use a butter knife to stir it in and bring the pastry together. Add a little more water if needed, then get your hands in the bowl, mould it into a ball and flatten to a disc. Wrap it in greaseproof paper (rather than cling film, which makes it sweat) and chill in the fridge for at least 30 minutes.

2. While the pastry is resting in the fridge, poach the pears. Pour the gin and water into a saucepan, add the sugar and bring to the boil, stirring to dissolve the sugar. Once boiling, turn down to a gentle simmer and slide the pears and vanilla pod into the liquid. Top with a cartouche (a circular piece of greaseproof paper the same circumference as the pan, with a small hole cut in the middle to let out steam) and poach the pears for 15 minutes, then turn off the heat and allow them to cool in the syrup. Once cool, strain the pears, reserving the syrup. Pour the syrup back into the pan, add 20g of the elderberries and boil it to reduce the syrup to a glaze.

3. Preheat the oven to 200°C/180°C fan/gas 6 and line a baking sheet with baking parchment.

4. Remove the pastry from the fridge and unwrap it. Dust a clean surface with flour and roll the pastry out to a circle 30cm in diameter. Use the rolling pin to transfer it to the lined baking sheet. Spread the remaining elderberries out in a circle in the middle of the pastry, leaving a 2cm border around the edge, then arrange the poached pear slices on top. Brush with the reduced elderberry syrup then gently lift the border of the pastry up and around the filling. As you lift the dough and place it against the filling, it will pleat naturally. Patch up any tears, then chill in the fridge for about 20 minutes, until the pastry is hardened. Brush the pastry with egg wash and sprinkle with a little more sugar. Bake in the oven for 40 minutes, then remove from the oven and serve.

TIP: Use quince when they are in season. They are harder and will take a bit longer to poach, so keep checking them.

Secret
Ingredients

Though it sits towards the end of the book, Secret Ingredients is a place I hope you'll visit with some regularity. As well as a hugely versatile Wild Garlic Pesto (page 263) which is great for the Cheese Straws (page 45), the Yoghurt Flatbreads (page 39), and the Asparagus and Goat's Curd Tart (page 108), you'll find a lush but incredibly simple Labneh (page 256) that can be adapted with the seasons. I've also included a whole host of flavoured butters (pages 257-61) to bring some extra oomph to your cooking: try frying some cod in kimchi butter, or stirring the dried mushroom butter into a wild mushroom risotto.

Making fresh curd cheese (page 254) is super-easy and really fun to do, and results in delicate, fresh cheese to use to fill pasta, allotment pasties or strawberry tarts. You'll also find my go-to stocks in this chapter (pages 266–67), which form the building blocks of so many dishes I cook at home. Make a big batch of chicken or veg stock, freeze what you don't use that day, and you'll always have the wherewithal to whip up a soup, stew, braise or risotto.

Fresh curd cheese

Makes about 500g

This is not ricotta, but it shares many of its characteristics – a fresh, crumbly texture and neutral yet creamy taste. Fresh curd cheese is easy to make at home – just add acid to good-quality whole milk – and it's a fun process which yields a versatile and delicious light cheese. Play around with different milks, too: get hold of some raw milk for a more interesting flavour or have a go with sheep's or goat's milk if you can find some. This is the perfect for filling the filled pasta on page 89 or using in the Allotment Greens and Anchovy Orecchiette on page 68, or in salads (like the Peach, Prosciutto and Celery Leaf Panzanella on page 106).

1.5 litres organic whole milk
½ tsp sea salt
50ml distilled spirit vinegar, white rice vinegar or lemon juice

1. Put the milk and salt in a non-reactive, ceramic or stainless steel saucepan and heat to just below boiling point – small bubbles should be rumbling to the surface. Add the vinegar or lemon juice and remove from the heat, stirring slowly. You should immediately see the milk curdle and curds starting to form – if you don't, add a dash more acid – lemon juices vary in acidity so you might need to use more if you're working with lemon juice. Stir the mixture slowly with a wooden spoon for a minute or so, then cover the pan with a clean tea towel and leave for 30 minutes.

2. Line a sieve with a double layer of muslin or cheesecloth and rest it over a bowl. Pour the curdled milk into the sieve and place the sieve and bowl in the fridge. How long you hang the cheese depends on the texture you are looking for because the longer you hang it, the more whey drips out and the firmer it becomes. If you're after something quite firm, hang it for a good 6 hours, or overnight, but if you prefer it loose and creamy, a couple of hours of hanging should suffice. Put the curd cheese in a jar or airtight container in the fridge and use within a couple of days (this is not difficult). Also, do not discard the whey – put it in a jar in the fridge and use it to make my Whey-brined Lamb Chops (page 115), to add tang to pasta sauces, braises, dressings and soups.

TIP: If you can't wait to try your cheese, toast some sourdough or other good-quality bread until golden, rub it with a raw garlic clove, then spoon over the curd. Drizzle with extra-virgin olive oil, scatter over a few salt flakes or an oil-packed anchovy, season with freshly grated nutmeg or black pepper and enjoy the fruits of your labour.

Sort-of silk weaver's brain (*curd cheese dip*)

Serves 4

200g Fresh Curd Cheese
     (page 254)
1 garlic clove, grated
1 spring onion, trimmed, or
     shallot, finely chopped
handful of fresh herbs from
     the garden, such as parsley,
     tarragon, chive, mint and
     lovage, finely chopped
4 tbsp olive oil
freshly ground black pepper,
     to taste

I've eaten *cervelle de canut*, which literally translates to 'silk weaver's brain', in markets and bouchons in Lyon and it's so delicious. Its name is a reference to Lyon's heritage as a silk-weaving capital, and the low opinion held of silk workers by the city's rich. This is my version, which is great served with little toasts made from thinly sliced, toasted French baguette, or with good-quality potato crisps.

Combine all the ingredients in a bowl, taste for seasoning and serve as a dip.

Labneh

Makes 500g

Labneh is one of those things that you make for the first time and then wonder how you ever lived without it. I make this on repeat. A staple of Middle Eastern cuisine, it's simply natural yoghurt that has been strained through muslin to remove the whey and give it a wonderfully thick, creamy texture with that distinctive yoghurt tang. Use the best yoghurt you can find for this – I favour a live, full-fat, probiotic, natural yoghurt, and you can play with adding goat's yoghurt too, if you're a fan of the flavour. Labneh can be used in so many different ways, drizzled with olive oil and stirred with a tablespoon or two of Wild Garlic Pesto (page 263), or chopped seasonal herbs, or spread onto a plate and topped with roasted veg (as in the Squishy Aubergine, Crispy Chickpea and Broccoli Salad on page 59). I love it topped with Savoury Granola (page 262) and homemade ferments (pages 146–47) and scooped onto warm flatbreads.

500g full-fat live probiotic
     Greek or natural yoghurt
salt

1. Mix the yoghurt with a good pinch of salt. Line a sieve with a piece of muslin or a clean J-cloth and rest over a deep bowl. Spoon in the yoghurt, cover and put in the fridge to strain for anything between 3 and 8 hours (or overnight).

2. How long you strain it will determine how firm it is, because the more moisture it loses the firmer it becomes. If you're looking for something a bit looser and creamy for dips or to spread on toast, then just strain it for a couple of hours. If it's a firmer consistency you're after, leave it for longer. You'll be left with a fresh, soft cheese-like substance – this is your labneh – and liquid in the bowl. The liquid is the whey. Do not discard this as it's great used in sauces, ferments and brines (see Whey-brined Lamb Chops on page 115).

Flavoured butters

If my years of bothering chefs and eating out has taught me anything, it's to never underestimate the flavour-enhancing power of good butter. I can't count the number of times I've been left speechless by a mouthful, and on asking the chef, been met with an insouciant shrug and the words, 'just a bit of butter'. Butter is fat, and fat carries flavour, and as well as providing an irresistible, mouth-coating richness. It's the ultimate flavour enhancer: a fantastic vehicle for other flavours. Making your own flavoured butters, and keeping them on hand in the fridge and freezer, ready to be sliced and used as and when, equips you with a secret weapon that will never fail to enhance your cooking. The only rule is to start with good-quality butter; I go for unsalted so I can adjust the seasoning according to the saltiness of whatever I'm adding.

Brown butter

Makes 200g

If ever there was a secret ingredient, this is it. We all know that a knob of butter can work wonders to add flavour and luxury to cooked dishes, but imagine what it can do when the butter has been gently caramelised, adding an irresistible nutty dimension. Try this spread on hot toasted Sourdough Crumpets on page 27, or swirled into freshly boiled pasta or gnocchi along with some lemon juice and Parmesan. Brown butter is best friends with fish too – use it for frying scallops or add it to the Dover Sole on page 80. It's also fab in mashed potatoes or celeriac purée – use it to pimp up the topping of the Sheepless Shepherd's Pie on page 179.

200g unsalted butter
pinch of sea salt
2 tbsp cold milk

1. Preferably use a light-coloured saucepan so you can watch the butter change colour. Set the pan over a medium heat, add the butter and melt it gently, swirling the pan: it will foam, then the milk solids will turn nut-brown and it will smell nutty. Use a silicone spatula to stir the butter and cook it evenly, being careful not to burn it. Once it's smelling good and nutty, pour the butter into a clean heatproof bowl, leaving as much of the solids as you can in the pan.

2. Stir the pinch of salt into the butter in the bowl and allow it to cool, then transfer to the bowl of a stand mixer fitted with the whisk attachment with the milk and whisk on a low speed for 2–3 minutes, turning it up to medium and whipping for a further 4 minutes, until fluffy and peaks form (alternatively whisk it in a bowl using an electric hand-held whisk, starting on low speed and increasing to medium speed).

3. Lay a piece of baking parchment or greaseproof paper (about 22 x 30cm) or a double layer of cling film on the surface and use a spatula to scoop the whipped butter out onto the paper or film, forming it into a sausage shape down the middle. Wrap the paper or film tightly over the butter and roll it into a neat log, twisting the ends to seal. The butter will keep for up to a week in the fridge.

Homemade butter

While it's not something you'll want to do every day, there is something utterly joyful, sensual and disarmingly simple about making your own butter: watching as the whipping cream collapses from stiff peaks into miraculous nuggets of golden butter. I love how tactile this process is. After all, how often do we actually get to hold and squeeze great hunks of silky yellow butter in our hands and feel like a dairy farmer for a day?

If you're going to the effort of making your own, seek out special cream for the job – you want the highest welfare dairy you can find: organic cream from grass-fed cows at the very least. Jersey cream is easy to find in supermarkets and has a superb richness, while Guernsey cream has a wonderful lush golden hue thanks to the fact Guernsey cows can't process beta carotene from their graze, which means it passes into, and colours, their milk. If you live in the vicinity of dairies or dairy farms, go on the hunt for extra-special cream. You can play with the flavourings once you've given it a go: I love to add a couple of tablespoons of really good-quality crème fraîche or sour cream when I churn the cream, to give the butter a sour tang, or 'cultured' flavour. Try adding smoked salt for an irresistible hint of smokiness.

800ml Jersey double cream
1 tsp sea salt

1. Sterilise the bowl of a stand mixer according to the instructions on page 2.

2. Pour the cream and salt into the sterilised bowl, fit the stand mixer with the whisk attachment and beat on a medium-high speed until the cream is over-whipped and collapses. This will take longer than you might think, but keep beating until it splits into butter solids and liquid is sloshing around the bowl then strain through a muslin-lined sieve. Return the butter to the mixer and beat again on a low-medium speed to extract any remaining buttermilk, then drain through the sieve again.

3. Fill a large bowl with iced water and lower the butter into it, kneading and pressing it with your hands and squeezing out more buttermilk. You may need to do this two or three more times, changing the water each time until it's clear. It's important to get out as much liquid as possible as retained liquid can turn the butter sour more quickly. Lay a piece of baking parchment or greaseproof paper (about 22 x 30cm) or a double layer of cling film on the surface and use a spatula to scoop the butter out onto the paper or film, forming it into a sausage shape down the middle. Wrap the paper or film tightly over the butter and roll into a neat log, twisting the ends to seal. The butter will keep for 2–3 weeks, if all the liquid has been removed (around a week if it's still a little wet).

Kimchi butter

Makes 260g

The sour, fiery flavours of your homemade kimchi are mellowed and balanced by this butter, which is transformative for frying fish like cod, adding to a pan of mussels, melting on top of seared steak, slathered onto roasted chicken wings or tossed through stir-fried or steamed veg or greens. You get the idea.

60g My 'Kind Of' Kimchi (page 145), or shop-bought kimchi
200g unsalted butter, at room temperature, diced
¼ tsp salt

Drain the kimchi in a sieve (reserving any juice to put back in the jar), then chop it very finely. Whip the butter and salt in the bowl of a stand mixer fitted with the whisk attachment until fluffy (or whisk it in a bowl using an electric hand-held whisk, starting on low speed and increasing to medium speed), then stir through the kimchi until thoroughly combined, adding a little of the juice to season it. Taste the butter to check that it's nice and sour. Lay a piece of baking parchment or greaseproof paper (about 22 x 30cm) or a double layer of cling film on the surface and use a spatula to scoop the whipped butter out onto the paper or film, forming it into a sausage shape down the middle. Wrap the paper or film tightly over the butter and roll it into a neat log, twisting the ends to seal. The butter will keep for up to a week.

Wild garlic butter

Makes 240g

This butter is wonderful spread on the just-grilled Yoghurt Flatbreads on page 39, or stuffed under the skin of chicken before roasting. It's also lovely to fry mushrooms in, fry gnocchi with, to top a grilled steak, seafood or roasted veg. You can use any seasonal green herb if wild garlic isn't available. It's great made with tarragon, parsley, chives or lovage.

30g wild garlic leaves
juice of ½ lemon
1 tsp sea salt
1 tbsp olive oil
200g unsalted butter, at room temperature, diced

Put the wild garlic, lemon juice, salt and olive oil in the bowl of food processor and blitz until really finely chopped. Add the butter and pulse again to combine. Lay a piece of baking parchment or greaseproof paper (about 22 x 30cm) or a double layer of cling film on the surface and use a spatula to scoop the butter out onto the paper or film, forming it into a sausage shape down the middle. Wrap the paper or film tightly over the butter and roll it into a neat log, twisting the ends to seal. The butter will keep for up to a week.

Dried mushroom butter

Makes 250g

The umami woodland flavours of this butter are brilliant for cooking all manner of savoury dishes. Use it to baste pan-fried chicken, fish or wild mushrooms, or stir into risottos and pasta dishes. It's also incredible for pushing under the skin of chicken or game before you roast it.

30g dried mushrooms
2 tbsp roasted hazelnuts (see method on page 80), chopped
1 garlic clove
200g unsalted butter, at room temperature, diced
1 tsp sea salt

Blitz the dried mushrooms in the bowl of a food processor until very finely chopped – ground almost to a powder. Add the hazelnuts and garlic and pulse to finely chop, then add the butter and salt and pulse to combine thoroughly. Lay a piece of baking parchment or greaseproof paper (about 22 x 30cm) or a double layer of cling film on the surface and use a spatula to scoop the butter out onto the paper or film, forming it into a sausage shape down the middle. Wrap the paper or film tightly over the butter and roll it into a neat log, twisting the ends to seal. The butter will keep for up to a week.

Seeded dry-store crackers

Makes 15–20 crackers

These tasty little crackers are perfect with the dips on pages 46–49, and are a brilliant way to use up all the end of packets of flour, seeds and spices you might have lurking in your cupboards. Change them up according to what you've got to hand, and try serving them with cheese, too.

100g spelt flour, plus extra for dusting
50g wholemeal flour
50g rye flour
20g polenta flour (or 220g flours of your choice)
1 tsp salt
30g pumpkin seeds
1 tsp fennel seeds
1 tsp cumin seeds
1 tsp white sesame seeds
1 tsp smoked sweet paprika
100ml rapeseed oil, or melted and cooled coconut oil
1–2 tbsp iced water

1. Combine the flours, salt, seeds and paprika in a large bowl until evenly mixed. Pour over the oil and use a spoon or blunt knife to incorporate it into the dough, then rub it in until the mixture has the consistency of breadcrumbs. Sprinkle over the iced water, a tablespoon at a time, working it in until it forms a smooth dough. Knead it briefly in the bowl, mould it into a ball, then chill it in the fridge (uncovered, in the bowl) for at least 20 minutes.

2. Preheat the oven to 200°C/180°C fan/gas 6 and line a baking sheet with greaseproof paper.

3. Lightly dust a clean surface with flour and roll out the dough to a thickness of 5mm. Use a 4-cm cookie cutter or small dish to cut out rounds from the dough and place them on the lined baking sheet. Bake in the oven for 15–20 minutes, until crisp and golden. Remove from the oven and leave to cool on a wire rack. They will keep in an airtight container for a few days.

Savoury granola

Makes 450g

Trust me that Future You will love Present You for making a big jar of this savoury granola. Crunchy, nutty, toasty and fragrant with whole spices and rosemary, it's an incredibly versatile ingredient to have, and fantastic scattered on almost everything savoury. It's particularly good for bringing texture, protein and seasoning to veggie dishes, and where an ingredient is soft, sweet or creamy – with roasted veg, on soups, salads, dips or grilled flatbreads. Build a little breakfast or lunch meze plate with a swoop of Labneh (page 256), some roasted veg, a spoonful of hummus, some homemade ferments and a handful of this granola.

150g jumbo oats
100g whole, skin-on almonds
50g pine nuts
60g pumpkin seeds
50g buckwheat groats
1 tbsp mixed spices (smoked
   sweet paprika, coriander
   seeds, fennel seeds,
   caraway and cumin seeds)
1 tsp sea salt flakes
½ tsp dried chilli flakes (I love
   Urfa or Aleppo chilli flakes
   for this)
½ tsp garlic granules
2 sprigs of rosemary, leaves
   picked and finely chopped
3 tbsp coconut oil, melted
1 tsp runny honey or maple
   syrup

1. Preheat the oven to 200°C/180°C fan/gas 6 and line a large roasting dish or baking tray with baking parchment.

2. Put the oats, almonds, pine nuts, seeds, buckwheat groats, spices, salt, chilli flakes, garlic granules and rosemary in a large mixing bowl and stir to combine. Pour over the coconut oil and honey or maple syrup and use your hands to thoroughly incorporate everything and make sure the dry ingredients are evenly coated. Spread the mix out on the lined roasting dish or baking tray in a single layer and bake for 15–20 minutes, stirring occasionally, until the oats and nuts take on a deep golden colour and crisp up nicely. Remove from the oven, leave to cool completely then keep in a sealed container for up to 1 month.

Wild garlic pesto

Fills 1 x 300ml jar

Preserve the fleeting joy of wild garlic season in this simple pesto, which can be used for slathering onto hot flatbreads (page 39) Sourdough Pizza (page 62), stirring through pasta or rippling into homemade Labneh (page 256).

40g hazelnuts (skin off), roasted (see method on page 80)
100g wild garlic leaves, chopped
30g Parmesan, finely grated
grated zest and juice of ½ unwaxed lemon
100ml extra-virgin olive oil (the best you can afford), plus extra to top up the jar
sea salt and freshly ground black pepper

1. Sterilise a 300ml jar according to the instructions on page 2.

2. Put the hazelnuts, wild garlic, Parmesan and lemon zest and juice in the bowl of a food processor and blitz briefly, until coarsely chopped. Season with salt and pepper, then slowly add the olive oil and blitz until you have a pesto. Pour it into the sterilised jar and top with a little more olive oil, so no air can get to the pesto. Chill in the fridge for up to a week. It also freezes well (in an ice-cube tray or plastic container).

Cobnut salsa verde

Fills 1 x 300ml jar

Cobnuts are a variety of hazelnut traditionally grown in Kent and harvested from August while fresh and green, rather than dried. Their flesh has a unique moist, creamy consistency and they are worth seeking out to use in salads, baking (see the Rhubarb and White Chocolate Blondies on page 248) and savoury dishes. They grew in our garden as a kid and my dad used to have an annual turf war with the squirrels to get to his fill. He couldn't really compete, but occasionally came back triumphant with a plastic bag and would sit at the table cracking them and dipping them in salt. This salsa verde is a great way of making the most of them and contrasts their creamy freshness with salty capers, bright herbs and a punch of mustard. It's fantastic with lamb, or drizzled over roasted veg. In fact, it makes the perfect accompaniment for the Whole Roast Cauliflower on page 192.

2 tbsp capers, chopped
1 garlic clove
sprig of rosemary, leaves picked and chopped
pinch of sea salt
20g flat-leaf parsley, leaves picked
1 tbsp mint or tarragon leaves
100g cobnuts, shelled (50g shelled weight) and chopped
1 tbsp Dijon mustard
grated zest and juice of ½ unwaxed lemon
1 tsp good-quality honey
1 tbsp water
100ml extra-virgin olive oil
1–2 tsp red wine vinegar

1. Sterilise a 300ml jar according to the instructions on page 2.

2. You can make this salsa verde in a food processor or mini chopper, simply by blitzing all of the ingredients to a green sauce, but if you have a pestle and mortar go for that because you can control the texture a bit better. This salsa is nice when it's a little chunky, allowing you to make the most of the lovely creamy texture of the cobnuts.

3. Place the capers, garlic, rosemary and salt in a mortar and gently pound them with the pestle until you have a green paste. Add the other herbs and grind them down too, then add the cobnuts and crush them into the herb mix, being careful to leave some chunks and not crush them too finely. Add the mustard, lemon zest and juice, honey and water and stir and grind with the pestle, to combine the whole lot, then gradually add the olive oil. Mix until well blended, then taste for seasoning and add a teaspoon or two of red wine vinegar to sharpen it, if you think it needs it. Pour into the sterilised jar and chill in the fridge for up to a week. It also freezes well (in an ice-cube tray or plastic container).

4. Bring it out of the fridge 30 minutes before you want to use it to loosen it up, as the olive oil will solidify in the fridge.

TIP: If you can't get hold of cobnuts, use hazelnuts instead.

All-purpose chicken broth

This is one of the most cooked recipes in our kitchen. There are just so many ways to use chicken stock, and making your own from either a roast bird's spent carcass or a fresh bird whose poached meat you can also eat, is resourceful and comforting. There is always a tub of chicken stock in my freezer, ready to defrost and turn into the Restorative Ginger Chicken Soba Noodle Soup on page 171, or slosh into a risotto, braise or gravy. It might seem like an effort to make it, but really it's a case of getting everything into a pot, covering it with water and letting time do the rest. The thing to remember is that your work will be rewarded, tenfold – homemade chicken stock is always going to get used and it's always going to improve the flavours in your cooking. You can make it with spent chicken carcasses, too.

1–1.5kg whole organic chicken
    (if you've used the legs and
    wings for confit, these will
    have been removed)
4 litres cold water
1 leek, washed and chopped
1 celery stick, washed
1 carrot, washed
1 onion, halved (skin on)
2 bay leaves
6 black peppercorns
salt

1. Thoroughly season the chicken with a couple of teaspoons of good-quality salt and leave it to sit for 30 minutes at room temperature.

2. Place the chicken in a large pot or casserole dish and cover with the cold water. Add the other stock ingredients (apart from the salt) and bring to the boil over a medium heat. When small bubbles start to appear on the surface of the stock, turn the heat down to a simmer and skim the surface of any scum, trying not to remove the fat that will be floating on the top of the liquid because this carries flavour.

3. Put a lid on the pot or casserole dish with a slight gap to allow some steam to escape, and set a timer for 35 minutes. After this time, lift the chicken out of the broth and onto a plate, allow to cool for a couple of minutes then carefully remove the breasts (to use in soups and salads – try the soup on page 171) and return the chicken back to the pot. Cover with the lid and cook for 20 more minutes, then, like you did with the breasts, remove the legs to use in salads etc. (this won't apply if you're using a chicken whose legs you've used for the confit recipe on page 100). Return the carcass to the pot and continue to simmer with the lid slightly ajar for 2–3 hours, adding a bit more water if it's reduced too much. Taste the broth for salt and add a little more if you think it needs it. It should have a lovely balanced flavour and not taste salty. When you're happy with how it tastes, strain, leave it to cool, then cover and chill. It will keep in the fridge for up to a week or freezes really well for up to 6 months.

Fish stock

Makes 1 litre

If you go to the trouble of making your own fish stock, you will be enchanted by the way it elevates all the fishy dishes you cook. It's quicker to make than chicken stock and lasts well in the freezer. If you're not a fan of fennel you can leave it out or replace it with carrot. Get fish heads, bones and offcuts from your fishmonger – they are usually happy to throw some in a bag free of charge.

600g fish offcuts (bones and heads, gills and eyes removed) – I like flat fish bones such as Dover sole or brill; avoid oily fish
2 bay leaves
1 onion, thinly sliced
1 celery stick, thinly sliced
2 fronds or heads of wild fennel (or ¼ fennel bulb, chopped)
pinch of fennel seeds
a few sprigs of flat-leaf parsley
200ml white wine
6 black peppercorns
1 litre cold water
3 tsp fish sauce

1. If you need to, cut the fish bones down so that they fit into your pan, then put them in a medium saucepan with the rest of the ingredients (except the water and fish sauce). Cover with the water and turn the heat to medium-high. Bring the stock to the boil, then immediately turn it down to a simmer, skimming any scum from the surface. Simmer for 25 minutes, then remove from the heat and leave to sit for 20 minutes – this will allow the impurities to settle.

2. Strain the stock through a fine-mesh sieve lined with muslin or use a pour-over coffee filter. Season with the fish sauce, cover and chill. The stock will keep in the fridge for 2–3 days or in the freezer for up to 6 months.

Fridge forage vegetable stock

Makes 1 litre

This is a staple at home, made using odd bits of veg from the bottom of the fridge and dregs of white wine. It makes a really lovely, flavourful stock which is a great base for soups, risottos and stews. Change up the recipe according to what's in the fridge, adding parsley, turnip, celeriac or any other veg that might be lurking around.

1 tbsp rapeseed oil
1 bay leaf
6 black peppercorns
½ leek, thinly sliced (use the green half)
2 carrots, finely chopped
1 onion, finely chopped
1 celery stick
1 garlic clove, chopped
¼ fennel bulb
100ml white wine
2–3 litres cold water
4cm piece of dried kombu or dulse (optional)
a couple of mushrooms, sliced
large pinch of sea salt

1. Heat the rapeseed oil in a large (preferably ceramic) casserole or stock pot over a medium-high heat. Add the bay leaf, peppercorns and all of the vegetables (except for the mushrooms) and sweat, stirring, for 8–10 minutes. When some of the veg are starting to brown and create a caramelised crust on the bottom of the pan, pour in the wine and use a wooden spoon to rub the crust from the pan – this will incorporate all that flavour into the stock. Now cover with the water, add the seaweed (if using) and mushrooms and bring to the boil. Skim the surface to remove any scum, reduce to a simmer and taste for seasoning, adding a little more salt if you think the flavours need coaxing out a little more. Simmer for 40 minutes–1 hour, until you're happy with the flavour.

2. Strain the stock through a fine-mesh sieve and leave to cool. The stock will keep in the fridge for up to a week and freezes really well for up to 6 months.

Index

Acknowledgements

Books are wonderfully creative, collaborative, all-consuming projects and I could not have created this one without the help of a crack team of incredibly talented, patient and good-humoured people. I'd like to start with the fantastic team at HarperCollins, without whom this book would never have been born. Katya Shipster, you picked up my book proposal with a zeal and positivity that was utterly heartening, and it was wonderful to feel that you really understood what I was trying to do and had such vision for this project. Thank you so much for the opportunity, for your support and encouragement, for cooking my recipes for your family and raving about them, for putting up with my dad jokes and for your boundless enthusiasm. It's been really wonderful collaborating with you and I feel so privileged to have joined a food list that you're putting so much heart and soul into.

George Atsiaris and James Empringham, it's been a pleasure working with you both on this project, you've both worked so incredibly hard and it is gloriously reflected across these pages: thank you so much. Also huge thanks to Julie and Jasmine in marketing, Rosie in PR and Tom, Alice, Dom and Anna in the sales team for all your brilliant hard work in getting this book out there. Laura Nickoll, you are a fantastic copyeditor and I was so thrilled to have you on the team for my 'difficult second album'. Thank you for all the hours you worked on making this book the best it could be.

Helen Cathcart, you are, quite simply, the best, and I feel so incredibly lucky to have worked with you on yet another beautiful book. It's our third book baby together, but you shot like an absolute trooper throughout your own actual pregnancy, going above and beyond. No one sees or captures the beauty in my food quite like you, and I'm endlessly inspired by the way you create such glorious images.

The gorgeous visuals in this book are down to an amazing team of creative women who collaborated with me on the shoot. Linda Berlin, your props and unparalleled eye for styling have played a massive part in this. Becks Wilkinson – you are an unbelievable chef and food stylist, thank you so much for all your hard work on our seriously pressurised shoots, you are an absolute legend and a true inspiration. Cissy Difford, you are such a grafter and a calm, twinkling presence, thank you for all your assistance; I'm so excited to see what the future holds for you – I just know it's bright! Also thanks to Helen's assistants Jen and Kinga, you both rule and I love how much you like to eat – my kind of women.

Liz Marvin, you know how crucial your support, both emotionally and professionally throughout the writing process has been to me. You're such an incredible human being and I feel very smug that I realised that at the tender age of what – 14? – and haven't let you go since. You are unbelievably good at what you do and I love you. Mina Holland, you have been such a supportive friend and guide, thank you for your valuable input and for your ongoing kindness and encouragement. You are a truly amazing writer and editor – an all round bit of a genius really, and I'm so lucky to count you as a friend. Chris Hayes, you know how much I value your ongoing support, friendship and kindness, and the fact you didn't write me off all those years ago despite my gallingly naive advances in a black velvet romper suit. CW is very lucky indeed to have such a smart, witty and inspirational woman in her life. And thanks to Jonathon Cook (aka Jon the Poacher) for helping reignite my love of foraging.

A wonderful team of friends and colleagues has helped me with the recipe testing for this book – massive shout out to Nena Foster, Anna Higham, Peter and Maggie Barker, Ann-Marie Booth. To Joe McCanta for providing me with an endless supply of booze and for supplying the two excellent cocktail recipes in the book. Huge thanks to my manager Holly Arnold for her ongoing hard work and and to Jon Elek at United Agents for your help with shaping my proposal, for introducing me to Katya and also to Rosa Shierenberg for her help and management throughout the process.

To my wonderful husband Jamie. Thank you for picking me up whenever I need it, for your ongoing bolstering and endless love, support, patience and kindness all of which are tested to the max while I'm in book mode. You are my angel and I adore you and couldn't do this without you. Thank you for always washing up, clearing up and eating with gusto. I love you with all my heart.

To my family – I love you beyond the ends of the earth, thanks for all your love, laughs and help – my love affair with food began at home and I have so much to be thankful for. To all of my wonderful friends – you know who you are and I am so unbelievably lucky to feel so loved and supported throughout all that I do, you know I couldn't do any of this without you, and I will feed you forever. I'd also like to thank everyone who follows me on Instagram (rosiefoodie) and Twitter and reads my blog and articles – your kindness, engagement and feedback keeps me motivated, fulfilled and striving to be better at what I do everyday.